Native Americans

Native Americans

Enduring Cultures and Traditions

Trudy Griffin-Pierce

MetroBooks

MetroBooks

An Imprint of Friedman/Fairfax Publishers

Library of Congress Cataloging-in-Publication data available upon request.

ISBN 1-56799-389-3

Editor: Tony Burgess
Art Director: Lynne Yeamans
Designer: Susan Cox-Smith
Photography Editor: Dorian Romer
Production Associate: Camille Lee

Color separations by Bright Arts Graphics (s) Pte Ltd
Printed in the United Kingdom by Butler & Tanner Limited

Grateful acknowledgment is given to authors, publishers, and photographers for permission to reprint material. Every effort has been made to determine copyright owners of photographs and of reprinted textual material. In the case of any omissions, the Publisher will be pleased to make suitable acknowledgment in future editions.

For bulk purchases and special sales, please contact:
Friedman/Fairfax Publishers
Attention: Sales Department
15 West 26th Street
New York, NY 10010
212/685-6610 FAX 212/685-1307

Visit the Friedman/Fairfax Website:
http://www.webcom.com/friedman

ACKNOWLEDGMENTS

It takes many to bring a book into being. Deepest appreciation goes to Keith Pierce, the team at Michael Friedman Publishing, and all those who are working to communicate the message of sustainable change based on Native American spiritual principles, most notably: Vine Deloria, Jr., Norbert Hill, Jr., and the people at AISES and *Winds of Change*. Important sources include W. Richard West, Jr. and others at the National Museum of the American Indian, *Native Peoples* magazine, *News From Indian Country,* and Duane Champagne's edited volume *Native America: Portrait of the Peoples*. The purpose of this book is not only to strengthen cross-cultural understanding, but also to further the realization that truly we are all one, and must work together to restore balance to the earth we all share.

Contents

Foreword

For most of the twentieth century, a great intellectual barrier existed in the literature about American Indians. Almost every book on the subject recounted the history, culture, religion, and art of a tribe as they were from first contact with Europeans up to 1890. When the American frontier closed, the books also concluded, with barely a few paragraphs describing what had happened to the Indians thereafter. People's knowledge of Indians, therefore, was severely restricted to the classical period when Native Americans roamed, hunted, and fished in relative comfort and freedom. No wonder, then, that many otherwise well-educated citizens devoutly believed that when you left Buffalo, New York, your stagecoach was liable to be attacked by Apache war parties anywhere between there and Cleveland, Ohio.

In recent decades, this condition has been altered somewhat. A continuous stream of books by sincere non-Indians has poured from the presses, usually explaining that times have changed and that Indians now speak for themselves. The current generation of Indians is producing an unusual number of writers who devote a considerable amount of space and energy to explaining how difficult it is to be an Indian. We are, in fact, overwhelmed by books of poetry recounting the hardships of modern Indian life. Even this mournful situation seems to be changing, and a few books now describe some of the more positive, successful aspects of modern Indian life.

Trudy Griffin-Pierce has marched into the field with a new concept—that of matching historical Native American traditions with the modern expressions of those traditions as people live them today. Covering the traditional culture areas, she brings a new dimension to the old data by showing systematically how the different tribes have brought their dances, ceremonies, and customs into the modern world with them. We are reminded that while outward appearances may indeed change as technology changes, behavior and values must remain pretty much the same within Indian

■ 8 ■

communities. People preserve the meaning of traditions even though the situation in which they live has been radically altered.

This book makes a lot of sense because events of recent times do not appear as radically disruptive activities once they are seen in this broad cultural and historical context. Underlying all of the customs and practices, from aboriginal times until today, are the glimpses of spirituality that served as the foundation of tribal life. Depending on the geographical area, the spiritual may manifest itself in basket making, First Salmon ceremonies, beadwork, cooking, planting ceremonies, or simply taking a respectful attitude toward the neighborhood.

Too often we read about Indians' religious practices as if they were simply abstract theological propositions designed to ensure a temporary kind of salvation from the cares of the world. Trudy Griffin-Pierce shows us that the traditional Indian reverence for all forms of life and expression produced customs that can assist us in making a better adjustment to the world in which we live today. Ultimately, of course, spirituality involves mastering the details and intimacies of the world around us. Thus the casual becomes rare and the unusual often becomes commonplace. As we read in these chapters how the different tribes were able to achieve such a precise fit with the lands on which they live, the thought occurs that perhaps we can learn from each other.

I applaud Trudy for weaving so many details into the stories of these regional cultures. Each chapter is a gold mine of facts blended with a consistent and substantial interpretation of the great variety of ways that groups of people adjusted to the various environments on this continent. Here we see the true meaning of Indian life—the satisfaction that comes with the experience of participating in the struggle to understand the greater fabric of life.

Vine Deloria, Jr.
University of Colorado, Boulder

Two Worlds Collide

When Europeans set foot on the North American continent in 1492, two worlds collided. Until the billowing sails and curved bows of Columbus's ships arrived in the islands of the Caribbean, time had been reckoned in cycles of the seasons, and the people had regarded themselves as an integral part of nature.

Two profoundly different worldviews clashed in 1492. Only the Americas, Australia, and Oceania were still outside the enormous trade network of the so-called Old World, which consisted of Europe, Africa, and Asia. Until this time, the native peoples of North America had existed in isolation.

Perhaps as many as forty million people lived in hundreds of Indian nations that stretched from the Atlantic to the Pacific and from Central America to the Arctic. Shaped by the availability of resources, each nation developed its own means of adapting to the local environment, its own

political system, its own kind of family, household, and village structures—in short, its own culture.

For example, in Nevada, the harsh, arid environment had taught the Northern Paiutes to live in small groups of several families, ranging seasonally over the terrain, gathering pine nuts in September, and wading into chilly waters in March to pull up the young shoots of cattails. In contrast, the Tlingits of the Northwest Coast built permanent villages of up to one thousand people who were supported by such bountiful supplies of salmon and other marine resources

Above: Willard Price, of Sheep Springs, Arizona, painted this figure of Thunderbird.

Opposite: People are realizing that there is another side to the battle depicted in this 1896 lithograph at what is now known as the Little Bighorn National Monument. In 1995, warrior tribes including the Lakota, Northern Cheyenne, and Arapaho; scout tribes such as the Crow; and representatives of the 7th Cavalry celebrated a five-day reconciliation ceremonial at the site of the battle.

A Sarcee woman holds the reins of a horse harnessed with a travois. Before Plains tribes acquired horses, they had to rely on smaller travois carried by dogs; horses could haul four times the load and travel twice the distance each day in comparison to dogs.

that they had to work only a few months each year to accumulate a year's food supply and a considerable trading surplus. With such abundance, the Tlingits developed a high standard of living, a distinctive style of art, a rich ceremonial life, and a highly ranked society based on great wealth.

From the rich diversity of Indian cultures came prophets, sculptors, poets, warriors, spiritual leaders, orators, and healers. Each nation expressed its unique identity through its

myths, worldview, art styles, relationship to the sacred, and forms of dance, sport, and recreation.

We tend to think of Europe as a dominating world force because the technological advances associated with the Industrial Revolution eventually led to European military, political, and economic dominance. This dominance in turn created a hunger for expanded territory and economic gain that propelled Europeans into the New World. However, in 1492 Europe lagged behind Asia technologically, politically, and culturally; China led the Old World in terms of technology, art, architecture, and in the development of a common writing system.

Ball-playing was just one of many forms of recreation enjoyed by Prairie peoples.

In a very real sense, when the peoples of the Caribbean encountered Columbus, they were facing not only the superior technology of the Europeans but also the larger knowledge accumulated through the centuries from the entire Old World. Marco Polo had brought back gunpowder from China. European guns, crossbows, iron weapons, armor, and horses gave the Europeans significant advantages over the stone-tool military technologies of native peoples.

The Europeans unknowingly brought with them an even more devastating arsenal of conquest: smallpox, measles, influenza, bubonic plague, diphtheria, typhus, cholera, malaria, and scarlet fever. The isolated peoples of the Americas had no natural immunity to these diseases, which swept through entire tribes like wildfire. In 1496, Father Bartolome de las Casas reported 1.1 million Indians over the age of fourteen years in Hispaniola; by 1535, less than forty years later, only five hundred Indians were still alive on this island. The Taino and Ciguayo Indians had completely vanished by the 1550s.

Blinded by their technology and wedded to their notions of architecture, land ownership, and religion, the newcomers were largely unable to see the validity of Native American culture. Indeed, the Europeans saw the inhabitants of the New World as barely human. Such an attitude helped to justify the seizure of Indian land and the conquest, slavery, and genocide of Native Americans.

Contrary to European belief, however, native peoples of the Caribbean lived in huts not because of their inability to build more substantial homes, but because they lived in a mild climate and had no need to develop sturdy European-style architecture. Their intimate knowledge of the land, accumulated by trial and error over many generations, along with the natural abundance of their surroundings, meant that they had little need to extend their technology. Their relatively low population densities, in comparison to Europeans, had enabled the native peoples to survive for millennia without depleting their resources. In fact, they were so well adapted to their landscape that the native peoples of the Americas had a standard of nutrition higher than that of most Europeans. Ironically, many colonists later came to America so conspicuously unfit for survival that they lived on the edge of starvation. Indeed, the Jamestown colonists of 1607 lacked hunting skills, were afraid of the forests, and knew nothing of the strange plants and animals that surrounded them. Without the help of the Algonquians of the Atlantic seaboard, these new settlers would not have survived their first winter.

European misconceptions of native cultures were worsened because first contact occurred far from the central points of Native American civilization. The main concentrations of population were in Mesoamerica and Peru, where intensive farming had created ideal conditions for the blossoming of large multiethnic empires, such as the Aztec and Inca. Some estimates place the Aztec civilization of Mexico at more than 25 million people, whereas the Inca Empire may have reached 12 million people.

Underlying obvious differences in military technology and material culture lay even more profound differences. Europeans, bent on exploration, conquest, and settlement, brought their portable, institutionalized spirituality with them. Although Descartes had not yet been born, Europeans were already beginning to embrace a scientific consciousness based on the notion of human mastery over nature. They had lost their notion of nature as living and organic; territorial expansion made one piece of land as valuable as another if it contained equal resources or was strategically located.

For the original inhabitants of the Americas, however, land was not mere property; rather, the land and the people were one. Native Americans considered their surroundings to be the repository of mythic events and ancestral origins. So secure were Native Americans in their relationship with their homeland that they met these newcomers more with a sense of puzzled curiosity than serious apprehension. Only later, after word had spread from tribe to tribe, did the impact of these white-skinned men become evident. By then, it was too late.

Opposite: A Plains Indian medicine man prepares to minister to a patient in this George Catlin painting. Traditional healers specialized in specific forms of intervention, including diagnosis, herbal treatments, and particular ceremonies. Native Americans understood the intimate relationship between body, mind, and spirit; most healers were also acknowledged spiritual leaders.

Above: Anasazi ancestors of today's Puebloan peoples painted this kiva mural.

THE JOURNEY OF CREATION

The Europeans wondered where the peoples of the Indian nations could have come from. The newcomers assumed that such civilizations lacked the intelligence to have evolved independently, and so concluded that the natives must have had Old World origins; they must trace their descent to seafaring Welshmen, or perhaps Egyptians, or even to one of the Lost Tribes of Israel.

Today, most scientists agree that the Indians crossed the Bering Strait from eastern Asia to Alaska on a land bridge formed by huge glaciers during one of three periods of the Ice Age: between seventy and thirty thousand years ago, between twenty-five and fifteen thousand years ago, and between fourteen and ten thousand years ago. Following herds of mastodons, families traveled back and forth across an undistinguishable plain, unaware that they were entering a new land. Physically, they resembled ourselves. Although they sought shelter in caves, these men and women were *Homo sapiens*, endowed with an intelligence and spirituality that led them to establish ties with the supernatural, the land, and with one another.

However, archaeologists disagree on how long ago the first Americans arrived. By twelve thousand years ago, long before any nation known to history, people were already living in all parts of North and South America. Some scientists even believe that people lived in the Americas as long as fifty thousand years ago. Archaeologists are investigating finds from both continents, and controversy continues concerning the precise date when humans began populating the Western Hemisphere.

Indian people have never puzzled over their origins. They know with the certainty of faith and spiritual truth that they emerged from another, lower world, migrated from elsewhere, or were created on their own land by Holy People. Much like the biblical narrative of Genesis, Native American stories of creation have been handed down through generations, forming the basis for behavior and belief. However, unlike Christianity and Judaism, which concentrate power in the hands of a supreme being, Native American spirituality emphasizes the interdependence of all beings; people must honor all other living creatures and

Every year when the first snow fell, Ojibwa (Chippewa) men celebrated the Snowshoe Dance, as depicted in this 1835 painting by artist George Catlin.

forces of the universe with responsible human action if they are to survive. Furthermore, native traditions do not seek to dominate ways of thinking or worship under the guise of religious orthodoxy. Each person is responsible for his or her relationship to the Creator and the other beings with whom the earth is shared.

According to some tribal peoples, when the Creator brought the world into existence, the story of his Creation was so far beyond human comprehension that he gave each religion a part of this story upon which to base their spiritual beliefs and practices. Thus, each group must practice its own faith to keep the world in balance.

Tribal languages lack a word for "religion"; the term "sacred" is more appropriate because it conveys the reverence for all living beings that underlies native rituals. Traditional Hopis and Navajos begin the day by greeting the sun with thankfulness, because its light and warmth make life possible.

One of the main objectives of Native American ritual life is the establishment and maintenance of what Navajos call

hózhó—an untranslatable term that expresses harmony, well-being, and all that is good in life. Through right thinking, responsible action, and the performance of rituals, they keep their earthly lives in balance. Stories associated with the natural world—with stars, animals, plants, and mountains—remind the people of the right way to live their lives. By keeping their lives in order, humans fulfill their responsibility to the maintenance of order in the universe.

Native American beliefs center on the concept of reciprocity. Because of the interdependence of all forms of life, every being in the universe has the responsibility to contribute its own unique gift or ability to keep the world in balance. The sacredness of all life is embodied in the use of such kin terms as "Grandmother Spider" and "Mother Earth." This reminds humans that they are related to all beings and forces in the universe. Kinship is based on responsible cooperation stemming from respect and affection.

Spirituality has always been the foundation for tribal life. Political leaders were often spiritual leaders. Councils—and even conferences today—were spiritually guided; such meetings were initiated with prayers of thankfulness to the Creator for life, an acknowledgment of the sacredness of all living things, and a request for mutual understanding.

On an individual basis, sacred beliefs permeate every facet of daily life. This means leaving an offering to a yucca plant that will be woven into a basket and honoring an animal with a prayer as it gives up its life for human benefit. Rituals must be conducted with faith, love, and devotion—tu'i hiapsimak, "with good heart," as the Yaqui Indians say—to ensure the proper outcome. Although such actions benefit the entire community, the determination of "good heart" has to do with one's personal relationship with the sacred. Life is considered to be a journey that must be undertaken with a good and whole heart; the spirit in which each step is taken determines the destination. Rather than emphasizing the reward of personal salvation in the next life, traditional Native American beliefs focus on "seeking the path of life" in the here and now—on being rather than on becoming.

THE POWER OF THE LAND

"Look on all land as our land. All things on it and all people that are on it are in our care. Our songs and ceremonies call us caretakers of this land for all people. We have been taught to take care of this land in this way so that all people will benefit and all living things."

—*Mina Lansa, a Hopi from Old Oraibi*

Native Americans believe the land is Mother Earth, which cannot be sold. Each group's origin story tells how the Creator, or another Holy Being, meant for them to live in their particular territory.

Each feature of the landscape—every mountain and lake, every valley and meadow—holds its own unique place in an integrated whole in which humans are but another part. They have a sacred relationship to all animals and plants that, in turn, provide both physical and spiritual sustenance. Thus tribal histories, the

Above: Before the arrival of the Europeans, Hopewellian artists created this copper plate manatee.

Left: According to anthropologist Claire Farrer, during the Mescalero Apache girls' puberty ceremony, the singers not only "sing women into their adult roles," but they also ensure the continuation of the Mescalero themselves by singing "the people into their concerted existence." During the ceremony, these powerful holy men recount tribal history "from the time of the beginning by the shores of a big lake far to the north."

Comē leuyndæ bourguant ou rotissem le poisson
et la chair

Les Indiens font vng grand feu de bo023, et le bois est cōsomē en
charbon prengnem quatre fourchette debois et les fichem en terre de mether
plufra batons de franera dossua tops pour ogetter de hauteur du feu d'b
pied et demy et prez a' estendem leur poisson et chairs nand ils sont
la challeur du feu la fumet de la graisse qui tombe dans le feu fait
bouçauer ou rotir lay chair et poisson dicet vng boy menger se ly
xurut sonnem chr pour quil ne bruste dy estam lay chair et poisso
cuite setur a la waûeur de harono sor

survival of future generations, and the afterlife are intimately intertwined with the land upon which each tribe has lived for centuries. By understanding and caring for the resources of their particular territory, native peoples have been assured that those resources would take care of them.

Opposite: Smoking and roasting fish and meat enabled native peoples to store what they did not immediately eat. Native Americans were so well adapted to their resource base that they had a standard of nutrition higher than that of most Europeans.

Above: A Santa Clara Puebloan woman baking bread in a traditional adobe oven.

SPIRITUAL HEALING

"Our philosophy of life sees the Great Spirit's Creation as a whole piece. If something in the environment harms man, it is reasonable that the Creator provided a specific herb to cure the sickness or has given some person the wisdom to heal....Prayer is an essential part of all medicine; it puts the person troubled by illness into a proper relationship to the Great Spirit and his Creation."
—*John Snow, chief of the Stoneys of Alberta*

American Indian beliefs about health and spirituality were so intertwined that spiritual practices have always played an important part in their health care systems. Annual observances, such as the Sun Dance of the Plains peoples and the Green Corn ceremony of Southeast and Northeast peoples, were tribalwide purification rituals that maintained the balance between the natural and supernatural worlds. On both a communal and an individual basis, humans were expected to fulfill their ritual responsibilities by giving thanks to the great beings who make life possible. Neither higher nor lower than other animals, people were called upon to demonstrate respect for the animals and plants that sustain life. A natural outcome of ritual participation was a sense of connection to other humans and to the forces of the universe. People emerged from ceremonies reassured of their place in the cosmos.

When illness did occur, native peoples used herbal remedies that were ingested, inhaled, or applied externally. In the case of serious illness, they held healing ceremonies designed to restore harmony in the universe. Native peoples often use various symbols to express the balance they are seeking to restore, such as a circle to emphasize wholeness, because it has no beginning or end. Jennie Joe, a Navajo professor, explained that "within the symbolic circle other elements of life...represent the equilibrium that is needed to maintain health and well-being." An example would be the four directions, which contain within them sources of knowledge, power, and energy. At another level of understanding, these four elements symbolize the innate qualities of a person's being—physical, mental, emotional, and spiritual. A person can only maintain health if these elements are in balance within as well as without. The Navajo emphasize "right thinking" and believe that what humans think and speak about, they draw into their lives.

One of the main differences that Dr. J.T. Garrett, a Cherokee health professional, has found between traditional Indian medicine and modern Western medicine is that Indian medicine is wellness-oriented, whereas modern medicine is illness-oriented. Healers are called upon to offer thanks for an abundant harvest or a successful hunt, to bless a new home or a girl coming of age, to provide protection on a journey, or to ensure success in an undertaking. The annual ceremonies previously mentioned help to ensure the well-being of the entire community. Garrett also reported that Indian medicine focuses on why illness occurs, including natural and supernatural causes. Treatment is thus approached holistically because multiple causes are expected; both spiritual and physiological means are used to heal the patient. Another major difference is that the Indian patient is treated in a family or community setting with personalized treatment. In contrast, modern medicine emphasizes the "how" behind illness, focuses only on "natural" causes, prefers to link illness to a single cause, and approaches treatment impersonally and physiologically.

THE CREATIVE PROCESS AND ART

"The transformation of natural materials through [the] creative process is...a sacred transition. Wood, stone, antler, bark, leather, feathers, cornhusks, shells, porcupine quills, metals, and natural pigments are parts of a living universe; each has a spiritual essence. The artist and the object harness the spirits of these materials, increasing their power."

—*Seneca Tom Hill, in* All Roads Are Good

Native languages do not have a word for "art," just as they have no word for "religion." There is no separation in Indian cultures between art and the living spirit in nature; these values are inherent in daily life. The artistic process was always considered to be a creative ritual, a way of bringing the intangible and spiritual into physical form. Seneca Tom Hill described the vision-inspired images that Plains Indians painted on their clothing as "visual prayers...a way to pay tribute to spirit forces. Designs became metaphors for beliefs."

Puebloan women wash freshly harvested wheat.

Native Americans created utilitarian objects, such as the Northwest Coast canoe, house posts, and box seen here, that were as beautiful as they were useful. Today, such traditional arts are undergoing a remarkable artistic renaissance accompanied by a renewed dedication to traditional ceremonies.

Native peoples understood that the process of creation was just as important as the finished product and that an object's beauty comes from the spirit in which it is made. Designs protected and blessed the person who made them, and the completed object was imbued with power and effectiveness by the songs sung during its creation. Without prayers and a respectful attitude during the creative process, the finished object was lifeless, spiritless.

Thus, the being of the maker became an essential part of the object itself. Although they appreciated the artistry of a well-made basket and the symmetrical lines of a seagoing canoe, Native Americans never created art for the purpose of contemplation. Everyone followed some form of creative self-expression by making and decorating their clothing, weapons, utensils, tools, or shelter. Utilitarian objects were as beautiful as they were useful, such as the finely made birch-bark baskets decorated with quillwork made by

Canadian Micmac women or delicately carved elk-horn spoons from California. Karuk men carved these spoons to use when they ate acorn mush, a favorite dish. Beauty and function were never separated in the Indian worldview; art and life share that same interrelationship today.

TRIBAL LITERATURE AND HISTORY

Crazy Horse, a leader of the Oglala Sioux, once said, "A people without a history is like wind on the buffalo grass."

Through storytelling and ritual reenactments, Native Americans have transmitted their traditions and histories for centuries. Not only do myths convey traditional values, they also show people how to cope with the moral challenges of the present by reminding them that these values are still applicable in today's world.

A common misconception about oral cultures is that their traditions and their languages are less pure because they have not been written down. Their origin stories are considered less valid because they are not contained in a written sacred text like the Bible or the Torah.

However, this a gross misunderstanding. Native Americans have always retold their origin stories with great care. Each reenactment was actually a recreation of the beginning of the world and, as such, had to be recounted through song, dance, and prayer with immense precision. Sacred celebrations such as the World Renewal ceremonies of the Hupa, Yurok, and Karok of northern California ensured nature's renewal each year. Such sacred rituals provided answers to questions of existence and revealed the responsible actions required to meet the moral challenges of the present by maintaining the balance of the natural and supernatural worlds.

Oral traditions were highly developed into verbal art, which transmitted history, literature, spiritual beliefs, and ways of life. Tribal elders were repositories of their nations' histories. Oral literature also includes legends, ritual dramas, myths, chants, songs, prayers, speeches, and anecdotes. Both a means of education and a form of entertainment, such performances often included humor. Although origin stories formed the cornerstone of oral literature, it also included trickster tales, personalized stories such as the recitation of brave deeds in battle, ritual prayers for spring planting, courting songs, and oratory. In an oral culture, leaders were expected to be orators, endowed with the power to move the emotions of their people with compelling speeches that evoked confidence.

Without written language, meaning was greatly enhanced by the context in which stories were told. Grandfathers recounted stories to their grandchildren in

A young Indian boy wears an elaborate eagle-feather headdress for the annual powwow in Kamloops, British Columbia.

Fish played an important role in the diet of many Native Americans. The rivers, streams, and lakes of the Southeast region teemed with many kinds of fish, such as bass, crappy, catfish, mullet, brim, and rockfish.

the intimacy of their homes by crackling fires on bitterly cold winter nights. Because the spoken word was considered powerful enough to call forth the creatures themselves, it was vital to tell such stories when the animal protagonists were hibernating.

Other stories were recreated through ritual drama. Wearing intricately carved and ornately painted masks, Northwest Coast storytellers related stories connected with spirits or creatures drawn from mythology. Outside the large windowless communal house, rain poured down steadily, but inside, everyone focused their attention on the wondrous story that was unfolding by the central fire.

Among the peoples of the Northwest Coast, stories also took the form of spectacular dances. Fantastic masked and costumed figures cast dramatic shadows as they celebrated the powers of the spirits through a frenzy of chanting, dancing, screaming, and even mock combat.

Taken out of context, Native American oral literature appears as lines on a page; however, a story comes to life when a native speaker tells the same story to a native audience, because of their shared understanding and history. Although such stories provide a valuable glimpse into the life of native peoples for outsiders, it is important to remember that they are seeing only a part of a rich cultural heritage.

Because all Indian languages were originally spoken rather than written, each chapter in this book begins with a quotation so that readers can experience the beauty of Native American words and stories. These passages are meant to be read aloud. By reading the quotation before the chapter, you can begin to connect with the people of that culture area. The words will take on even greater meaning if you also read the opening quotation a second time, after you have finished the chapter.

CHAPTER I

The Southeast

Behold the wonderful work of our hands and let us be glad. Look upon the great mound; it is surmounted by the golden emblem of the sun; its glitter dazzles the eyes of the multitude. In it are inhumed the bones of our fathers and relatives who died on our sojourn in the wilderness, in a far-off wild country. They rest at Nunih Waiya. Our journey ends.

—*Choctaw Green Corn song*

Nunih Waiya, the huge platform mound built by the ancient Mississippian peoples, embodies the unbroken spiritual legacy that lives on in the Choctaw nation today. According to their origin story, foreigners forced the ancestors of the Choctaw to leave their old homeland in the west. The chief medicine man and prophet planted a fabussa (pole) in the center of the village to direct their journey. In the morning, the pole leaned toward the rising sun, so the people proceeded east, eventually crossing a great river, which they named Misha Sipokni ("That Whose Source and End Are Beyond

Knowing"), from which "Mississippi" was derived. The people wandered eastward for many years. According to tradition, they could not leave their dead behind, so they carried the bones. Weary from their migration, the people decided to rest. Winter was coming and they needed to plant their seed corn. They came to a great mound that seemed to lean toward a creek, so they named it Nunih Waiya, or "Leaning Mountain." They planted their corn and wintered there, later reaping such a bountiful harvest that they said, "Nunih Waiya really produced." When they set up the fabussa in the middle of their encampment, at the moment of sunrise, it began to dance, pushing itself deeper into the earth. When it settled without

Left: The Constitution of the Cherokee Nation was published in 1827 at New Echota, Georgia.

Opposite: In 1838, George Catlin painted a Seminole leader, The Cloud, dressed in the European-American finery adopted by his people. Several hundred Seminole eluded capture and deportation to Oklahoma; today, their descendants live in southern Florida.

CONSTITUTION

OF THE

CHEROKEE NATION,

MADE AND ESTABLISHED

AT A

GENERAL CONVENTION OF DELEGATES,

DULY AUTHORISED FOR THAT PURPOSE.

AT

NEW ECHOTA,

JULY 26, 1827.

PRINTED FOR THE CHEROKEE NATION,
AT THE OFFICE OF THE STATESMAN AND PATRIOT,
GEORGIA.

leaning in any direction, the chief said, "It is well, here we remain." After they buried the bones of their ancestors, the people sang the song that opens this chapter. They had found their home, the Great Mother.

The corn that supported both the prehistoric Mississippian and the historic Choctaw cultures grew abundantly in the rich alluvial valley of the Mississippi River's middle course, from the mouth of the Missouri south to Vicksburg. Beans, squash, and sunflowers also grew easily in the fertile soil, whose productivity was rapidly renewed by silt from seasonal floods.

The Southeast was a rich land of meandering rivers, broad valleys of oxbow lakes, and vast swamps of cypress and cane. Fish and waterfowl were easy to catch in the river backwaters and estuaries; deer, raccoons, and other mammals roamed the forests, which were filled with edible wild nuts, berries, and grasses.

This naturally favored area stretched from subtropical south Florida, where an abundant supply of fish and shellfish allowed the Calusa to develop a complex chief-dom without agriculture, to the low mountains of the Appalachian highlands, where the Cherokee grew crops in the fertile valleys, fished in the river shoals during the warm season, and hunted deer in the colder months. The Cherokee lived in woodlands of great variety: in their Appalachian homelands, the southern hardwood forests of chestnut, chestnut-oak, hickory, and poplar met the more northern birch, beech, hemlock, and sugar maple. South of the Appalachians, in a great crescent, lies the deep, fertile soil of the Black Belt. Most of the Southeast has mild winters, with as many as 240 frost-free days each year, and an abundant rainfall that exceeds forty inches (101.5cm) yearly in the Gulf area.

PEOPLES OF THE SOUTHEAST

Prehistorically, the Southeast was home to the Mississippian tradition, the most highly developed of Native American civilizations north of Mexico. In this complex, class-structured society, royalty lived a life of comfort and

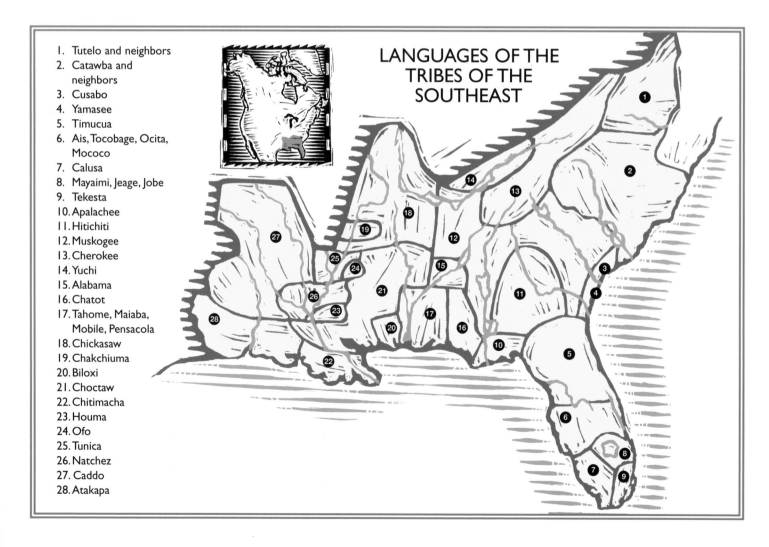

LANGUAGES OF THE TRIBES OF THE SOUTHEAST

1. Tutelo and neighbors
2. Catawba and neighbors
3. Cusabo
4. Yamasee
5. Timucua
6. Ais, Tocobage, Ocita, Mococo
7. Calusa
8. Mayaimi, Jeage, Jobe
9. Tekesta
10. Apalachee
11. Hitichiti
12. Muskogee
13. Cherokee
14. Yuchi
15. Alabama
16. Chatot
17. Tahome, Maiaba, Mobile, Pensacola
18. Chickasaw
19. Chakchiuma
20. Biloxi
21. Choctaw
22. Chitimacha
23. Houma
24. Ofo
25. Tunica
26. Natchez
27. Caddo
28. Atakapa

Left: The Hopewell celebrated elaborate mortuary ceremonies to honor their dead. This Hopewell pot, connected to Hopewellian "death cults," is decorated with hands across its surface.

Above: The Hopewell, whose culture flourished between 300 B.C. and A.D. 500, built large earthen mounds in the valleys of Ohio and Illinois, such as this one at Mound City National Historic Site, Ohio.

luxury complete with splendid houses and retinues of servants who carried the royals on litters through the streets. Several classes of citizens clustered in large cities; priests led the people in sun worship, and through a far-reaching trade network, a special class of artisans acquired the materials to create elaborately decorated and carved objects for ceremonial and burial use. This sophisticated civilization was supported by the agricultural labor of outlying villages. Its prosperity depended on the endless fields of corn planted in the rich alluvial soil along the Mississippi and its tributaries.

Many complex cultures developed within and just beyond the diverse and changing environment known as the Southeast. Beginning with the Paleo-Indian big-game hunters who moved into the area about 9000 B.C., through the Archaic and Woodland traditions that followed them, great Native American civilizations flourished long before the arrival of Columbus. Beginning perhaps as early as 800 B.C. and lasting possibly until A.D. 850, the Adena and then the Hopewell cultures

flourished in the valleys of Ohio and Illinois, just beyond the borders of the Southeast. The Adena buried their dead with their belongings on knolls and ridges, which they covered with dome-shaped mounds. After studying the life cycles of the wild plants they gathered, women began to experiment by planting their seeds. Over generations, they domesticated native North American seed plants, including squash, sunflower, goosefoot, little barley, marsh elder, and maygrass, lessening their reliance on hunting and gathering and providing a dependable food

SEMINOLE SURVIVAL

In the 1830s, the U.S. government, despite public pro-Seminole sentiment, forcibly removed most of the Seminole from Florida to Oklahoma, where their descendants live today. Small bands of Seminole survivors hid in the Everglades and other isolated areas, existing by trapping, hunting, fishing, and subsistence farming on small patches of land.

When the United States formally acknowledged the Seminole by setting aside reservation land in the 1890s, the government had trouble persuading the self-reliant Seminole to move. They continued to live in their remote camps, supplying their basic needs, but sometimes working seasonally for the money to buy a few goods such as coffee and ammunition.

By the 1930s, however, Seminole attitudes had begun to change as some Seminole developed successful cattle ranches. Many moved to reservations in ensuing years, and by 1992, most of the sixteen hundred enrolled members of the Seminole tribe lived on five reservations in south Florida.

supply that could be stored during the winter. This surplus made permanent village life possible.

Many different cultures and language groups shared Hopewell symbols and beliefs. A major part of their belief system focused on honoring their ancestors by holding mortuary activities and building elaborate ceremonial centers with burial mounds. Some of these mounds reached more than thirty feet (9m) in height and two hundred feet (61m) in circumference, thus elevating the spiritual above the everyday world. These centrally located sites played a role in Hopewell social lives as well—not only did the people lay their revered dead to rest there, but they also celebrated lavish feasts and thanksgiving ceremonies and conducted public meetings.

The Hopewell became increasingly dependent on agriculture, and the population of each village increased, leading to even greater complexity in social organization. The general population lived near their cultivated fields of corn, beans, squash, and other plants, and the elite—which included religious leaders—lived in the ceremonial center. The construction of such monumental earth mounds indicates the existence of centralized authority, with an underclass to build and a nobility to direct the construction. Their highly organized class structure included hereditary rulers, a priesthood, commoners, and specialists such as carvers, metalworkers, and traders.

For some members of Hopewell societies, trading was a full-time occupation. To gather materials that would become works of art to honor the dead, the Hopewell created one of the first major North American trade networks, a complex web of exchange that linked the Rocky Mountains to the Atlantic coast and the Great Lakes to the Gulf of Mexico. Traders obtained obsidian from Yellowstone, mica from North Carolina, and copper from

Below: In this 1938 photograph, Lilly Billy pieces fabric into sawtooth patterns and strips on her treadle sewing machine, while her sister Maggie makes dolls. Although the production of Seminole patchwork garments has become a commercial enterprise and an important source of income, this distinctive textile art continues to be an expression of cultural identity

Right: Seminole women devote much care and love to making the complex patchwork designs that are so distinctively Seminole.

On the Cherokee Reservation in western North Carolina, a mother carries her baby on her back. From mid-June through late August the Cherokees present Unto These Hills, an outdoor drama that portrays the history of the Eastern Band of Cherokee Indians. A federally recognized tribe, the Eastern Band is a sovereign unit of government that is neither an instrument of the U.S. federal government nor a political subdivision of the state government.

SEMINOLE AND MICCOSUKEE PATCHWORK

By the turn of the century, nearly every Miccosukee and Seminole family owned a sewing machine. Cecile R. Ganteaume, in *Creation's Journey*, has traced the development of Seminole and Miccosukee patchwork. During the first decades of the twentieth century, Miccosukee women began to incorporate simple, uncomplicated bands of patchwork into their husbands' shirts and their own long skirts. From the mid- to late-1920s, patchwork became popular among both Seminole and Miccosukee women; they developed more intricate designs, highlighting them with rickrack and piecing more colors of fabric into sawtooth patterns and stripes. When U.S. Route 41 between Tampa and Miami opened in 1928, tourists began buying dolls and patchwork clothing.

Instead of relying on a variety of highly nutritious crops, as had the Hopewell, the Mississippian peoples focused on maize, a new, highly productive strain of corn, which led in turn to a rapid population increase. To produce maize on a large scale, they relied on increasingly centralized economic and social controls. This greater centralization of authority meant that they had to produce even larger agricultural surpluses. Mississippian societies became increasingly stratified. Townspeople supported a royal class that presided over ceremonies from the central, flat-topped mounds. Unlike the mounds of the Adena and Hopewell, however, these were not burial mounds.

Aggressive, expansive Mississippian peoples dominated the river systems of the interior, bringing groups such as the Choctaw, Creek, and Chickasaw into their historic locations not too many centuries before Spain sent Hernando de Soto to conquer the land in 1539. Later, French explorers and settlers encountered the Mississippian-influenced Natchez, who lived along a tributary of the Mississippi River in nine towns with elaborate ceremonial centers, large plazas, burial mounds, dwellings, and temples for worship. Divided into four classes, Natchez society was composed of commoners, Honored Men, Nobles, and the

the Great Lakes. Artisans then carved the obsidian into blades and the mica into delicate silhouettes of birds, animals, and human hands. Over hot fires, specialists hammered the copper nuggets into sheets, which were then cut into ornaments, rings, and axes.

The Mississippian culture began to emerge by A.D. 700 and lasted for nine hundred years. As with the Adena and Hopewell, Mississippian civilization influenced many native societies, spreading a complex web of shared ceremonials, including elaborate mortuary rituals, art motifs and symbols, and practices such as the black drink ceremony.

Left: Charley, who lives with his family on Cherokee land in North Carolina, prefers sports to any other subject in school. Most public school curricula continue to be oriented toward non-Indians and fail to meet the needs of native children.

Above: The Choctaw were especially fond of ishtaboli, an ancestral form of lacrosse. Seeking to control the ball, a huge number of players stomped, tackled, hit, kicked, and trampled each other. Around 1834, George Catlin painted this scene of ishtaboli.

and to support an aristocratic class. An intricate web of social and political relations bound people together. However, the arrival of Europeans hastened the decline of these urban centers by decimating native populations through disease and warfare. In 1731, the French sold the survivors—except for the few who escaped to join the Chickasaw—into Caribbean slavery.

Between 1500 and 1700, at least thirty tribes lived in the broad coastal plain bordering the Atlantic Ocean and the Gulf of Mexico; but soon thereafter, European diseases, trade, warfare, enslavement, deportation, and the usurpation by Europeans of tribal lands decimated the native peoples. Entire peoples, such as the Calusa, were completely wiped out. In the 1560s, the Calusa may have included as many as ten thousand people; by 1750, none remained.

ruling class, the Suns. The Great Sun, venerated as a god, lived atop a grand mound and was carried on a litter.

Societies such as the Natchez required large numbers of people to construct the mounds, to celebrate mortuary rituals, to hold thanksgiving ceremonies for successful harvests,

SOUTHEASTERN LIFE: THE CHOCTAW

When the Choctaw reached Nunih Waiya, the Great Spirit divided them into clans, or iksa, which were then split into two groups called moieties, the Imoklasha and the Iholahata. Clanship became the foundation of Choctaw culture when the Great Spirit gave the people laws governing marriage. The Choctaw were forbidden to marry within their clan, and children belonged to their mother's clan. Choctaw family life was subordinated to the iksa. Children inherited their status from their mother and her clan. The matrilineal nature of clan membership meant that it was a boy's mother's brother—his maternal uncle—who taught him the skills he would need in hunting, warfare, and communal games. In turn, the boy's father taught such life skills to his sister's sons.

The Choctaw depended upon deer and bear as their main sources of meat; women made their husbands' breechclouts, leggings, and moccasins and their own skirts, shawls, and moccasins from tanned deer hides. Deer antler tips became arrowheads; the sinew and entrails became bowstrings and thread. Men caught fish with spears and arrows or by dragging nets of brush and vines through the water. They also poisoned fish with winterberries, buckeye, and devil's shoestring. As with hunting, the men shared their surplus with the rest of the village.

Although important sources of food, hunting and fishing were only secondary to agriculture. In addition to corn, the Choctaw raised beans, melons, pumpkins, peas, tobacco, and sunflowers in little plots around their cabins. They burned the underbrush and girdled the trees to clear the land and used a bent stick, the shoulder blade of a bison, or a piece of flint to make a crude hoe. The Choctaw were known as great farmers, producing such a surplus of corn and beans that they were able to sell these to neighboring tribes. Women and children cultivated their family's small cornfield and gathered fruits, seeds, nuts, and roots from the forest. Each family stored its supply of corn in a rude crib raised eight feet (2.4m) above the ground; other food was stored inside the family's home. Using wooden mortars and pestles, women ground corn into meal. They also boiled corn with pumpkins, beans, or bean leaves to make a nutritious stew.

SEMINOLE SURVIVAL

Based on differences existing in the Creek Confederacy dating back to the 1700s, the more conservative Miccosukee claimed a cultural origin and identity separate from the Seminole. When the Seminole organized in 1957 to receive federal recognition, a group of Miccosukee traditionalists followed a respected leader, Buffalo Tiger, in seeking their own identity. Not only do the more than four hundred Miccosukee speak a separate language, but they also continue to maintain more traditional ways of dress, religion, and life.

Without productive tribal economic development, however, the Seminole suffered from serious unemployment. They began selling state tax-free cigarettes in the 1970s under the dynamic leadership of Chairman Howard Tommie. In 1979, under Chairman James Billie, they introduced a high-stakes bingo game that offered a jackpot exceeding ten thousand dollars. The Seminole have since opened more bingo parlors, using the revenues to augment federal funds to improve the quality of life on the reservation. The tribe must provide its own fire and police protection, which costs approximately one million dollars a year. As government cutbacks diminish allocations to the tribe, bingo revenues help the Seminole to care for their elderly, establish a credit union, expand tribal cattle herds, and fund tribal scholarships.

Tribal leaders have also focused their energy on improving the quality of education for their people. By 1992, more than thirty Seminole held college degrees; many of these graduates work for the tribe and provide valuable role models.

THE GREEN CORN CEREMONY TODAY

In June 1983, anthropologist Harry Kersey, Jr., attended this several-day ceremony at the Miccosukee Reservation located on the edge of the Everglades National Park. As a guest of the Bird Clan, Kersey saw the camps of various clans arrayed in the traditional manner facing the dance area. A late rising new moon bathed numerous large chickees (open-sided wooden homes traditionally built atop platforms) in a pale silver glow, silhouetting their steeply pitched roofs against the treeline of a cyprus stand. Steamy rain showers, gnats, and mosquitoes made the oppressively hot, humid night seem interminable. Around 2 A.M. an exhorter roused the audience, calling for a traditional stomp dance. Thirty or so men and women of all ages formed pairs and began singing a rhythmic chant as they danced around the massive fire. The staccato sound of box turtle rattles fastened to dancers' legs punctuated the dance rhythm.

Ingraham Billie, a ninety-three-year-old medicine man, emerged from a small structure beside the dance ground. Kersey described Mr. Billie as "a stooped, frail figure.... He was only slightly above five feet [152cm] in height, and white hair fringed the turban he wore; his colorful garb sparkled in the reflected glow of the flames while he briefly prayed aloud, then abruptly returned to the seclusion of his shelter."

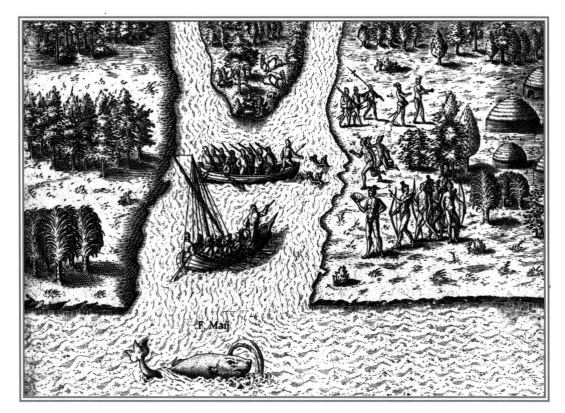

Based on a LeMoyne painting, this DeBry engraving depicts Hernando de Soto's encounter with the Timucuans on the St. John's River in Florida. News of European barbarism spread quickly as town after town was plundered of its valuables and the inhabitants seized, tortured, and forced into slavery.

The forest also provided material for spoons and dishes. Men covered pine frameworks with hickory siding to build cabins. The women wove baskets and mats from cane, which also provided the material for beds that were built several feet above the ground to minimize contact with fleas. With deerskins or bearskins for a mattress and bison skins or blankets for covering, these beds were quite comfortable. The beds were the Choctaw's only furniture, serving also as tables and chairs.

An infant felt secure wrapped in blankets inside a Choctaw cradle—ullosi afohka—which the mother carried on her back, hung from a tree, or rested upright on the ground. Once the baby began to crawl, the mother carried him or her on her back wrapped in a blanket. The next stage saw the child fastened to the back of a pony; by the age of four, children rode by themselves.

Choctaw children enjoyed an atmosphere of relative freedom. At his or her birth, the child was given a mare and colt, a cow and calf, and a sow and pigs. The child began adulthood with these animals and their offspring as the beginning of his or her stock.

Girls learned how to care for the household and the crops from their mothers. Maternal uncles taught boys how to use weapons, especially the bow and arrow, for hunting and warfare, as well as how to play traditional ball games. Boys developed their strength and skill by running races, wrestling, lifting weights, and participating in other contests.

Each Choctaw town had a chief; a war chief, or tascamingoutchy; two lieutenants under the war chief; and an assistant chief, or tichou-mingo, who arranged ceremonies, feasts, and dances, and who spoke for the chief. The people within each village belonged to one of four orders: the grand chief, village chief, and war chief; the beloved men,

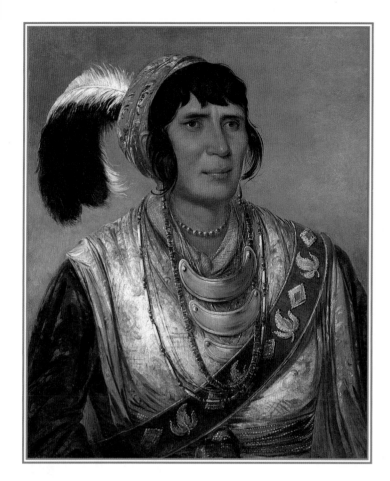

Seminole leader Osceola led an intense guerrilla war from the swamps of Florida. In 1837, soldiers seized him under a white flag of truce. The following year, shortly before Osceola's death, George Catlin painted this portrait of him at Fort Moultrie, South Carolina.

CHOCTAW BANDOLIERS

The everyday clothing of the Choctaw resembled that of their neighbors, but at traditional gatherings, they blended European-American styles with dress that was distinctively Choctaw.

On such occasions, men wore store-bought trousers, cotton hunting coats with ruffled collars and cuffs, glass-bead necklaces, and native-made silver earrings. Women embellished commercial or native-made shirts with stitched appliqué for their husbands and decorated their one-piece cotton dresses and ruffled aprons with appliqué. Shawls, ornamental hair combs, and several glass-bead necklaces completed their attire. But the true symbol of Choctaw pride came in the magnificently beaded bandoliers—sashes worn across the chest and over the shoulder or as belts.

Cecile R. Ganteaume of the National Museum of the American Indian, writing in *Creation's Journey*, described Choctaw bandoliers—eskofatshi—as symbolic of their determination "to retain not only land in their traditional territories, but their distinct cultural identity."

Native peoples throughout the Southeast made finely woven bandoliers and belts that incorporated beads, but Choctaw, Koasati, and Alabama Indian bandoliers were distinguished by their red wool tradecloth background and the fineness of their beaded embroidery in geometric designs.

or atacoulitoupa; the warriors; and the supporting people, or atac emittla.

A general council and three district chiefs joined the towns into the Choctaw nation. Each mingo, or district chief, represented one of the three geographic divisions of the nation: the Oklafalaya, or "Long People," lived in the northwest; the Ahepatakla, or "Potato-Eating People," lived in the northeast; and the Oklahannali, or "Sixtowns," lived in the southeast.

The men in each district elected their mingo; although those who were descended from a mingo were considered as successors, they also had to display leadership, courage, and ability, which were measured by achievements in a special field, such as warfare or healing. Both a mingo and a village chief persuaded their followers not by coercion, but by example and oratory. Scholar Arthur DeRosier, Jr., described the Choctaw political organization as an "amazingly efficient" system of "elected officials, unlimited debate, civilian rule, and local self-government."

Town councils discussed issues that were of common concern, such as making repairs on public buildings or tilling village fields. Each person was listened to with respect. Consensus was the goal, but if some individuals disagreed after the decision had been made, they remained silent. Choctaw councils used no coercion, nor did they punish dissenters.

Choctaw law was strict, especially concerning land ownership, theft, and murder. All land was held in common by the nation, but individuals had the rights of occupancy and use. Theft was punished by whipping and ridicule. When a man committed murder, he was brought before a group of warriors known as the "Light Horsemen," who had the power to arrest, try, and punish violators. If he was found guilty, the warriors designated the place and time of his punishment; the punishment for murder was death. The man was then expected to appear at the appointed hour and place. Sometimes a man requested a stay of execution to take care of family affairs or to participate in a hunt, dance, or major ball game. The condemned man always appeared; to have failed to do so would have brought disgrace to his iksa and to himself as a warrior.

Clan loyalty was so fundamental to Choctaw life that members of the iksa had the right to avenge a murder either by killing the murderer or one of the murderer's clansmen who had volunteered to die in his place. All murders were avenged, even if it took years of planning to do so. As a result, clan wars that involved entire chief-doms were not uncommon.

However, such retaliation was not allowed to blossom into war without careful consideration of the consequences. First, the general council conferred with the chief; only after formal debate and discussion did they decide to make war. With veterans of previous wars, a Great Warrior exhorted young men to join the battle. The volunteers then engaged in a three-day period of fasting and purification followed by a ritual feast before their departure.

Hunting and warlike games helped natives hone their fighting skills. Stalking deer, for example, required the stealth and patience of a successful warrior. The hunters enticed their quarry with animal cries. Using bows and arrows, axes, knives, tomahawks, and later rifles, Choctaw

men also killed bear, turkey, pigeon, otter, beaver, opossum, rabbit, and raccoon. For squirrels and birds, they used a blow cane—a hollow, straight cane about eight feet (2.4m) long from which hunters shot arrows by blowing in one end. An experienced hunter was so accurate with a blow cane that he seldom missed his mark at fifteen or twenty feet (4.5 or 6m).

A hunt might take men away from the town for several months, with a "big hunt" lasting an entire year. Sometimes more experienced hunters traveled to the other side of the Mississippi River into Osage country, land of the

THE RESURGENCE OF CREEK TRADITION

Today, most members of the Creek nation live in Alabama and Oklahoma. Formed when various tribal groups moved inland to escape settlers, the Creek nation settled along Ochese Creek and the Chattahoochee River. British traders from Charleston, South Carolina, gave the Creek their English name because they lived along interior waterways.

Once a huge inland confederacy, the Creek reached the height of their power just before the American Revolution: they could muster six thousand warriors from their hundred or so towns. After settlers and land speculators moved into their territory, the Creek split into two groups: the anti-American Upper Creek, who fought on the British side in the War of 1812, and the pro-American Lower Creek, who fought with the Tennessee militia under Andrew Jackson at the Battle of Horseshoe Bend. Despite their loyalty, the Lower Creek were forced by Jackson to cede two thirds of the territory of the entire Creek nation to the United States only months later.

Between 1820 and 1840, the Creek were forced to move west to Indian Territory; the Treaty of 1832 dissolved the Creek Nation in the east. Thousands died along the route west, and those who survived were forced to live in an alien climate without the necessities the government had promised them.

Although the dispossessed Creek struggled to rebuild their nation in the west, some remained in southwestern Alabama. Many intermarried with whites and were assimilated into the general population; others, however, fought to maintain a separate, distinct community at the headquarters of Perdido

Creek. In 1984, the Poarch Band of Creek became a federally recognized tribe; as of 1992, the band had approximately 1,850 enrolled members.

In 1985, the seventeen-hundred-seat Poarch Creek Bingo Palace opened, becoming the cornerstone for other economic ventures of the tribe. With federal funding, the Poarch Creeks have financed social and community services, fire and police protection, and adult education programs. They have also built family and senior citizen housing and a new tribal center, and they have equipped and staffed a health clinic. In 1988, the Poarch Band established a Creek Indian Arts Council.

One of the people who serves on the advisory board of this council is anthropologist J. Anthony Paredes, who has worked closely with the Poarch Creek since 1971. Paredes described the resurgence of Creek tradition among the Poarch. In 1987, the Alabama Creeks hired Sam Proctor, a traditionalist Creek from Oklahoma, to teach native heritage and Muskogee language classes.

Since then, some Alabama Creek have begun to participate in Creek ceremonies in Oklahoma; they are working toward reestablishing a traditional plaza with a properly sanctified fire in Alabama. Paredes believes that federal recognition brought "a broad-based sense of satisfying closure to processes of community transformation and ethnic intensification that began more than forty years earlier." Not only did recognition bring political and economic opportunities, it also "gave official reaffirmation to the Poarch people's long-standing awareness of their Indian identity."

warlike enemies of the Choctaw. Pushmataha, a great Choctaw leader made his reputation on just such an expedition. A few years later, Pushmataha went on a big hunt to Oklahoma, where a war party of Caddoes surprised the Choctaw warriors—killing everyone but Pushmataha. He remained in Oklahoma for months, befriended by a group of Spaniards who took him on trading expeditions. From these experiences, Pushmataha gained much knowledge of the land, which was to prove valuable in later negotiations with the U.S. government. After returning home, Pushmataha led many Choctaw parties west to hunt bison and to fight the Osage. One interpretation of his name, A push matahaubi, means "One Whose Tomahawk Is Fatal in War."

Of all community activities, the most popular was ishtaboli, an ancestral form of lacrosse that was the traditional Choctaw ball game. This game, widespread among the eastern woodland peoples, was played with special fervor by the Choctaw, whose playing field was filled with some seven hundred players. These men of status, warriors, and nobles were resplendent in egret feather costumes and their town, iksa, and moiety insignia. In 1899, scholar H.B. Cushman awaited their arrival, reporting that the players, "strong and athletic men, straight as arrows and fleet as antelopes…were heard in the distance

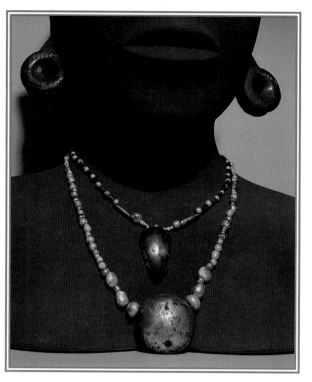

This jewelry was worn by a Hopewell male. The ear spools and necklaces are made of pearl beads from freshwater shellfish, and the pendants are of beaten copper.

advancing toward the plain from opposite sides, making the heretofore silent forests ring with their exulting songs and defiant hump-he! [banter]."

Once the game began, players stomped, trampled, tackled, and kicked their opponents to control the ball. The artist George Catlin described the melee: "In these desperate struggles for the ball, hundreds of strong young Indian athletes were running together and leaping, actually over each other's heads and darting between their adversary's legs, tripping and throwing, and foiling each other in every possible manner, and every voice raised to its highest key in shrill yelps and barks!"

Men approached ishtaboli with the same sense of anticipation and dedication that they brought to warfare; indeed, death and disfigurement on the playing field were not uncommon. Known as "the little brother of war," ishtaboli was not undertaken lightly; as with warfare, preparation for a game of ishtaboli included prayer, body painting, sacred medicines, dancing, and singing.

Good players were revered figures; Catlin painted Tullock-chisk-ko (He-Who-Drinks-the-Juice-of-the-Stone), the most distinguished ball player in the Choctaw nation, in 1834. Ishtaboli is so much a part of Choctaw culture that a towa (stickball) and kabucha (stickball sticks) appear on the emblem of the Mississippi Band of Choctaw Indians today.

Choctaw spiritual beliefs centered on the sun, which was endowed with the power of life and death; fire, which possessed intelligence, acted in harmony with the sun.

The Choctaw shared a traditional belief in the immortality of the soul. Until the 1820s, when Christian missionaries began to exert pressure to change, the Choctaw placed their dead on a scaffold, allowing the body to dete-

Noted for their elaborately decorated and carved objects for ceremonial and burial use, the prehistoric Hopewell people often depicted human hands in their artwork, as on this stone disk.

riorate into bones, which were then placed in a special house within the village until they were buried in a sacred mound. Once or twice a year, the Choctaw held a settlement-wide mourning ceremony.

The most important ceremonial feast was the annual Green Corn Dance, which lay at the heart of much of Southeastern ritual life, having been celebrated by the Seminole, Cherokee, Choctaw, and others. Mississippian beliefs live on in the Green Corn Ceremony, an elaborate thanksgiving and renewal festival that has been described as a combination of "Thanksgiving, New Year's, Yom Kippur, Lent, and Mardi Gras" by anthropologist Charles Hudson.

One of the best accounts comes to us from John Howard Payne, the author of *Home Sweet Home*. In 1835, Payne observed the Green Corn Ceremony at the Creek town of Tukabahchee, which led him to write, "I never beheld more intense devotion.... It was beginning the year with fasting, with humility, with purification, with prayer, with gratitude.... It was pausing to give thanks to Heaven, before daring to partake of its beneficence."

The Creek people also celebrated a corn ceremony, which coincided with the ripening of the first corn. Centered around the theme of spiritual renewal, this eight-day ceremony focused on the peoples' relationships with the plant and

Mounds such as this one in Ohio are the most distinctive legacy of the Hopewell culture.

animal worlds and with their fellow human beings. Part of this spiritual renewal included affording amnesty to criminals for all crimes except murder.

As with most ceremonies, the first requirements were purification and ritual cleansing. The women swept and cleaned their homes, extinguishing their hearth fires. Men refurbished community buildings. After they had finished these chores, everyone gathered at the town plaza. Village chiefs, medicine men, elders, and young warriors participated in the central, public rituals of this ceremony that ushered in the new year. Dancing and fasting were followed by the ritual eating of the new corn, a mock battle, a ritual deer hunt, ceremonial dancing, and feasting. Women took home coals from the sacred fire in the center of the plaza to relight their hearth fires for another year.

EUROPEAN CONTACT

When Europeans arrived, the old harmonies were shattered. Hernando de Soto arrived in Florida in 1540. The fatal European diseases that accompanied his expedition decimated the Indian peoples of that region, who died by the thousands. Many of those Indians who did not die from disease were slaughtered.

HAGLER

Hagler, born in 1690, became the principal chief of the Catawba Indians of South Carolina about 1748. By then the Catawba had been decimated by European disease and warfare with their traditional enemies, the Shawnee, Cherokee, and Iroquois. Hagler's diplomacy led to friendly relations with the British colonists, ensuring the survival of the Catawba people. In 1751, he traveled to Albany, New York, to attend a peace conference. In 1758, during the French and Indian War, Hagler helped the British to attack Fort Duquesne, which is located in present-day Pittsburgh, Pennsylvania. Hagler's support of the British led them to build forts along the Catawba River to protect the Catawba from other tribes, and to grant the people a reservation near what is now Rock Hill, South Carolina, in 1792. The Shawnee killed Hagler in 1763. The first memorial to an American Indian in the United States was a statue of Hagler, erected in 1826 by the state of South Carolina at Camden.

When de Soto's expedition arrived in Choctaw territory, a district chief, Tuscaloosa, met them. De Soto forced him to accompany the soldiers to Mabila, a town three days distant, but instead of fulfilling Spanish orders for provisions, Tuscaloosa sent a messenger to assemble warriors. When the Spaniards reached Mabila, Choctaw warriors attacked, killing twenty-two and inflicting nearly seven hundred arrow wounds on 150 of the survivors.

Europeans left the Choctaw alone for the next 150 years, until the French began settling the region around the lower Mississippi. They befriended the Choctaw with presents and honors, using them as buffers against other tribes. This common European strategy led to much inter-tribal bloodshed: in the early 1700s, the French used Choctaw mercenaries to help annihilate the Natchez.

By the early seventeenth century, French, Dutch, and English settlers had established outposts in the southeastern United States. In 1670, when Charleston was founded, the British captured and bought Indians for the slave trade. As massive depopulation broke aboriginal chiefdoms, survivors reorganized themselves into new towns, tribes, and confederacies.

As their traditional hunting grounds were restricted more and more each year, the Choctaw had to go farther to find game, relying increasingly on the Europeans' weapons and ammunition, which revolutionized the art of hunting and warfare. European traders offered farming implements that were also much more effective than the natives' own. The Choctaw were eager to obtain these superior tools and weapons, as well as clothing, domesticated plants and ani-

WILMA MANKILLER

"All of the people I encountered—the militants, the wise elders, the keepers of the medicine, the storytellers—were my teachers, my best teachers."

—*Wilma Mankiller in her recent autobiography,*
Mankiller: A Chief and Her People

Stepping down from her post in tribal government to teach at Dartmouth in the autumn of 1995, she left behind almost two decades of service to her people, first as a volunteer, later as the first woman elected deputy chief, and finally, in 1987, as principal chief of the Cherokee Nation. An inspirational leader, Mankiller says the key to the Cherokee's success is that they never give up. Tribally owned businesses, including defense subcontracting plants and horticultural operations, have come from community rebuilding. The Cherokee continue to thrive, undertaking such projects as the construction of a multimillion-dollar hydroelectric facility, while at the same time caring for the needs of families in small communities.

Mankiller's history and personal vision are deeply interwoven with the history and knowledge of her people: "Especially in the context of a tribal people, no individual's life stands apart and alone from the rest. My own story has meaning only as long as it is a part of the overall story of my people."

She grew up in rural and, later, urban poverty. Born in 1945 in the Rocky Mountain community in eastern Oklahoma, Mankiller moved to San Francisco with her family when she was eleven, under a Bureau of Indian Affairs relocation program. Mankiller got her first taste of the "fickleness" of the government's policy toward Indians when the pledge of oppor-

tunity turned out to be life in a housing project. In 1969, she participated in the occupation of Alcatraz Island, which, for her, became "a watershed experience," because it was "the first time I had seen people who had the nerve to stand up and challenge the system in that particular way."

These early experiences of Indian self-determination have inspired her present work for the revitalization of tribal communities: "It is my hope that those idealistic moments have blended with the perspective that luckily comes with maturity. It makes for a vintage mixture that has helped to sustain me against all odds, against real and imaginary foes, and even against death itself." These lessons, combined with her own innate tenacity, helped her to survive a devastating head-on collision that resulted in seventeen operations and two life-threatening diseases.

One quality that makes Mankiller remarkable is her ability to rise above the past and to work continually toward balance and harmony. Even though she vividly recounts the brutality of her people's history—most notably their forced relocation on the Trail of Tears—and her firsthand experience of racial prejudice, she rejects the role of victim, attributing these injustices to a lack of understanding. Most Americans were never taught "about the high degree of organization and democracy many tribal cultures had attained prior to the invasion of the Europeans."

Wilma Mankiller's life embodies the Cherokee way of "being of good mind. That means one has to think positively, to take what is handed out and turn it into a better path."

At the Battle of Lundy's Lane, a combined force of British, Canadian, and Shawnee warriors repelled a U.S. invasion force. Although the Indian fighters were instrumental in the victory, this painting is fairly typical in that no Indians appear in it.

mals, and foods such as sugar, coffee, and flour, and thus became dependent on traders—often going into debt. Indeed, trade became so widespread that for nearly a hundred years, the Choctaw language was the lingua franca among European traders and native peoples in the region.

The Choctaw quickly lost their economic independence as their wants multiplied but their means of satisfying those desires decreased. Choctaw reliance on trade goods led to the disappearance of traditional handicrafts and a dependence on European-made cloth, tools, and weapons. Traders also introduced alcohol, which further undermined the structure of tribal life.

In return for European goods, the Choctaw had only three important items to trade: skins and furs, their own skills, and land. First, European traders enticed native hunters to kill more deer than were necessary for the tribe to supply European demands for leather. Indian hunters had long been careful to avoid overhunting to maintain deer herds; they now disregarded their previous caution because of the massive commerce in deerskins. However, the Choctaw kept their deerskin monopoly for only a few decades; aggressive early American frontiersmen, driven by

acquisitiveness and a desire to make their fortunes, soon surpassed Choctaw hunters.

Next, the Choctaw bargained with the new U.S. government for food and clothing in return for their knowledge of the country as scouts and for their ability as soldiers, siding with the United States in the American Revolution and in the War of 1812. After the War of 1812, however, frontier warfare ended. With nothing else to trade, the Choctaw had to sell their land to live.

In the 1750s, European traders and settlers had brought African slaves to the Choctaw and Chickasaw. African-Americans performed labor, such as clearing fields and building roads, which enhanced the value of Choctaw property. Over time, the institution of slavery encouraged social stratification as the ownership of slaves became a marker of social status among the Choctaw.

By the nineteenth century, these and other factors had eroded Choctaw social structure, tearing apart the matrilineal clan-based structure of their society. The importance of men increased because of their dominant roles as hunters and traders, threatening the traditional status of women as providers in what had been an agricultural society. Traditional family structures weakened when traders married Choctaw women and settled in villages. Their mixed-blood sons and daughters tended to identify more with their European fathers than with their Indian mothers. Christian missionaries worked to undermine traditional

In 1982, more than one thousand Native Americans gathered in Philadelphia's Penn Treaty Park for a weeklong celebration commemorating the hundredth anniversary of the signing of William Penn's "Great Treaty." Forty-five tribes participated; Nordeen Nishone Luce (shown here) was among the Cherokee representatives.

native beliefs; they stressed the importance of the nuclear family over the clan and emphasized the value of men over women, reversing traditional values.

In 1811, a Shawnee chief named Tecumseh (1768–1813) and his brother, the "Prophet," traveled to the Southeast to enlist the Choctaw, as well as other groups, in a holy war to expel the Europeans. He hoped to form a great Indian confederacy, stretching from Canada to Florida, that would at best annihilate the newcomers and at least keep them contained to the east of the mountains.

The Creek, the most discontented of Southeastern Indian nations, received Tecumseh with admiration. They were the largest confederacy in the South and also the least acculturated and most warlike group. Caught geographically and politically in between the United States and Spanish Florida, they were subjected to the intrigues of these two countries, who tried to pit the Creek tribes against each other. Although the Chickasaw and the Choctaw were deeply bound as allies and spoke almost the same language,

the Creek and the Choctaw had been bitter enemies since the beginning of their history.

The Choctaw leader, Pushmataha, opposed Tecumseh's plans—not because he wanted the assimilation of his people, but because he knew that winning such a war was impossible. A realist who had observed the bad as well as the good aspects of European culture, Pushmataha knew that victory lay with the side that had the most men and arms. Pushmataha countered Tecumseh's compelling call to arms with firmness by pointing out the fallacy of Tecumseh's proposal: "A war against a people whose territories are now far greater than our own, and who are far better provided with all the necessary implements of war with men, guns, horses, and wealth, far beyond that of all our races combined forebodes nothing but destruction for our entire race."

Aware that the young Choctaw warriors were restless and eager to gain war honors, Pushmataha decided to support the Americans. He followed the ancient custom of summoning a general council, and several thousand Choctaw gathered to discuss the matter. In the War of 1812, the Choctaw joined their future to that of the growing American Republic.

Three years after the Battle of New Orleans, the Choctaw invited missionaries to come to their towns, not for their religious influence, but for the education they brought. Younger Choctaw, especially those of mixed blood, felt that the only hope for their people lay in education and the adoption of white customs. Divisions erupted between more traditional pure-bloods and mixed-bloods who adopted more assimilated lifestyles. Native Americans of mixed ancestry owned farms, trading posts, ferries, and inns.

Although Pushmataha and his warriors had made Mississippi safe for American settlers, by 1819 the mad rush for land—especially on which to grow cotton—put pressure on the Choctaw to give up all their land east of the Mississippi River.

Many leaders were convinced that tribal survival depended on the adoption of American ways. The Cherokee established a tribranch government with a bicameral council and a court system. The Cherokee Sequoyah (1770–1843), driven by the need for a written constitution and official records, developed a written Cherokee language.

The Choctaw, Chickasaw, and Creek also created constitutional governments and developed prosperous economies based on the most recent agricultural techniques. The Choctaw had extensive cattle herds and raised cotton, which they carded, spun, wove, and made into clothing. Choctaw finery at ball games included cotton dresses and shirts worn with traditional deerskin moccasins and leggings. Among these peoples, a class of affluent Indian elites emerged who lived in two-story plantation houses and owned slaves and fine carriages. This led Northern visitors to designate these nations, along with the Seminole, the Five Civilized Tribes.

But settlers still hungered for land; from 1828 on, climaxing in the Trail of Tears in 1838, hundreds of thousands of Indians were forcibly moved westward to Oklahoma. The main period of Choctaw expulsion occurred between 1831 and 1833. For the Choctaw, this meant a trek of 350 miles (563km) through a wild country of vast swamps, impenetrable canebreaks, swollen rivers, and dense forests. Those who were forced westward during

This sculptor, an Oconaluftee (Tennessee) Cherokee, carries on his people's ancient tradition of hand-carving ceremonial masks.

the winter of 1831–32 also endured one of the worst blizzards in the history of the South. A cholera epidemic swept down the Mississippi River, killing many the following summer. About eighteen thousand Indians were moved west during the 1830s, which does not include the enormous number who died on the trail and during the first few years in the new territory.

Some Choctaw successfully resisted two removal efforts, remaining in the Southeast. From the beginning of removal until after the Civil War, the Choctaw lived as landless and impoverished squatters and sharecroppers, barely eking out a living. By the turn of the century, however, they had formed rural communities with their own churches and schools. Finally, in 1944, the United States government acknowledged them with a sixteen-thousand-acre (6,400ha) reservation.

TOWARD THE FUTURE

The presence of Native Americans in the Southeast today is a powerful testimony to their cultural strength against overwhelming odds. Significant numbers of Seminole, Creek, Choctaw, Cherokee, and Catawba still live in Florida, Alabama, Mississippi, North Carolina, and South Carolina, 150 years after the first removal efforts. In 1990, these states, along with Georgia, Kentucky, Tennessee, Arkansas, and Louisiana, had a combined Indian population of 211,000 people.

The eastern Choctaw have their tribal headquarters at Philadelphia, Mississippi. There they have established a development company and created an industrial park, which houses greeting card plants and factories in which they made wiring harnesses and radio speakers for automobiles. Every year, they celebrate a four-day Choctaw Indian Fair that begins in the early morning of the first Wednesday after the Fourth of July. Begun in 1949 to revive and preserve Choctaw heritage, the Choctaw Indian Fair includes dancing, entertainment, pageantry, and crafts such as basket weaving, beadwork, and needlepoint on traditional styles of clothing. The highlight of the fair is the Choctaw Stickball World Series, the oldest field sport in America.

CHAPTER 2

The Northeast

✚

We thank our Creator that we are gathered here, healthy in body and mind. We thank our Creator for creating Mother Earth for us to walk on and enjoy…plant life on Mother Earth for survival; the weeds for healing, some weeds for eating, and also as Earth's decoration. We give thanks for the underbrush; saplings for healing; the trees, especially the maple, that are a haven for the animals and birds, and that also give us heat for comfort and cooking. We give thanks for the animals, especially the deer, that give us food; the birds, that give us pleasure through their singing in the early morning hours.

—*Iroquois Thanksgiving address, from* Creation's Journey

This prayer conveys the profound interconnectedness of the Northeastern peoples with the world around them, particularly with the great trees of the primeval forests. The foremost feature of the northeastern landscape, thick forests of broad-leaved deciduous trees, carpeted the valleys, and even denser forests of conifers reached up the sides of the hills and mountains. These trees provided physical and spiritual sustenance to Northeastern peoples, who collected the trees' nuts, fruits, and syrup and hunted the wildfowl, rabbits, and woodchucks who lived in or around the trees. From the trees' bark and timber, they built houses, canoes, and fortifications for their palisaded villages.

Iroquois children spent their infancy in cradleboards carved from trees. These cradleboards were decorated with carved and painted designs of a flowering tree holding a mother bird feeding her young, a representation of a sacred tree said to exist in the Sky World. The white pine was the symbol of the Great Law of Peace, the constitution of the Iroquois Confederacy. If a person grasps the white pine's roots and follows them back to the tree, he or she will find peace and unity.

The once-densely forested Northeast encompasses an immense area with three main divisions: the Coastal zone, which includes Canada's Atlantic Provinces and the U.S. seaboard down to North Carolina; the Saint Lawrence lowlands, which comprise southern

Left: Drums were often made of painted rawhide stretched to cover a wooden frame. This Ojibwa (Chippewa) drum bears a painted birdlike figure with raised wings.

Opposite: The Iroquois consider the stars of the Pleiades constellation to be seven men dancing in the heavens.

Ontario, upper New York State, and most of the Saint Lawrence and Susquehanna valley; and the Great Lakes–Riverine area.

The Coastal zone embraces the coastline as far north as the Gulf of Saint Lawrence, where many rivers flow into excellent harbors and an extensive river system allowed swift transportation by birch-bark canoe. Severe winters and a short growing season made the cultivation of grains or even root crops risky; subarctic winds might chill the air as early as September. The Coastal people lived hardy, wandering lives, searching the thick forests for moose, deer, bear, caribou, and rabbit, and the coasts and rivers for shellfish, salmon, smelt, and herring. Much farther south, the flat, breezy coastal plains were bordered by one of the world's richest fishing slopes. Amid thick forests teeming with game, lush growing areas were ideal for crops such as corn. The warmer climate and longer growing season in the south led to greater reliance on agriculture. As a result, denser populations, organized into rudimentary states, replaced the hunting bands typical of the north.

In the Saint Lawrence lowlands, mountains cradled low, luxuriant river beds and valleys, where people had easy access to a great variety of freshwater fish in the lakes and streams. Deer, bear, and small mammals abounded in forests of birch, beech, maple, and elm. Because of the fertile soil and long growing season, people here relied more on agriculture than did their neighbors to the northeast.

Farther west, the Great Lakes–Riverine area included deciduous forests, often of highly prized birch. In the Wisconsin-Minnesota region, the northern peoples gathered wild rice (*Zazania* sp.), while southern peoples relied on agriculture. Mostly hunter-gatherers, some of the peoples of the Great Lakes–Riverine area were able to grow squash, beans, and corn; those farthest west hunted bison.

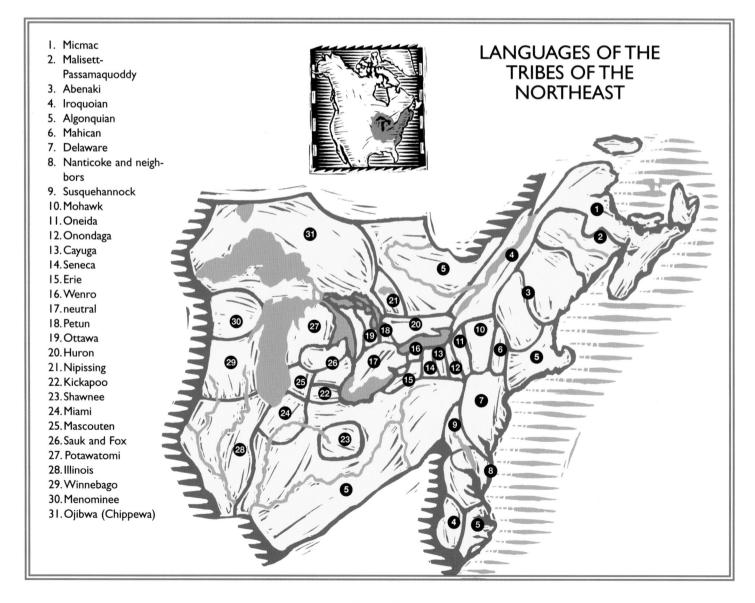

LANGUAGES OF THE TRIBES OF THE NORTHEAST

1. Micmac
2. Malisett-Passamaquoddy
3. Abenaki
4. Iroquoian
5. Algonquian
6. Mahican
7. Delaware
8. Nanticoke and neighbors
9. Susquehannock
10. Mohawk
11. Oneida
12. Onondaga
13. Cayuga
14. Seneca
15. Erie
16. Wenro
17. neutral
18. Petun
19. Ottawa
20. Huron
21. Nipissing
22. Kickapoo
23. Shawnee
24. Miami
25. Mascouten
26. Sauk and Fox
27. Potawatomi
28. Illinois
29. Winnebago
30. Menominee
31. Ojibwa (Chippewa)

PEOPLES OF THE REGION

An Algonquian woman lashes saplings together to make the framework for a wigwam. In the background, another woman covers a wigwam with skins.

Most of the peoples of the Northeast were Algonquian-speakers; some spoke Iroquoian languages; only the Winnebago of the Lake Michigan area spoke a Siouan language. The Eastern Algonquians lived from the Maritimes into North Carolina along the Atlantic coast and immediately inland from this area. The southernmost Algonquians, such as the Carolina Algonquian-speakers and those who belonged to the Powhatan Confederacy, were the first in the Northeast to experience sustained contact with Europeans. European diseases and warfare decimated their populations so quickly that they had no time to reorganize themselves into new groups. The northernmost Eastern Algonquians, such as the Micmac in Canada's Maritime provinces and the Maliseet of western New Brunswick, relied more on hunting and gathering than agriculture; they lived in hunting bands. Other Eastern Algonquians included the Passamaquoddy and Abenaki of Maine, the upper Connecticut valley, and Massachusetts; the Pocumtuck and the Nipmuch of central Massachusetts; the Massachusett of the coast and islands of southeastern New England; the Narragansett of Rhode Island; the Mohegan and Pequot of Connecticut; the Unquachog, Shinnecock, and Montauk of eastern Long Island; the Mahican of the upper Hudson; the

Delaware of New Jersey and Delaware; and the Nanaticoke and Conoy of Maryland.

The Saint Lawrence lowlands were home to the Iroquoian-speaking groups, who lived in fortified villages supported by intensive horticulture, fishing, and hunting. The Iroquois did not begin to feel the impact of European settlement until the 1760s, when settlers began to push north. The peoples of the Iroquois Confederacy included the Mohawk, Oneida, Onondaga, Cayuga, Seneca, and, later, the Tuscarora. Not all Iroquoian-speaking peoples belonged to the confederacy; others are the Huron—itself a nation of five tribes—the Wyandot, the Susquehannock, the Nottoway, and the Cherokee.

The Central Algonquians depended on horticulture, although not to the same extent as the Iroquois. Wild rice was such a major staple for the Menominee diet that they derived their tribal name from the Ojibwa word for wild rice—manomini.

Great leaders, including Pontiac and Tecumseh, emerged from this region to unify the nation. Central Algonquians included the Ojibwa, Potawatomi, Menominee, Sauk, Fox, Kickapoo, Miami, Illinois, Shawnee, and Cree.

THE MICMAC

"We are thy children; for we can know no origin but that which thy rays have given us, when first marrying efficaciously, with the earth we inhabit, they impregnated its womb, and caused us to grow out of it like the herbs of the field, and the trees of the forest, of which thou are equally the common father.... Sun! Be thou favorable to us in this point, as thou art in that of our hunting, when we beseech thee to guide us in quest of our daily support."

—*Micmac invocation to the sun*

In the sixteenth century, the Micmac lived in the region south and west of the Gulf of Saint Lawrence: the Maritime Provinces plus the Gaspe Peninsula. The four thousand or so Micmac, who relied primarily on inland hunting, were quite different from the Iroquois, who were intensive agriculturists. According to their tradition, the Micmac had knowledge of agriculture but had "forgotten" it; their short, cool summers precluded the cultivation of maize.

When the rivers froze and the bears retired to hollow trees, the Micmac year began. This was the Moon of Moose-calling (September), the time when people dispersed over their territory into hunting groups. Winter camps were small, with only one or two wigwams set up near a dependable source of water, in their owners' trapping or hunting territory. Each family, consisting of a chief hunter, his wife and children, and perhaps a dependent relative, lived in one wigwam, with each family member assigned a place.

After the husband had selected the wigwam's location and marked off the circular or elliptical floor plan, his wife and daughters covered a wooden framework with sheets of birch bark, animal skins, woven mats, or evergreen boughs. The women then erected an inner lining of swamp grass mats to provide insulation and to prevent leakage. Atop the dirt floor they laid fir branches covered with moose hides; they then shielded the entrance with a skin flap. After a family had children, they built a second entrance so that there was a hunters' door, through which the men entered, and a women's entrance, although widows could use either. The chief hunter and his wife slept at the center of the south wall. Nearby were their unmarried daughters and, at their left, the parents of either the husband or wife. Sons slept opposite their parents with a central hearth between them. Newly married couples built their own wigwams.

Either a nuclear family or two or more men and their families worked as economic units: women paddled fishing canoes and carried game into camp from where the men had killed it. In the Moon of Fat, Tame Animals (October) and the All Saints' Day Moon (November), men wore snowshoes as they stalked large game, such as elk, using stone-tipped arrows or lances to kill them. They also flushed beavers from their lodges, put deadfalls over beaver paths, and set split-log traps in the water near beaver dams. Men enticed bears with baited snares of boughs or bushes or speared them when the bears were hibernating.

The most important food animal was the moose. Men wearing decoy costumes with antlers would stalk moose (which travel singly). In the winter snow, men wearing snowshoes would run a moose down. During the moose's rutting season, hunters made and used a moose call—a conically shaped instrument that imitated the sound of the call made by a solitary moose to attract a mate. Birch-bark moose calls were indispensable in the harsh, cold woods of the north. After luring a moose, hunters would trap it with overhead snares made of twisted birch branches.

The Moon of Frost-fish (January) was the time to harpoon seal and to fish for ponamo (tomcod), which had spawned

The divine ancestor of the Iroquois sits on the Great Turtle's back in this illustration of the Iroquois creation story.

CREATION

According to the Iroquoian Creation story, the world was once a chaotic water world. When a pregnant woman fell from the Sky World, ducks and geese flew up to break her fall with their wings and carried her to the Great Turtle, master of all animals. The Great Turtle sought the assistance of the water animals, such as beaver, otter, and muskrat, to dive deep into the almost bottomless sea to bring up bits of earth that had fallen from the sky with the woman. He then asked the woman to dance upon the magic earth on his back to bring the island of earth into existence. The Great Turtle then generously offered his back as a foundation to hold up the earth island, creating a haven of order.

In some Iroquois nations, the Turtle clan is the most prominent political and religious clan because it symbolically holds up the society just as their mythic ancestor supports the earth. This story conveys an essential Native American value: all beings are related and interdependent, and each being has the responsibility to contribute his or her unique power to the continuation of life. Today the Iroquois continue to practice these values. Seneca Tom Hill said, "Our culture is not static but dynamic and ongoing, and we were placed on Turtle Island to re-create the good works of creation."

under the ice during the Chief Moon (December). The great hunt for beavers, otters, moose, bears, and caribou began in the Snow-blinding Moon (February) and lasted until the middle of the following month.

Spring was a joyous time for the Micmac because they returned to their permanent encampments, gathering in groups of two hundred or more. Months had passed since they had seen their friends and relatives, and there was much news to share. The rivers swarmed with spawning fish beginning in the middle of the Spring Moon (March). Using bone fishhooks, nets, and weirs, the men caught smelt, followed by herring, then sturgeon, and salmon at the end of the Moon of Egg-laying (April). The women gathered abundant shellfish and searched through the islets for the eggs of Canadian geese and waterfowl.

During the summer, from the Moon of Young Seals (May) until the Moose-calling Moon (September), the Micmac had no concern about food because it was so easily collected. The men caught abundant cod on the coast, and women continued to gather many kinds of shellfish, as well as the eels that spawned in September. Throughout the Moon of Leaf-opening (June),

Above: The painting on this Cree man's shirt depicts a battle between warring tribes on foot and on horseback; strips of porcupine quillwork decorate the shoulders.

Below: An Algonquian child wore this elaborately decorated caribou-skin coat.

the Moon when Seafowl Shed Their Feathers (July), and the Moon When Young Birds Are Full-fledged (August), the people remained in their summer settlements, spread out along a section of the coast or riverbank. Family groups feasted, danced, and socialized together, giving young people an opportunity to meet. During the summer festivities, an official "Watcher of the Young People" informed the chief and the community of the names of marriageable young people and created matches among them.

A boy who wanted to marry a girl might arrange to work with her father for a given period of time. Although couples were free to live where they chose after marriage, many Micmac believed that it was best to live with the bride's family for the first year or more.

Newborns were washed, wrapped, and placed in cradleboards that mothers carried on their backs. Children learned from imitation and from admonition to treat elders and parents with respect; in turn, parents treated their children with great tenderness and affection. From their fathers, boys learned how to hunt and to make implements and weapons out of wood, stone, bone, and shell. A man held a feast when his son took his first step or killed his first game, however small. But only when he hunted and killed large game, such as moose, was a boy considered to be a man. Girls helped their mothers by gathering firewood and carrying water, cooking, processing skins, making clothing, fashioning bark containers, and fetching game into camp from the woods. They also learned how to decorate with porcupine quills and embroider with moose hair.

Complex ceremonials surrounded death. Those who were dying dressed in their finest clothes, sang their death song, and recited their adventures. They might have a feast for all who came to visit, if supplies were available. When death occurred, formal mourning began; the corpse was carried out through a special opening instead of the door. The body was tightly wrapped in the fetal position and buried in a deep grave. At the house of the deceased,

mourners gave a funeral feast that included orations for the deceased man or woman. Because the Micmac returned to their permanent villages each year, they did not remove the bones of the dead.

Micmac beliefs and values centered on the Great Spirit, a creator who was the same as the Central Algonquian Manitou. However, the Micmac differed from other Algonquians by identifying the Great Spirit with the sun and by offering the sun invocations, such as the prayer at the beginning of this section.

The hero Gluskap, the transformer, was a mythic figure associated with the Eastern Algonquians. He was not a divinity, but like Coyote in the west, Gluskap changed elements in the world largely for his own amusement. He

BIRCH BARK

For the Algonquians who lived in and along the shores of the western Great Lakes, the bark of the white birch, also known as the paper or canoe birch, provided the material for their physical and spiritual needs. The Algonquians used birch bark for transportation, shelter, utensils, hunting and fishing tools, and as a writing device. From birch bark, they fashioned durable wigwams and maneuverable canoes; created cooking pots, dishes, needle cases, winnowing trays, and leak-proof containers for maple syrup and water; and made moose calls and fishing nets.

The Abnaki considered the birch to be sacred material, naming it Gluskabe, after one of their hero gods, who asked the tree to take care of them. According to myth, birds migrated back to their northern forests in the spring when they were released from the birch-bark containers in which they had been caged. Because these birds were thought to bring summer warmth and regrowth, the Abnaki said that life emerged from the birch-bark container along with the migrating birds.

Ojibwa women created birch-bark cutouts in the shapes of people, animals,

and familiar everyday objects. Some of these cutouts served as patterns for beadwork designs on moccasins. The Ojibwa also carved birds, plants, and shrubs into the outer surface of their birch containers. Frances Densmore, who spent more than twenty years in close contact with the Ojibwa, described snowy evenings spent sitting around a brightly burning fire inside a warm winter wigwam. Young men reclined near drums, while old women told stories, illustrating their tales by running around the fire to act out different characters. As they listened to the stories by the firelight, younger women fashioned birch-bark cutouts and dishes on which they carved away a layer of bark to create intricate designs.

Birch bark also provided the material for pictographic scrolls, which were used for recording songs and teachings of the sacred Midewiwin. The Midewiwin, or Great Medicine Society, was the heart of the spiritual life for the peoples of the western Great Lakes, such as the Ojibwa, Menominee, Sauk, Fox, Kickapoo, and Winnebago. Midewiwin teachings held

that long life and good health were attained through a combination of ceremonial practices and ethical conduct in everyday life. An Ojibwa apprentice of the powerful Midewiwin Society often inscribed memory scrolls on birch bark to help him learn sacred songs and stories to be recited at ceremonies. The paperlike qualities of the bark made it an ideal surface on which each individual could record his own mnemonic devices for help in remembering song and story sequences.

The Ojibwa knew how to remove bark without destroying the tree. The bark came off in large sheets, and its resinous quality made it impervious to shrinking or stretching. Furthermore, because its grain runs around the tree trunk, the sheets are easy to sew together along the length of a canoe. White cedar was used for the canoe's framework, and hard maple for the paddles and the thwarts that held the gunwales together. From the black spruce came resin to waterproof the seams, which were sewed together with the roots of the same tree.

OJIBWA BANDOLIER BAGS

Speaking of spiritual expression in daily life, Earl Nyholm, a renowned Ojibwa canoe maker whose canoes are in the collection of the American Museum of Natural History, said that he puts his spirit into every canoe he makes. Ojibwa women, reflected Nyholm, go through this same spiritual process in making their heavily and intricately beaded bandolier bags. A respectable Ojibwa would not consider himself properly dressed for a formal occasion unless he wore at least one of these bags, with its wide strap across his chest. Nyholm, in *All Roads Are Good*, described these bags as "a labor of love, almost like giving birth to a child. Just to make one bag would be a year off from her whole life." Inspired by the feeling of the Woodlands, women covered the bags with stylized designs of flowers and fruit. More geometric designs depicted other aspects of their world, such as the formation of geese flying overhead.

who lived in each of these three main areas. The geography of this region also played a major role in Indian-European interactions. Although French and British explorers and fishermen frequented the coasts of the Northeast, their smaller numbers meant they had less impact than the Spanish farther south, whose diseases and brutality decimated the native population. In the northern regions, the fur trade remained the basis of Indian-European relations until the nineteenth century. Although whites did not seize their land, the growing demand for furs eventually pitted tribes against each other in economic competition, leading them to develop confederacies to protect hunting territories and trade routes from encroachment. Farther south, the longer growing season and abundance of good soil brought an influx of land-hungry settlers.

could bring rain or change the wind, turn people into frogs, give the beaver his tail, and help the Micmac fight the Europeans.

The Micmac based their actions on four general principles. First, they believed life was everywhere, in both visible and invisible forms. Various forms of life could change into one another; thus, some kinds of animals and people were not what they appeared to be. Second, the behavior of the ancestors, who were great hunters and who generously shared their kill, was a guide for their descendants; it was important to emulate this dignity, resourcefulness, and courage. Third, although chiefs had exceptional abilities, everyone was equal and should practice being generous, courageous, and fair. With only occasional exceptions, moderation was always better than excess. Finally, in comparison to non-Indians, Indians possessed unique powers, such as supernatural helpers and "Indian luck," or keskamizit, which enabled them to accomplish things with great ability or speed.

The great variation in geography, vegetation, drainage, and climate, as well as the availability of natural resources, strongly influenced the character and cultures of the Indians

Opposite: In this 1836 painting by George Catlin, Iroquois Chee-ah-ka-tchee holds her child, swaddled on a cradleboard.

Right: French explorers encountered the Winnebago in present-day Wisconsin, south of Green Bay and as far inland as Lake Winnebago. Many Winnebago still live in their Wisconsin homeland, but others were forced to move to Iowa; later they moved to Minnesota and then again to Nebraska. This 1971 photograph shows a Nebraska Winnebago dancer celebrating the annual powwow.

The year 1979 marked the fiftieth annual Winnebago powwow at Wisconsin Dells, Wisconsin. Here, two boys in full ceremonial regalia await their turn to dance.

THE IROQUOIS CONFEDERACY

Best known of all Iroquois nations were the Five Nations of the Haudenosaunee, whose confederacy took its name from the longhouses in which they lived. These five nations came to think of themselves as embodying an enormous longhouse that stretched 250 miles (402km) across what is now New York State. The Onondaga, who lived in the center of the region, near the Haudenosaunee Trail—their principal communication route—were said to represent the central corridor of the Great Longhouse and were the Firekeepers for all five nations. The westernmost group, the Seneca, were the Keepers of the Western Door, and the Mohawks were the Keepers of the Eastern door. Together with the Oneida and the Cayuga, these five groups formed the Iroquois Confederacy, later expanding to include the Tuscarora. The actual date when the confederacy was founded is unknown, but historians agree that it existed before Columbus' arrival.

The tribes created the confederation as a means for the peaceful resolution of conflict among the member nations. Before the existence of the League of the Iroquois, when a man murdered someone of another nation, the victim's people sought revenge through raids, which often erupted into war between the nations.

Deganawidah, a Huron spiritual leader, had a vision of a great spruce tree that reached through the sky to communicate with the Great Spirit. His vision also showed him how to put these ideals into practical application through the Great Law, a set of rules and procedures for settling hostilities. Yet few people accepted his message, perhaps because of Deganawidah's speech impediment. In his travels, he met the compelling Mohawk orator, Hiawatha. Together, Hiawatha and Deganawidah were able to communicate effectively the Great Spirit's message of peace, unity, and clear thinking to the Five Nations. When they finally convinced the nations to relinquish warfare among

themselves, they planted the Great Tree of Peace on Onondaga land near present-day Syracuse, New York.

The Iroquois put these ideals into practice by forming a confederacy of forty-nine chiefs. These representatives settled their disputes peacefully through agreements and ceremonies at annual gatherings, with each decision requiring unanimous consensus among all member nations.

The women of each matrilineal clan chose their most respected woman to be Clan Mother who, in turn, chose a clan chief, called a sachem, to represent the lineage on the basis of his integrity, wisdom, vision, and oratorical ability. The Clan Mother also had the power to depose the chief if he did not conform to the will of his lineage.

Iroquoian values of unity, democracy, and liberty and the effective ways in which the nations of the confederacy put these ideals into action quickly attracted the attention of American leaders. Even before the American Revolution, these leaders sought the help of the Iroquois in their attempt to replace the British monarchy with a democratic alternative; in 1755, they formulated the Albany Plan of Union based on Iroquoian ideals.

In Philadelphia, in May and June 1776, American leaders asked Iroquois chiefs to attend the weeks of debate on the Declaration of Independence. Impressed with the sincere efforts of the Americans, an Onondaga sachem gave John Hancock, who presided over the debates, the name Karanduawn, which means "The Great Tree." In 1790, Thomas Jefferson led others in a toast to the United States Constitution as an "[Iroquois] tree of peace" that sheltered the Americans "with its branches of the union."

In 1777, the Iroquois Confederacy allowed each nation of the League to follow its own path in the war between the British and the Americans. This division of allegiance ended the League's military power.

The Iroquois were fortunate because their inland location and the buffer of their Algonquian neighbors to the east protected them from the initial onslaught of European intrusion. The Eastern Algonquians, on the other hand, had to bear the brunt of the impact of the first European encroachment.

Unlike the heavy oceangoing canoes of the Northwest peoples, the canoes of the Algonquians had to be light enough to be easily carried from one stream to the next.

In the 1500s, during sporadic contact with European fishermen, the Micmac began to prize trade items such as metal knives, axes, and kettles. Contact with Europeans, however, left them susceptible to diseases, leading to a sharp decline in the Micmac population. By the middle of the seventeenth century, smallpox, alcoholism, and warfare further reduced the population to about two thousand.

Beginning in the seventeenth century, the Micmac joined other tribes for mutual defense against the English and the Iroquois Mohawk. The Abnaki, Malecite, and Micmac formed one of the first federations by exchanging plans, news, and embassies. In traveling from tribe to tribe, ambassadors carried wampum as a form of identification, a badge of accreditation. These strings of tubular beads, made originally from the purple sections of hard clamshells, symbolized treaty-making throughout the Northeast. Although the Iroquois later used them as a form of compensation, wampum strings were never used as money.

The French period (1600–1760) brought many changes to Micmac culture, notably their involvement in the fur trade and an alliance with the French against the British. British colonists arrived soon after hostilities ceased in 1760, taking over Micmac lands. Under a variety of treaty arrangements, the British established Indian reserves, which became smaller over time because of settler encroachment. British colonists took over the fur trade, the number of fur-bearing animals decreased, and Micmac lands declined, leading the Micmac into a semisedentary lifestyle.

Most men used their traditional knowledge to work in lumbering, guiding, and commercial fishing. By the mid-nineteenth century, Micmac men became a rural proletariat working at seasonal jobs that no one else was willing to accept for minimum wages. They were excluded from permanent jobs with the lumber mills and railroads. The year 1910 brought improved medical services and schools on some reserves. During World War I, some Micmac served in the Canadian army. After the depression and World War II, government assistance for veterans brought renewed, although short-lived, prosperity. Other federal programs helped to modernize the reserves with electricity, television, and educational programs. However, discrimination led to unemployment, even for educated Micmacs. In the 1960s, Micmac men, like the Mohawk, discovered an occupational niche in "high steel." Although dangerous, this construction work on high-rise buildings paid well; furthermore, it was compatible with Micmac values and concepts of social time.

THE LENNI-LENAPE

In the century before European contact, the Lenni-Lenape—as the Delaware call themselves—numbered between nine and twelve thousand and lived in a loose network of villages that stretched from what is now Delaware to areas much farther west and north. They located their villages on river meadows surrounded by sovereign hunting territory that belonged to that particular village. The Delaware covered their domed wigwams, oblong arched buildings, and rectangular longhouses with bark. At least once a week, men, women, and children physically and spiritually purified themselves by steaming in the village sweathouse, located beside a creek.

The Delaware nation was more a loose federation of lineages than one large tribe. Like the Iroquois, they were matrilineal, and when a tribal sachem died, his rank passed to a close relative in the sachem's mother's bloodline, such as his sister's son or brother. Delaware sachems had little political power and led by persuasion rather than force. Tribal elders had to reach a consensus before the sachem could negotiate treaties or commit his people to war. Children learned the ways of their elders by sitting silently on the fringes of adult gatherings.

The spiritual world of the Delaware revolved around the Great Spirit, the Creator and the spiritual force that lives within all things. The world was alive with spirits who heard and answered prayers through sunrises and spring rains, bountiful hunts, and plentiful harvests. All things—humans, animals, rocks, and trees—had souls. The forces warmed, fed, and healed human beings; in return, humans had the responsibility to keep a natural balance.

The Delaware, like other nations, made smoke bags of deerskin to carry tobacco and pipes. Smoking had both social and spiritual aspects: the smoke had the ability to send prayers skyward. When people made a smoke bag, they often decorated it at the top and bottom, with two identical bands of quillwork bordered by tin cones fringed with feathers. According to Seneca Tom Hill, the symmetry of the bag's design reflected the Delaware's belief that "human beings were to maintain a balance between physical and spiritual needs."

Delaware educator Linda Poolaw, writing in *All Roads Are Good*, compared traditional ways of learning with those of today. Instead of learning by silently observing their elders at council meetings, "the white man's education wants us to hurry up and find something...pop it up on a computer...read it and go take a test and pass it and, suddenly, you know it and you're smart." When she was growing up, she was taught not to demand immediate answers. Instead, "you just have to stay around

Two Winnebago men playing checkers in 1842. Today, the Winnebago live both in Wisconsin and in northeastern Nebraska. Siouan speakers, they were the only tribe in the Northeast that did not speak an Algonquian or Iroquoian language.

NORBERT S. HILL, JR.

"Many people, in their attempts to build their lives, lose touch with their own sense of belonging and of being a part of something greater than themselves. Indian leadership can facilitate this, and our dream of recovery and reemergence can facilitate Indian leadership. Great things are accomplished by ordinary people who are consumed with a dream. With no dreams and no vision, there can be no development. But energy and persistence will conquer all obstacles."

—Oneida Norbert Hill, in an article on American Indian leadership in Winds of Change

These words were intended to inspire Indian students, but they have a universal meaning that bridges ethnic boundaries. As executive director for the American Indian Science and Engineering Society (AISES), Hill raises millions of dollars for scholarships for American Indian students in engineering and science. He remembers beginning his education at the University of Wisconsin-Oshkosh in the early 1960s "as a frightened, academically insecure seventeen-year-old with a determination to do what some people were telling me I couldn't do." At that time, the college dropout rate for Native American students nationwide was 95 percent. Hill succeeded thanks to his energy and persistence and a supportive campus community.

Hill has become an eloquent voice for effective Indian leadership: "Two words that best describe Indian people and our concerns today are 'recovery' and 'reemergence.' Recovery relates to the issue of physical and cultural survival, which is never far from an American Indian's mind. Reemergence means Indians want to survive without being assimilated into the American melting pot. Indian people seek to contribute to a greater America from within our own cultural contexts, centers and identities. Ours is a multicultural vision involving land, values, community, education, economic stability and modern skills. Grassroots commitment and creative leadership are required in order for a people to survive and then to prosper. We need to listen to our own song and feel the rhythm of our future."

Hill points out that Native Americans must lead themselves. "After a century of mostly ineffective paternalistic government intervention, American Indians are realizing that leaders from among our own people are our best representatives in the American political scene," says Hill. He emphasizes that "our greatest chances for success lie within our own grassroots efforts." In his father's words, "Speak softly, walk humbly, and act compassionately."

The key to success is reviving the spirit of community. Hill agrees with Mohican Don Coyhis, a leader in Indian community development work, who "emphasizes that spirit and intent must be aligned in order for community development to be successful. If community spirit returns, then the intention of all our programs and projects gains a hidden source of energy."

In 1992, Hill advised President Bill Clinton's education transition team. He has also been director of the Native American Educational Opportunity Program at the University of Colorado, Boulder, an education policy fellow at the Institute for Educational Leadership in Washington, D.C., and a member of the board of the National Center for Native American Studies and Policy Development at George Washington University. He has been the executive director of AISES since 1983.

His family provided successful role models. In 1899, his grandmother, Rosa Minoka Hill, was the first Indian to earn an M.D. from Women's Medical College of Philadelphia. In the 1960s and 1970s, his father, Norbert Sr., served as tribal chairman. Hill once headed the Oneida tribe's education committee, and he returns to the reservation several times a year to lecture and to visit.

Hill says that the Oneida are "building the infrastructure of the community, but they aren't there yet." It will take "at least another three to five years of continued investments in industry and the education of young people."

Hill concludes his article on American Indian leadership by quoting Lillian Roybal Rose, a Latina working to encourage crosscultural leadership, who says, "We need to learn how to make a shift, to find the creative alternative. You have to let go of the hopelessness that keeps you angry. If you're stuck in the anger, you may never see what you need to change. The creative alternative is on the other side of your anger." Hill adds, "Our work as Indian people lies on the other side of rage and despair. Individuals, communities, and leaders alike must understand how internalized oppression has affected us as Indians. This is an important first step in rebuilding Indian community."

and listen, and the answer will come to you. Just keep thinking about it, and you'll get your answer." Poolaw observed, "It's all here, we just have to take the time to find it. That will be the beauty and balance of the learning process."

This sense of reflection, of taking the time to sit and allow one's surroundings to speak to the spirit, emerges in Delaware art. Poolaw, whose father is a Kiowa, a Plains culture, and whose mother is Delaware, a Woodlands culture, said that each tribe's beadwork design is indicative of its cultural origin. Kiowa designs, which are "geometrical and sometimes based on dreams and visions," reflect their nomadic lifestyle. In comparison, Delaware designs reflect "a more sedentary Woodlands lifestyle, in which people had time to sit and observe nature, and thereby copy or imitate it more realistically."

THE HURON

Of the sixteen different Iroquoian peoples in the Northeast, the Five Nations of the Iroquois Confederacy are best known. The term "Iroquois" has thus come to refer to the Mohawk, Oneida, Onondaga, Cayuga, and Seneca, whose confederacy extended from Schoharie Creek west of Schenectady, New York, to the Genessee at Rochester, New York. After 1722, the Confederacy expanded to become the Six Nations when these nations were joined by the Tuscarora, who had come north from North Carolina a decade earlier.

Little is known about the early history of any Iroquois-speaking groups in this region, except for the Huron, a group that did not join the Iroquois Confederacy. In the 1630s, the French developed a fascination with Indian lifeways and customs; this was attributed to accounts of Huron life by French writers. After the midcentury, when any Huron survivors, along with the Iroquois-speaking Petuns, Neutrals, and Eries, had been dispersed among the Five Nations, literate Europeans had lost their fascination with native peoples. Thus, the richest accounts of earliest times describe the Huron, who called themselves Ouendat.

Five tribes—the Attignawantan, Attigneenongnahac, Arendaronon, Tahontaenrat, and Ataronchronon—made up the Huron Confederacy or Nation, which included thirty to forty thousand people by the time the French arrived in the early 1600s. Even before then, the Huron had joined with many of the Algonquians to create alliances for offense and defense against the Iroquois Confederacy, with whom they were constantly at war.

Each Huron tribe had representatives to the league council and village chiefs. At least once each year, they held confederacy councils to renew and strengthen ties of friendship and to plan offensive strategies against their enemies.

In 1855, a group of Winnebago moved to a small reservation at Blue Earth, Minnesota, where they became expert farmers. However, whites responded to the 1862 Sioux uprising in Minnesota by demanding the removal of all Indians, including the Winnebago, who had not participated in the uprising. Of the 1,934 Winnebago taken from Blue Earth, only 1,382 survived the removal, carried out during the harsh winter of 1862.

canoes and pine for resin, firewood, and palisade posts. In times of famine, they gathered acorns from oaks.

Even more important than the species of trees was the size of the secondary forests near their village. The Huron were unable to use heavy timber because of their limited technology and instead relied on ten- to twelve-inch (12.5 to 30.5cm) diameter logs for the construction of their villages. For a six-acre (2.4ha) single palisaded village that would house one thousand people in thirty-six longhouses, they needed a minimum of twenty thousand poles and 162,000 square feet (15,066 sq m) of bark roofing. Most villages, however, had double or triple palisades.

Huron longhouses, similar to those of the Iroquois Confederacy, varied in size depending on the size of the families who lived there. Average longhouses were about twenty-five by one hundred feet (7.5 by 30.5m) and about twenty-five feet high. Hearths were set in the central passageway, a corridor about ten to twelve feet (3 to 3.5m) in

Many Native American objects are in European museums. This Algonquian hide painting, collected in 1786 by A.M. Fayolle on behalf of French royalty, was displayed in 1934 in the Ethnological Museum of the Trocadero in Paris.

Located between Lake Simcoe and Georgian Bay, an arm of Lake Huron, Huron country was a land of moderate fertility surrounded by tangled cedar swamps and alder. Small rivers and steep, boulder-strewn, recessional shorelines separated the four major upland areas of Huron territory.

Because agriculture provided three-quarters of their food supply, the Huron settled in permanent palisaded villages spaced fairly closely together. They carefully selected a site for a village based on its proximity to a spring or other water source, arable soils, available firewood, and young secondary forest, as well as the defendability of the location. A defensive village position, preferably one bordered with steep slopes, was essential because Iroquois warfare depended on surprise attacks rather than sieges.

The Huron used cedar and elm bark as roof material for their longhouses; they used birch bark for utensils and

width in front of the longhouse sleeping platforms, which stretched the length of the lodge. Every two nuclear families on opposite sides of the central corridor shared a fireplace; each family lived in an area twelve to twenty feet (3.7 to 6m) long. Women stored corn casks and firewood in vestibules at both ends of the longhouse.

Men built new longhouses in the spring when the sap was rising, making the bark and wood more pliable, which enabled them to construct the slightly rounded ends and vaulted roofs of Huron longhouses more easily. A double row of staggered posts two to four feet (61 to 122cm) in diameter comprised the outer walls. For insulation against the cold winters, the Huron wove sheets of elm, cedar, or ash bark between the posts. Smoke escaped through roof openings, and doors opened at either end or on the sides near the ends; in cold weather, these openings were closed with sheets of bark or skins.

To the Huron, the longhouse embodied the values of family solidarity, economic cooperation, and rule by mutual agreement. They projected these longhouse values onto the village, the tribe, and the Huron nation.

The Huron relied on hunting more to provide hides for clothing than for meat; they began their year's activities in early March, when men tracked deer to places where the deer had sought shelter from the deep, ice-encrusted snow of late winter. From the time they returned from the deer hunt until mid-May, the men fished for spawning walleye, sucker, pike, and sturgeon. Women prepared the fields for planting by burning the brush to the ground; men burned off brush only when they were clearing new fields. At the end of May, women planted soaked corn kernels— nine to ten in each hole— placed several feet apart.

Although some men stayed home to defend the village, most left on trading or war expeditions. Both trading and warfare provided adventure so that Huron men could gain prestige and prove their manhood. Most men traded to acquire goods that they could convert into social status through ritualized gift-giving. Gifts were expected during participation in ceremonies and to take part in gambling. Men fulfilled their social obligations by providing for their extended families and by sharing with the needy; generosity increased a man's social standing.

Before the French brought the fur trade and introduced European goods, the Huron traded most extensively with Algonquian peoples such as the Ottawa. The Ottawa, who traded over distances of eight hundred to fifteen hundred miles (1,287 to 2,413.5km), exchanged fish, fur, dried berries, reed mats, and other products for Huron wampum, nets, and pigments. Although the Ottawa were their primary trading partners, the Huron traded their pottery to groups as far away as the Ojibwa, who lived on the east shore of Lake Superior. The Huron controlled the aboriginal trade from the Saint Lawrence Valley into Ontario and traded so extensively that Huron became the lingua franca of the region, which meant that Algonquian tribes and the Winnebago, who spoke a Siouan tongue, had to learn the Huron language for trading purposes.

The two major reasons Huron men undertook warfare were to gain prestige and to avenge the murder of blood relatives. Only in the late 1630s, after the introduction of the fur trade, did they begin to fight wars for territorial gain or hunting rights.

In the late 1640s, intent on acquiring the fur-bearing areas controlled by the Huron, the Seneca, Onondaga,

IROQUOIS ANTLER CARVING

Tuscarora Richard Hill, Sr., writing in *Creation's Journey*, described native artists as "bridge-builders" because "by making things of beauty and belief," they "keep their people's values, ethics, and ways of thinking alive." Art bridges differences between ancient worldviews and modern realities.

Hill's father spent thirty-five years as an iron worker, a different kind of bridge builder, who built long bridges and tall buildings with steel. But at the age of fifty-five, Hill's father discovered his artistic side when he began carving deer and moose antler, an art his ancestors had practiced centuries before. Hill's father belongs to the turtle clan: identifying with these animals, he primarily carves turtles in addition to deer, bear, eagles, and corn.

Hill says that his father believes that the Creator is guiding his hand as he carves and that he is simply freeing the form that rests within the material. He still marvels at his father's gift, which he developed only in the last twenty years. "His gift," concluded Hill, "has become my reason to believe in the power of the living spirit that connects us to the land, the animals, the plants, the celestial beings, and all our relatives."

Cayuga, and, at times, Oneida destroyed entire Huron villages to gain control of the fur-bearing areas.

While men were fighting and trading during the summer, women spent much of their time in the fields weeding and protecting the corn from pests, at times staying in small shacks in their fields for days. During these stays, however, they had to be wary of Iroquois warriors, who often attacked small parties working away from the village.

Women spent the end of August and the beginning of September harvesting, drying, and storing the corn. They hung harvested corn on poles under the roofs of longhouses. Once the corn was dry, the women shelled and stored it in large, corn storage casks.

Men returned from trading and warfare in time to prepare for the large autumn deer hunts. Deer congregated for the rutting season—the last half of October—in the oak areas of Ontario, a few days' journey to the south of Huron territory. In early November, the men came back from deer hunting only to leave immediately for fish stations: bark houses near the fall spawned runs of whitefish, lake trout, and cisco. Each fishing house had a "fish preacher" who ritually addressed the fish, telling them that the Huron honored them and did not burn their bones. In a brief ceremony, the men offered tobacco to the water. They dried, smoked, and stored the fish for winter.

The Huron celebrated their success in harvesting, fishing, hunting, and trading with ceremonies, feasting, and social

Although there were some formalized political and religious offices with limited authority, on the whole, Native American societies were basically egalitarian. Few positions were hereditary, and most leaders were chosen on the basis of personal qualities and individual merit.

activities. They practiced onderha—a spiritual relationship with the land—to maintain the balance and harmony in their world. This included ceremonial practices and beliefs that Huron elders controlled and transmitted to their descendants. All things—animals, plants, people, rocks—had a soul or spirit; the most powerful spirits controlled the daily affairs of human beings. Of all spirits, the sky was considered to be the most powerful, because it was in charge of all natural phenomena. The Huron burned tobacco in its honor and invoked the presence of the sky when they concluded a treaty or gave a promise. All living things were in the care of Sun, the grandson of Moon.

THE IROQUOIS TODAY

Today, the Iroquois are forging a lifestyle that blends ancestral wisdom with modern technology. They work as ironworkers, steelworkers, artists, teachers, and other professionals. Yet they continue to teach and speak Iroquois languages, to celebrate great ceremonies of thanksgiving, and to recite the Great Law of the Haudenosaunee before meetings of the Great Longhouse on the Onondaga Reservation. Many urban Iroquois return to the reservation to renew their spiritual and cultural ties with their families.

In the struggle for sovereignty, Iroquois people have actively participated in many international treaty forums related to the rights of indigenous peoples. For nearly a century, the Iroquois Confederacy has issued its own passports, which are honored by many nations.

TOWARD THE FUTURE

Community Healing and Cultural Resurgence
"In the kind of Indian community-building that is happening for us here in Maine, people have to know that your spirit and intent are in line...[then] there are many bold things you can say, because people know where you're coming from. They know what you're feeling and that you care for them. They know they can trust you."

—Pam Francis, director of the Pleasant Point
Passamaquoddy Reservation Housing Authority

The Passamaquoddy people have suffered cultural destruction for more than two hundred years, beginning in 1794, when they ceded a land mass of approximately two thirds of what is now Maine. What was then the Commonwealth of Massachusetts, which received the land, acted in violation of the Indian Nonintercourse Act of 1790, which was designed to protect Indian land claims. The tribe did not receive federal recognition until 1978; finally, in 1980, the U.S. government paid partial restitution in the form of an $81.5 million land claims settlement split between the Passamaquoddy and the Penobscot tribes.

But the serious damage of two hundred years of history left high alcohol and drug abuse, vandalism, and unemployment rates. Angry and frustrated children broke windows at the reservation's school; when the tribe could not keep up with expensive repairs, the school was boarded up.

Writer Richard Simonelli of *Winds of Change* (summer 1995, vol. X, no. 3) described how the tribe began a program known as "Healing Wind"—Kiketahsuwiw Wowcawson in the Passamaquoddy language. At the heart of Healing Wind lies the talking circle, a tradition practiced by many Native American peoples in which a sacred object—in this case, an eagle wing—empowers the holder to speak his or her heart and mind while others listen with respectful silence. Through the continued practice of the talking circle, members of the community have established relationships with each other based on mutual trust and respect, replacing conflict with understanding and, in the process, developing an ever-greater ability to work together for the good of the entire tribe.

A few years ago, tribal member Vera Francis learned about the Colorado Springs–based White Bison organization, which is designed to facilitate community wellness based on consistency in the way community members speak and how they behave, that is, the alignment of spirit and intent. Such traditional principles promote the kind of balanced life of physical, mental, emotional, and spiritual well-being essential to community healing.

In 1993, tribal members spoke with White Bison representatives, who told them the next step was the formation of a core group. Pam Francis sought out forty people committed to four things: a substance-free lifestyle; a personal program of spiritual, emotional, physical, and intellectual wellness; a commitment to leadership opportunities; and two years of service in the program. Despite a history of conflict within the community, they eventually formed a core group based on the need for community change and commitment to their tribe.

Many activities are a part of the Healing Wind effort, including talking circles, the medicine wheel and community teachings, the smudging ceremony, outreach to the wider reservation community, the formation of Native Brothers, and the Visioning Process. In the Visioning Process, people

THE FALSE FACE SOCIETY

When Seneca Tom Hill was growing up, family elder Ezekial Hill was a member of the False Face Society. As Tom relates in *Creation's Journey*, Ezekial told him how medicine people carved masks from living trees "that consented to sacrificing a part of themselves." Tom found that "the masks had the power to focus the attention of all who saw them on natural forces that we experience but cannot understand." During the ceremonies, "the masks' power was integrated with the energies of those who wore them in a timeless ritual of healing." They taught him about "good and evil, the Creation, healing, and respect. They gave me a sense of history, too, a feeling of being part of a long chain of life."

An Algonquian word, pauau, refers to any gathering of people; today, Euro-Americans use the term derived from this word, powwow, to signify any kind of meeting, caucus, or social event. Native Americans use this term to refer to any tribal or inter-tribal event with dancing, singing, honoring ceremonies, and giveaways, as well as prayers and speeches in native languages or in English.

share their hopes, fears, and dreams; next they capture these ideas on paper. Native Brothers is a group of community men who make it possible for the children to play basketball, baseball, kickball, and floor hockey as well as to go on fishing and camping trips. By spring 1994, the windows were unboarded and natural light returned to the school. As Native Brother Sappy Lewey said, "We feel that the youth are our present. Deal with them today, not tomorrow; tomorrow will be better if we work with them today."

Today, community members have made positive changes in their lives, which have spread to community organizations. Tribal departments now cooperate for the benefit of the people. The Housing Commissioners, the Tribal Council, and the School Committee have passed leadership commitments to live by and to support the community vision.

The Passamaquoddy have written a booklet about their healing journey that documents some of the process; it is available at cost, in the hope of inspiring others to set up programs similar to Healing Wind.

The Honor the Earth Powwow

"The powwow is not a showcase or tourist attraction. It's part of the vital living culture of the people. It's important to remember what happened here many years ago. And it's important to share that with our neighbors and the non-Indian people who come here to be with us. It's that act of sharing.... this is who we are, this is what we are.... that's the reason we do this.
—*a powwow spokesman, speaking to Dave Hurley for* Native Peoples *magazine*

The Honor the Earth Traditional Homecoming Powwow has been held every summer for the last twenty-one years on the Lac Courte Oreilles Reservation near Hayward, Wisconsin. A traditional powwow rather than a contest powwow, this event includes more than 540 adult and child dancers in the dancing and Grand Entry processions, and twenty-four drums with more than 150 singers from many tribes, making it the largest traditional powwow in the Great Lakes area.

The Lac Courte Oreilles people held the first Honor the Earth Powwow to protest "the injuries to the earth and the disrespect and injustices to the tribe" caused by the dam built by the Northern States Power Company on tribal lands fifty years earlier. The tribal council unanimously rejected all the offers from the power company to build the dam on the East fork of the Chippewa River near Winter, Wisconsin, because the dam would create a vast flow that would submerge thousands of acres of forest land, tribal wild rice beds, blueberry fields, timberlands, and cemeteries.

Nevertheless, the Federal Power Commission issued a license to the Wisconsin-Minnesota Light and Power Company. The completed dam flooded a much larger area than predicted. Instead of 315.4 acres (126ha), water covered 525.5 acres (210ha) of tribal land.

Eddie Benton, an Ojibwa (Chippewa), told writer Dave Hurley about growing up "among the more traditional

THE HAUDENOSAUNEE DECLARATION

"The Haudenosaunee, or Six Nations Iroquois Confederacy, is among the most ancient continuously operating governments in the world. Long before the arrival of the European peoples in North America, our people met in council to enact the principles of peaceful coexistence among nations and the recognition of the right of peoples to a continued and uninterrupted existence. European people left our council fires and journeyed forth into the world to spread principles of justice and democracy which they learned from us and which have had profound effects upon the evolution of the Modern World....

"Brothers and Sisters: When the Europeans first invaded our lands, they found a world filled with the bountiful gifts of creation.... Everywhere the game was plentiful, and sometimes the birds darkened the sky like great clouds, so great were their numbers. Our country teemed with elk and deer, bear and moose, and we were a happy and prosperous people in those times.

"Brothers and Sisters: Our Mother the Earth is growing old now. No longer does she support upon her breast the teeming herds of wildlife who once shared this place with us, and most of the great forest which is our home is gone today. The forest was butchered a century ago to make charcoal for the forges of the Industrial Revolution, most of the game was destroyed by sport hunters and farmers, most of the bird life has been destroyed by hunters and pesticides which are common this century. Many of the rivers flow thick with the effluence of great population centers throughout the country. We see the 'scorched earth' policy has not ended.

"Brothers and Sisters: We are alarmed at the evidence that is before us. The smoke from industrial centers in the Midwest around the Great Lakes rises in a deadly cloud and returns to earth in the form of acid rains over the Adirondack Mountains,

and the fish life cannot reproduce in the acid waters. In the high country of the Adirondack Mountains, the lakes are still, the fish are no more.

"The people who plant the lands that we have occupied for thousands of years display no love for the life of this place. Each year they plant the same crops on the same land and they must then spray those crops with poisons to kill the insects which naturally infest their fields because they do not rotate crops or allow the land to rest. Their pesticides kill the bird life, and the runoff poisons the surface waters.

"They must spray also the other plant life with herbicides, and each year the runoff from the fields carries these poisons into the watersheds of our country and into the waters of the world.

"Brothers and Sisters: Our ancient homeland is spotted today with an array of chemical dumps. Along the Niagara River dioxin, a particularly deadly substance, threatens the remaining life there and in the waters which flow from there. Forestry departments spray the surviving forests with powerful insecticides to encourage tourism by people seeking a few days or weeks away from the cities where the air hangs heavy with sulphur and carbon oxides. The insecticides kill the black flies, but also destroy much of the food chain for the bird, fish and animal life which also inhabit those regions.

"The fish of the Great Lakes are laced with mercury from industrial plants, and fluoride from aluminum plants poisons the land and the people. Sewage from the population centers is mixed with PCBs and PBS in the watershed of the Great Lakes and the Finger Lakes, and the water is virtually nowhere safe for any living creature.

"Brothers and Sisters: We are alarmed that a string of nuclear power plants is being built around our country and that

Indians, people with the old ways," on the Lac Courte Orielles Reservation. "I often heard them talk of the flood and the inundation of the graves…. grown men had tears in their eyes when they talked of it. This had a profound and deep effect on me."

Nearly fifty years later, in February 1970, when the Northern States Power Company (who had succeeded the Wisconsin-Minnesota Power and Light Company) applied for a renewal of the license, the Lac Courte Oreilles asked that the Federal Power Commission reject their request for renewal. When the lobbying efforts of the power company proved too powerful, Eddie Benton, then executive director of the St. Paul chapter of the American Indian Movement (AIM), recruited help from AIM members.

They decided to stage a protest demonstration at the power dam before the license was scheduled to be renewed. More than four hundred people celebrated the first Honor the Earth Powwow on the shores of Little Round Lake on the reservation on July 31, 1971. The next morning, a hundred of them took over the Winter Dam and held it for four days. Wisconsin governor Patrick Lucey, who had been against the relicensing, met with representatives of the

at Three Mile Island in the southern portion of our ancient territories an 'accident' has occurred which is of a type of accident which could hasten the end of life in this place. We are dismayed that a nuclear waste dump at West Valley [N.Y.] upstream from one of our communities is releasing radioactive substances through our lands and into the watershed of Lake Erie. We are offended that the information about the nature of these plants is known only to the highest officials of the United States, leaving the people unarmed to defend themselves from such development and the development of nuclear power is encouraged to continue.

"We are concerned for the well-being and continued survival of our brothers and sisters in the Southwest and Northwest who are exposed to uranium mining and its inherent dangers. The mining end is the dirtiest portion of the nuclear fuel cycle and has progressed beyond questions of whether or not the machinery is dependable. Already vast amounts of low-level radioactive uranium tailings have been dumped in cities and used in building materials of dwellings and public buildings over a wide area of the Southwest. People have died, and many more can be expected to die.

"Proponents of the Nuclear Fuel Cycle issue statement after statement to the people, urging that the nuclear reactors are fitted with safety devices so sophisticated that a meltdown is only the most remote of possibilities. Yet we observe that no machinery or other invention made by human hands was a permanent thing. Nothing humans ever built, not even the pyramids of Egypt, maintained their purpose indefinitely. The only universal truth applicable to humanmade devices is that all of them fail in their turn. Nuclear reactors must also fall victim to that truth.

"Brothers and Sisters: We cannot adequately express our feelings of horror and repulsion as we view the policies of industry and government in North America which threaten to destroy all life. Our forefathers predicted that the European Way of Life would bring a Spiritual imbalance to the world, that the Earth would grow old as a result of that imbalance. Now it is before all the world to see—that the life-producing forces are being reversed, and that the life-potential is leaving this land. Only a people whose minds are twisted beyond an ability to perceive truth could act in ways which will threaten the future generations of humanity.

"Brothers and Sisters: We point out to you the Spiritual Path of Righteousness and Reason. We bring to your thought and minds that right-minded human beings seek to promote above all else the life of all things. We direct to your minds that peace is not merely the absence of war, but the constant effort to maintain harmonious existence between all peoples, from individual to individual and between humans and the other beings of this planet. We point out to you that a Spiritual Consciousness is the Path to Survival of Humankind. We who walk about on Mother Earth occupy this place for only a short time. It is our duty as human beings to preserve the life that is here for the benefit of the generations yet unborn.

"Brothers and Sisters: The Haudenosaunee are determined to take whatever actions we can to halt the destruction of Mother Earth. In our territories, we continue to carry out our function as spiritual caretakers of the land. In this role as caretakers we cannot, and will not, stand idly by while the future of the coming generations is being systematically destroyed. We recognize that the fight is a long one and that we cannot hope to win it alone. To win, to secure the future, we must join hands with like-minded people and create a strength through unity. We commemorate two hundred years of injustice and the destruction of the world with these words."

After their forced removal from Minnesota, the Winnebago's enthusiasm for farming had been permanently diminished. Here, dancers participate in the annual powwow at Winnebago, Nebraska.

tribe and Northern States Power Company to listen to a list of grievances. The result of the meeting was that the disputed land was returned to the tribe.

This event brought a new sense of community and self-determination to the Lac Courte Oreilles people, leading them to build a new school, a community college, and a shopping center, and to pursue compensation from the power company through the courts. Today, thanks to its persistence and determination, the tribe owns the power generating plant at the Winter Dam and sells power to the Northern States Power Company.

To honor their new beginning, Eddie Benton and others organized a reunion powwow in 1972. A sense of homecoming pervades what has become an annual event as many peo-

JOANNE SHENANDOAH

"If you believe you can do something and your heart and your mind are in the right place and you're not doing it for gain or greed or recognition, all these things come into play—they really come into play, and I'm learning that. It's a wonderful lesson."

—*Oneida JoAnne Shenandoah, quoted by Jill O'Brien in* News from Indian Country

The world-renowned singer/songwriter was describing how she and her husband had amassed the largest collection of Iroquois music since the 1930s, but she was also referring to her decision to give up working for other corporations and people and to devote herself completely to her music. Since then, she has recorded numerous records on many independent labels, as well as soundtracks. She has been on four different segments of the television show *Northern Exposure*, and in 1993, the First Americans in the Arts Foundation named her the Native Musician of the Year. She tours the world often with her daughter and journalist husband.

Recently, she sang with her sister at Woodstock '94, as part of the thirty-five-member Iroquois delegation, who "came out on stage at the beginning, all dressed in Native dress, and Jake Swamp said prayers...and talked about the earth, and it was wonderful." She summed up the experience: "What better way than to have a festival for peace, love and music start with a spiritual beginning?"

JoAnne Shenandoah never loses sight of her identity as a member of the Oneida Nation, Wolf Clan, Haudenosaunee (Iroquois) Confederacy. Her parents are Maisie Shenandoah, an Oneida Clan Mother, and the late Clifford Shenandoah, an Onondaga Chief, jazz guitarist, and ironworker.

Her songs range from love songs (because, as she jokingly puts it, "Native people fall in love, too") to songs such as "To Those Who Dream," which is about following the path of the elders in being true to one's dreams. Her album *Once in a Red Moon* includes "struggle songs" that center around issues that have to be addressed: "[As Native people] we have the highest rate of suicide; we have things that are affecting us like grave desecration, so a lot of those songs are very heavy. The really good thing about music is we can communicate what we really would like to say but can't."

She lives on the original land where Chief Shenandoah lived, the leader who saved George Washington's starving army in Valley Forge with three hundred bushels of corn from upstate New York. "Word has it," she said, "that if it weren't for this one saving act, we'd probably be under British rule today." Her song "Blanket Days" recalls Chief Shenandoah's life when, after the war, Washington "ordered General Sullivan to burn all the villages when the Oneidas were promised that they'd be able to keep their houses and fields. It's a grim part of my history.... obviously, it's not in a history book."

At present, JoAnne Shenandoah has many concerts coming up as well as two albums. One is an intense-message symphonic album. "I have two pieces orchestrated for a fifty-piece orchestra, and they surround Iroquois history, mythology, and legends, but it's done more in a more pop vein....The other album I'm working on is...a little similar to *Once in a Red Moon*, but that still has more of a country flair to it."

A project that is near to her heart is on CD-ROM so that "kids can learn more about Iroquois history. There's so much of a culture to reach. We can do it in one song or through video. I'm really happy that the population is ready to start learning more about Native music and Native life." Shenandoah keeps the spirit of her people alive, sharing it with the world through her music and her life.

Most modern powwows are not exclusive to any one tribal group or nation; rather, Indians and non-Indians alike are welcome to enjoy the celebration of the cultural resurgence represented by these gatherings.

ple schedule their annual vacations around the powwow, and many Lac Courte Oreilles tribal members who live off the reservation return each year to remember the time when a determined group of Ojibwa took a stand for their people.

The Oneida Health Promotions Department

"All people shall love one another and live together in peace. This message has three parts: peace, righteousness and power. Each part has two branches. Health means soundness of mind and body. It also means Peace, for that is what comes when minds are sane and bodies are cared for."

—Peacemaker, *a messenger of the Creator, according to* Barbara Kawenehe Barnes *in* Traditional Teachings

These traditional Oneida teachings inspired the leaders of the Oneida Health Promotions Department to open the Oneida Healthworks Fitness Center on their reservation in March 1987. Designed as a corporate fitness center that is open to the public, the center exists primarily for the three thousand employees of the Oneida tribe and their families. The fitness center has an employee incentive program that pays ten dollars a month to those who meet the minimum points set out by the fitness center each month.

The program centers on six major areas of wellness: social, emotional, intellectual, physical, spiritual, and occupational. In addition to providing exercise facilities, the center conducts miniworkshops in weight reduction, nutrition, lifestyle changes, stress management, and special exercise programs for diabetics. During the year, the fitness center sponsors runs, golf outings, ski trips, and activities to coincide with National Employee Health and Fitness week.

In December 1993, Healthworks Fitness Center director Oneida Scott Webster began the Elder Exercise Program. On Monday and Wednesday mornings, elders come to the center for an hour-long program that includes a warm-up, stretching, weightlifting, and aerobics. The progress of the twenty-five members has been remarkable: two elders who once needed a wheelchair and a cane are now walking independently.

Today, the Oneida and other peoples of the Northeast are building stronger, healthier nations as they fulfill traditional teachings that emphasize the interdependence of all aspects of being. As the Creator said through Peacemaker, "Peace...is what comes when minds are sane and bodies cared for." By honoring the earth and by honoring themselves, they have embarked on a healing journey that will benefit all peoples.

Powwows provide Native Americans with a link to their past, but in many other ways Indians today are looking forward, building stronger and healthier communities on a foundation of historical and cultural self-awareness.

CHAPTER 3

The Southwest

✚

What you strive for in this world is hózhó (beauty, balance, harmony). How you live, how you treat one another, the way you cook, how you arrange your home, how you live in your surroundings—in the Diné [Navajo] way this would be art and religion....your home and environment are your church, your place of prayers.

—*Conrad House, Navajo/Oneida, in* All Roads Are Good

These words from Conrad House, a Navajo/Oneida artist, express the commitment Southwestern peoples have to keeping the universe in balance through proper living. As with all Native Americans, the sacred is interwoven into daily life.

The landscape of the American Southwest, with its broad sweep of open sky and vast canyons, inspires a sense of the infinite. It is easy to see why the spiritual pervades all aspects of life among groups such as the Hopi, who live atop windswept mesas high above the surrounding plain, next to the sky itself, or their Navajo neighbors, who herd sheep against a horizon

of bare-boned mesas and brilliantly colored buttes. Farther west, the Havasupai live beside their sky blue waterfall cradled deep within the Grand Canyon. And, in the southernmost part of Arizona, the Tohono O'odham live under a sky that cracks open with deafening thunder, and suddenly washes of dry sand are transformed into rushing torrents within minutes. The power of nature is never forgotten in the Southwest, a land of great extremes in temperature, terrain, and access to life-giving water. The grandeur of the land is so overwhelming that it is hard to see how anything else could form the basis of belief for those who live there.

Water defines the Southwest, both geographically and practically. The Colorado River winds its way southwestward from the Rocky Mountains toward the Gulf of

Left: A beautiful example of traditional Hopi pottery.

Opposite: The people of Acoma Pueblo celebrate their feast day, dedicated to Saint Stephan, on September 2. Known as the Sky City, Acoma is perched atop a dramatic 365-foot (111m) -high mesa and is one of the oldest continuously occupied villages in the United States.

California; the Rio Grande meanders south from the Colorado Rockies, splitting the state of New Mexico. Together with the Pecos River in eastern New Mexico, these rivers demarcate the borders of the Southwest.

Primarily semiarid and alpine arid desert, the Southwest is a land in which water is life. Although Southwestern peoples have had to live with the ever-present reality of drought, which could easily bring starvation, the harsh and seemingly inhospitable nature of the Southwest has also worked in their favor, delaying the onslaught of outsiders that overwhelmed the Indian nations farther east. Southwestern peoples have kept their cultures alive in unbroken traditions that span centuries.

Native Americans were living in the Southwest by at least twelve thousand years ago, when the climate was cool and wet. These nomadic hunter-gatherers lived in small family bands and hunted mammoth, tapir, and giant bison.

Two thousand years later, as the climate became drier and warmer, woodlands became desert grasslands, forests of ponderosa pine retreated to the Colorado Plateau, and the saguaro cactus and other desert plants took their places. Large game began to die out, and forest animals moved to higher elevations. Smaller animals, such as deer and rabbits, flourished. Between 3000 and 2000 B.C., southern Arizona became a desert land.

The peoples of the region responded to these changes by harvesting wild plants—agave, cactus, acorns, piñon nuts, and juniper berries—which ripened at different times of year and at different elevations. Between 3500 and 3000 B.C., Southwestern peoples began to experiment with growing food; remains of a primitive variety of maize date to 3500 B.C. By 1000 B.C., the peoples were able to supplement their hunting and gathering with the corn and squash they had planted. Gradually, as with the Adena and

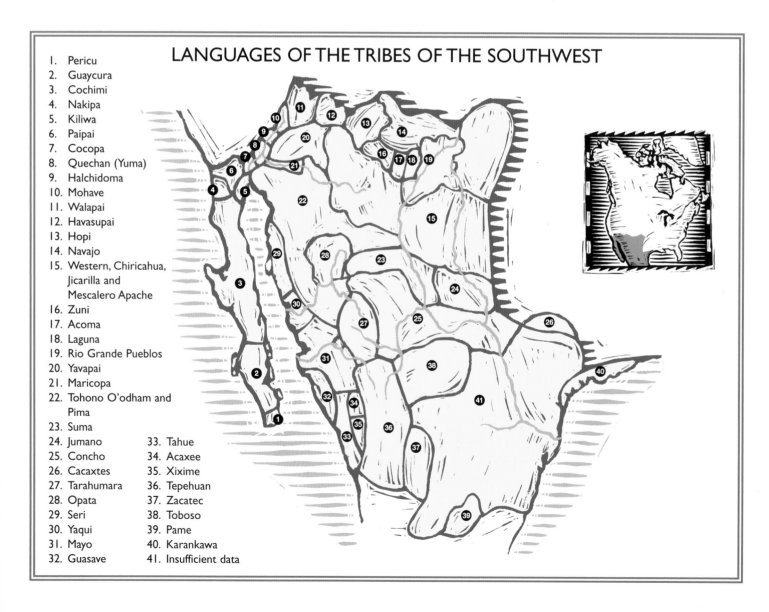

LANGUAGES OF THE TRIBES OF THE SOUTHWEST

1. Pericu
2. Guaycura
3. Cochimi
4. Nakipa
5. Kiliwa
6. Paipai
7. Cocopa
8. Quechan (Yuma)
9. Halchidoma
10. Mohave
11. Walapai
12. Havasupai
13. Hopi
14. Navajo
15. Western, Chiricahua, Jicarilla and Mescalero Apache
16. Zuni
17. Acoma
18. Laguna
19. Rio Grande Pueblos
20. Yavapai
21. Maricopa
22. Tohono O'odham and Pima
23. Suma
24. Jumano
25. Concho
26. Cacaxtes
27. Tarahumara
28. Opata
29. Seri
30. Yaqui
31. Mayo
32. Guasave
33. Tahue
34. Acaxee
35. Xixime
36. Tepehuan
37. Zacatec
38. Toboso
39. Pame
40. Karankawa
41. Insufficient data

subterranean, ceremonial
chambers called kivas,
which are similar to those
the Hopi use today.

In southern Arizona, the
Hohokam—probably
ancestral O'odham—creat-
ed a civilization based on
irrigation and agriculture,
which allowed them to
flourish in the intense and
unrelenting summer heat.
They dug hundreds of
miles of canals around present-day Florence and
Phoenix, Arizona, to irri-
gate between 65,000 to
250,000 acres (26,000 to
100,000ha) of land.

The third major South-
western pre-Hispanic
culture, the Mogollon,
ranged across southeastern
Arizona, southwestern
New Mexico, and northern
Mexico. Like the Anasazi
(with whom some
Mogollon groups later
merged), the Mogollon
organized many of their

Hopewell peoples who lived farther east, agriculture
allowed denser concentrations of people to live together.
Settled village life followed, and by the first millennium
A.D., the great regional civilizations of the Southwest had
begun to take shape.

The Anasazi, ancestors of today's Pueblo people, lived
on the Colorado Plateau. In addition to massive multisto-
ried pueblos, the Anasazi built round and rectangular, often

communities around great kivas. A southern Mogollon
group that flourished between A.D. 1000 and 1150, the
Mimbres left behind a legacy of distinctive black-on-white
pictorial pottery. Mimbres artists transformed utilitarian
vessels into art with their active portrayals of stylized
humans wrestling with bears and of rounded fish struggling
against elegant, long-necked cranes. More static Mimbres
designs were isolated figures centered at the bottom of wide

KACHINA CARVING TODAY

"It's breathtaking when the kachinas come to the plaza to dance and sing their songs... They bring...kachina dolls for the children. These are usually tied to long stems of deep green cattail, still moist from the distant waters. It's truly a wondrous sight, especially when the kachinas give them out after the dance. You can feel the excitement radiating from the children, and you can see the anticipation in their eyes. I remember those feelings when I was that age. Hopeful that I, too, would be befriended by a kachina who might've brought something for me. When I stand on the rooftop above the plaza watching the girls admiring their dolls—and the boys, too— it reminds me of a pond that's full of life down there, with all the cattail around the edge of the plaza, reaching up, swaying in the light breeze. There's a happiness all around."

—*Hopi Ramson Lomatewama in an article for* Native Peoples *magazine*

Katsinam, or kachinas, are the spirit beings who bring spiritual well-being into the physical world. Kachina dancers are the masked impersonators who embody the spirit of a particular kachina while dancing at a ceremony. Kachina dolls are the carved cottonwood figures used as spiritual and educational instruments.

The kachina dolls that are carved today take many forms and styles. Some kachina doll carvers favor realism; others, however, prefer to allow the natural

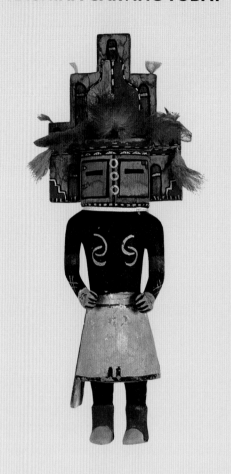

curves of the wood to determine the shape of the figure.

Some carvers, such as Manfred Susunkewa, make kachina dolls in the old style because of a personal conviction that kachina dolls should maintain a strong connection to Hopi religion and culture. His carvings resemble the old-style tihu, the ancient blocky, unelaborated figures—very different from today's kachina doll sculptures. He uses the old methods, designs, and materials, such as plants, volcanic ash, and other natural colors for paint.

Susunkewa emphasizes, "The kachina doll was never art. They were not rich in style, but rich in spiritual terms." Unlike many modern kachina dolls, the ones that Susunkewa carves do not stand on bases;

they are hung from the wall or held by a string around the figure's neck.

Ramson Lomatewama sings when he carves, and, he says, "Often times, I pray for strength through humility. After that, you pick up your knife and talk to the root—you ask the root to cooperate and help you along." As he carves, he sings various kachina songs. Eventually, "the songs pare themselves down to a few. Eventually, I find myself singing one particular kachina's song.

"Where does creativity come from? Every design, every product of human creativity, is born out of our affinity with nature and the spirit—that higher power which we need not comprehend…. It is not the monetary benefits, nor the prestige that is important. It is the belief that my creations, the kachina dolls that I carve, are manifestations of my attitudes toward life itself. And, if I radiate those positive feelings, somehow or other, my carvings will become the vehicle for those feelings to be carried and further radiated in someone else's life."

Although kachina carvers have different ideas about the form kachinas should take, they share an underlying philosophy of what the kachina doll means to Hopi culture. As Susunkewa told Tom Wallace of *Native Peoples* magazine, "The translation of the word Hopi means 'blameless.' To be blameless, we never wrong another or create conflict with mother earth or anything that comes from the earth, including fellow humans…. We are not born Hopi; Hopi is earned."

bowls: graphic turtles with delicately crosshatched interiors, scorpions with swirling tails that echo the circular surface, aesthetically pleasing rabbits with crescent-shaped banded bodies.

More local groups such as the Salado and Sinagua added their rich heritage to the Anasazi and Hohokam. Meanwhile, the Patayan people, from whom the Yumans are probably descended, settled along the Colorado River. Finally, sometime before the arrival of the Spaniards in 1540, Athabascan-speaking groups migrated into the Southwest.

THE VILLAGE FARMERS

"Po-wa-ha ('water-wind-breath') is the creative energy of the world, the breath that makes the wind blow and the water flow. Within Mimbres pots...wonderful, billowing cloud forms swirl with the wind around the mountains. You can... sense the breath that gives everything its energy.
—Rina Swentzell, a contemporary Tewa-Santa Clara educator and writer, in All Roads Are Good

The sense of unbroken cultural continuity, from the prehistoric Mimbres people to the present-day Puebloans, is part of what makes Pueblo cultures so strong and vital in today's world. The dwellings of their ancestors lie scattered through the canyons of the Four Corners area, where Utah, Colorado, New Mexico, and Arizona meet. Living in two- and four-storied apartmentlike buildings, Anasazi women made elaborate pottery, decorated with bold asymmetric birdlike Sikyatki designs, elegant black-on-white Mesa Verde zigzags, hatched and solid Tularosa spirals, and fine-line, black-on-white Chaco hatching.

When the Spaniards arrived in 1540, however, they found the Anasazi villages deserted and the Pueblo people living where they do today—along the Rio Grande in northern New Mexico, in western New Mexico, and on the Hopi mesas of northern Arizona. The Spaniards found more than forty thousand Pueblos living in about ninety villages; as warfare, drought, and disease decimated their numbers, the peoples of these villages consolidated themselves into the nineteen pueblos that exist today.

Impressed by their distinctive stone and adobe multi-chambered houses and settled village lifestyle, the Spaniards named them "town-dwellers" or Pueblo Indians. Each Puebloan village was, and is, an independent political entity, but today all the pueblos belong to a loose federation called the All Indian Pueblo Council.

Puebloan peoples express the central values of their worldview—that people must live in harmony with nature and with each other—through their ceremonies, architecture, dances, poetry, pottery, songs, and legends. The kiva, a ceremonial chamber located at the spiritual and physical heart of the pueblo, is a place where men perform private and communal rituals on a daily and annual basis to ensure the continuation of human, plant, and animal life. Nearly all Pueblo ceremonies occur on a calendrical basis and focus on weather control, healing illness, village harmony, and success in hunting and warfare.

Although they share many cultural similarities—similar architecture, settled village life, agriculture, pottery making, and a rich ceremonial life—Puebloan peoples speak several different languages. Most Puebloans speak one of three Tanoan languages: people from Taos, Picuris, Sandia, and Isleta speak Tiwa dialects; the people from Jemez are the only remaining Towa speakers; and Tewa is spoken at San Ildefonso, Nambe, Tesuque, San Juan, Santa Clara, Pojoaque, and at the village of Hano, on First Mesa. (After the reconquest that followed the Pueblo Revolt of 1680, many Tewa families moved to join the Hopi on their mesas in northern Arizona. Although they adopted many Hopi customs, they maintained their Tewa language.) The Keresan language can be heard in the villages of Santo Domingo, Cochiti, San Felipe, Santa Ana, and Zia along the Rio Grande and its tributaries, and farther west in Laguna and Acoma. The people of Zuni speak a language unrelated to any other spoken in the Southwest. In Arizona, the Hopi speak a language from the Uto-Aztecan family; a non-Pueblo group, the O'odham (Pimans) of southern Arizona are their linguistic cousins.

Access to the Rio Grande and its tributaries created a major difference between the Eastern and Western Pueblos that was reflected in nearly all aspects of culture, from ceremonial concerns to methods of food production. This river and its tributaries enabled the Eastern Pueblos—Santa Ana, San Felipe, Santo Domingo, Cochiti, Zia, Jemez, Sandia, Isleta, Picuris, Taos, Tesuque, Nambe, Pojoaque, San Ildefonso, Santa Clara, and San Juan—to practice irrigation agriculture. The peoples of the Western Pueblos of Zuni, Hopi, Hano, Acoma, and Laguna lacked a dependable supply of water and had to rely on runoff from seasonal rains to raise their crops.

Living in an arid, inhospitable environment without a permanent water source, the Western Puebloans emphasize weather control, especially rain production, in their ceremonies. The faith it takes to bring rain, however, is inextricably interwoven not only into public ceremonies but also into the private lives of all individuals.

For the Hopi, corn is life, requiring the diligent care and love that parents lavish on their children. Hopi George Nasoftie explained, "When one goes [to tend the plants]...one can humbly encourage the plants, saying, 'You will exert yourselves.' One says this to his plants as he reflects on his children and his grandchildren. For them, one sacrifices in his fields."

The Hopi say that corn is the human life span. They believe that the Hopi emerged upward from previous worlds just as corn sprouts from the earth. Both humans and corn take sustenance from the earth; the corn plant reaches maturity when it develops "eyes" or kernels that enable it to "look out on the world" just as a person is considered to be fully alive only after their eyes can see. In its final stages of life, the corn plant relies on its leaves that bend and touch the ground, supporting the plant like the canes that older people use to support themselves.

O'ODHAM DANCES BY OFELIA ZEPEDA

...It is the time for the ritual.
To dance, to sing so that rain may come,
so that the earth may be fixed one more time.
Throughout the night,
a night too short for such important work,
the people converge energies.
They call upon the night.
They call upon the stars in the darkness.
They call upon the hot breezes.
They call upon the heat coming off the earth.
They implore all the animals.
The ones that fly in the sky.
The ones that crawl upon the earth.
The ones that walk.
The ones that swim in the water and
The ones that move in between water, sky, and earth.
They implore them to focus on the moisture.
All are dependent.
From the dry darkness of the desert,
On that one night the call of the people is heard.
It is heard by the oceans, winds, and clouds.
All respond sympathetically.
Throughout the night you hear the one who is assigned yelling:
     before it becomes light
         there are still songs to be sung
         before the sun comes up
             there is still a little bit of night left.
With the dawn we face the sunrise.
We face it with all our humility.
We are mere beings.
All we can do is extend our hands toward the first light.
In our hands we capture the first light.
We take it and cleanse ourselves.
We touch our eyes with it.
We touch our faces with it.
We touch our hair with it.
We touch our limbs.
We rub our hands together, we want to keep this light with us.
We are complete with this light.
This is the way we begin and end things.

Above: The Anasazi ancestors of the present-day Puebloans left many petrogylphs on rock faces in the Four Corners area. Petrogylphs are pecked into the surface of the rock, while pictographs are painted on the surface.

"To grow corn is to know how to behave, to know the nature of human life and its purpose in the scheme of things," according to one Hopi man. "To commit oneself, one's lineage, to growing corn in a place that receives but a few inches of rain or snow each year, and to do so in dry washes...only with old knowledge embedded in magical digging sticks, is an utmost act of faith."

Fortunately, the Kachinas—supernatural beings who have the power to bring rain and are masters of the art of raising corn and other plants—come to the aid of the Hopi. Through ceremonies, these intermediaries between the Creator and humankind visit the Hopi villages from about the time of the winter solstice until just after the summer solstice, when they return to their homes atop the San Francisco Peaks, near Flagstaff, Arizona. According to Hopi belief, when a priest of the Kachina cult wears a mask and dances, the spirit of that Kachina temporarily replaces his human spirit.

Hopi Emory Sekaquaptewa explained that the songs of the Kachinas evoke the kind of reverential attitude that it takes to grow corn: the Kachinas "help the people to experience a renewed faith in the good and long life, and to aspire to Hopi ideals of compassion, cooperation, and humility."

Young girls learn how to become nurturers of their people by first caring for the kachina dolls given to them by the dancers. It takes a concerted village effort to ensure that the Kachinas bring their blessing of rain when they come; everyone in the village contributes by living their lives with generosity of spirit, compassion toward others, and prayer.

The peoples of the Eastern Pueblos, assured of a permanent water source and a greater chance of reaping a good harvest, focused their ceremonies on curing, village harmony, hunting, and war. Tanoan-speaking Puebloans often sojourned with Plains Indians while they were trading and hunting buffalo; some of their ceremonies echoed the Plains Indians' ceremonial focus on ensuring success in hunting and warfare.

Among their Keresan neighbors, medicine associations are the strongest institutions. The Eastern Pueblos lived closest to Spanish population centers and felt the full brunt of attempts by the Spaniards to repress their ceremonies (unlike the Western Pueblos, who lived in more remote and less desirable areas). The Spaniards forced harsh laws upon the

Above: Traditional Native American foods from the Southwest included sunflower seeds, prickly pear cactus fruit, and many varieties of corn, chilis, squash, and beans. Also depicted is piki, a delicious paper-thin bread that Hopi women make from blue corn meal.

Below: The distinctive patterns decorating Hopi pottery are instantly recognizable, despite the wide variety of specific forms that these patterns may take.

European diseases, took on greater governmental and ceremonial functions. They responded to the repression of their spiritual beliefs and practices by making it a priority to preserve their ancient traditions and protect the culture from outside influence. Today, these societies are so important that the town chief, or cacique, must be a member of the highest ranking medicine association in the pueblo.

THE RANCHERIA FARMERS

Rancheria farmers lived along rivers or in the well-watered mountain and desert areas of southern Arizona and northern Mexico. They relied on flood water and irrigation from rivers to help them grow crops. Each family within a rancheria settlement owned a home and fields that were separated by as much as half a mile (805m). Most of them shifted to another location during the year as they supplemented their diet with hunting and gathering.

The rancheria peoples spoke languages from the Uto-Aztecan and Hokan families. Although they are both in the Uto-Aztecan language family, the Yaqui and Pimans speak mutually unintelligible languages and have very different cultures. The Hokan-speakers live both along the Colorado River and its tributaries and in the upland region of western and northern Arizona.

Eastern Pueblos, outlawed their ceremonial practices, destroyed Kachina masks and paraphernalia, demanded the people's conversion to Catholicism, and forced them to labor on the ranches of Spanish officers and political land grantees. Puebloan peoples dealt with such repression by keeping the two faiths separate. They practiced their traditional ceremonies in secret, and to appease the early Franciscan missionaries, they publicly celebrated Catholic services.

PUEBLO INDIAN PRAYER

Hold on to what is good, even if it is a handful of earth.
Hold on to what you believe, even if it is a tree which stands alone.
Hold on to what you must do, even if it is a long way from home.
Hold on to life, even when it is easier letting go.
Hold on to my hand, even when I have gone away from you.

The Yaqui

"We believe that our ancestors the Surem could actually talk with the animals that lived in the wilderness....the Surem spoke to saila maso, our brother the deer, because they needed him to survive in this world....[they asked] the deer's forgiveness for having to kill him.

—*Yaqui Felipe Molina*

The Yaqui homeland was some of the most fertile farmland in Mexico. The Yaqui lived in eight towns clustered around the Rio Yaqui. Their tribal organizations were strong enough that they were able to defeat the Spanish forces who invaded

When the United States annexed the region after 1848, the officials from the American government continued to pressure the Pueblos to assimilate to another way of life. The powerful medicine societies, which had originally focused their work on curing because so many of their people were dying from

their lands in 1617. Much to the surprise of the Spaniards, the Yaquis then asked that Jesuit priests be sent to them to teach them more productive agricultural methods. Instead of separating Catholicism from their traditional ceremonial beliefs and practices, the Yaqui fused the two together, creating an entirely new religion.

A peaceful 120-year period of integration of Yaqui and Spanish cultures followed; it was shattered when Spanish settlers began encroaching on Yaqui land in the 1730s. Fighting desperately to protect their land, the Indians were slaughtered; more than five thousand died in a single revolt. From the late 1880s to the early 1900s, Mexicans took over most of Yaqui territory, deporting the Yaqui people to forced labor camps in the Yucatan peninsula. Many Yaquis escaped to build Yaqui communities near Tucson and Phoenix, Arizona. They sought political asylum in the United States and officially received this status in 1906. In 1978 they finally received tribal recognition and reservation land.

Yaqui names often reflect both personal and tribal history. A Yaqui elder named Refugio Savala—his name means "refugee"—escaped with his parents from their home in Sonora, Mexico, in 1904 at the height of deportation and persecution of the Yaquis by the Mexican government.

The major Yaqui ritual is their forty-day Easter ceremony, which culminates in the symbolic triumph of good over evil. Flowers are an important symbol to the Yaqui because they believe that through a miracle, Christ's blood mingled with the earth and was transformed into flowers. The Flower World is one of several supernatural worlds in which the Yaqui believe. Home to the deer, the beautiful and sacred Flower World lies beneath the dawn in the east.

A young Pima boy rides a bull at the youth rodeo event of the annual O'odham Tash All-Indian Days celebration in southern Arizona.

The Pimans
The ocean wind from far off overtakes me.
It bends down the tassels of the corn.
The ocean hurts my heart.
Beautiful clouds bring rain upon our fields.
—*Tohono O'odham Salt Pilgrimage Song*

As with the Eastern and Western Puebloans, the cultural differences among the three different groups of Pimans resulted from access to a river. They think of themselves as three distinct groups and take their names from the different environmental niches they occupy within their desert world: the Sand People, the Desert People, and the River People.

"We are from the sand, and known as Sand Indians, to find our way of life on the sand of the Earth. That is why we go all over to seek our food to live well," the late Miguel Velasco told writer/photographer Stephen Trimble. He was describing the traditional life of the Hia C-ed O'odham—the Sand People—called the Sand Papago by outsiders. These nomadic hunter-gatherers lived in the most extreme reaches of the desert and depended on natural stone tanks in the mountains that stored water from infrequent summer cloudbursts. Their intimate knowledge of the land and its plants and animals allowed them to survive in a land where most would die quickly: for food and drink, they relied on more than sixty species of plants and forty species of animals. At certain times of the year, they

Anthropologists emphasize the Navajo ability to incorporate, integrate, and adapt non-Navajo aspects of culture into distinctly Navajo products. Here, a Navajo mother and her sons blend the old and the new.

fished in the Gulf of California. Only in the mid-1980s did the Hia C-ed O'odham receive recognition from the Tohono O'odham nation, which brought with it access to health benefits, education, and social services. Today some twelve hundred Hia C-ed O'odham continue in their struggle to obtain land of their own.

> *Where on Quijotoa Mountain a cloud stands*
> *There my heart stands with it.*
> *Where the mountain trembles with the thunder*
> *My heart trembles with it.*
> —*Tohono O'odham song recounted by Chona to*
> *Ruth Underhill*

The Tohono O'odham sing many songs for rain, reflecting the vital importance of moisture to the Desert People, as they call themselves. The Spanish called them Papago, in reference to their reliance on the mesquite and tepary beans—Papago means "bean eater." In the 1980s, they officially became the Tohono O'odham Nation.

Traditionally, they lived in a slightly more bountiful desert niche than did the Hia C-ed O'odham, although they still had no permanent streams or rivers on which to rely. They spent the winter in villages near wells or permanent springs in the mountains. At other times of year, they cultivated fields of desert-adapted varieties of corn, beans, squash, cowpeas, and melons. By building brush dams at the mouths of arroyos, they were able to spread the water from summer thunderstorms over their adjacent fields. In July or August, as soon as the fields were wet, they planted; they harvested their crops in October and November. They stayed in the field villages only during the summer rainy season and as long as the water lasted in the reservoir. They were able to raise about one-fifth of the food they ate.

The Tohono O'odham supplemented their crops with deer, mountain sheep, mountain lions, doves, rabbits, and other rodents. Some of the wild plants they collected included prickly pear fruits and pads, mesquite, agave, amaranth greens, acorns, cholla buds, and saguaro fruit.

The Sonoran Desert is the only region in the world where the saguaro cactus grows. It is sacred to the Tohono O'odham, whose ceremonial year begins with the ripening of the saguaro fruit. They say that saguaros are people, too. Standing upright with humanlike arms that reach upward in supplication, saguaros give barren and immense mountain ranges a reassuringly human scale.

In the searing heat of midsummer, the saguaro blossoms ripen into pale pink fruits that split open to expose juicy red flesh. At just the right time, the women harvested this precious resource with long poles made from the ribs of dead saguaros. They boiled the fruit to make syrup and jam; they dried and shaped it into cakes; and they also dried, ground, and converted it into meal. The people also ate the sweet crimson flesh of the fresh fruit; saguaro fruit has a taste and consistency similar to kiwi fruit. The medicine men fermented some of the syrup into ceremonial wine called nawait.

The four-day saguaro wine ceremony was the most sacred of Tohono O'odham traditions. Then the men gathered in the round house to "drink down the clouds" with saguaro wine and to "sing down the rain" with special prayers. They prayed that the rain would saturate the earth just as the ritual wine saturated their bodies.

In previous generations, Tohono O'odham men undertook a dangerous eight-day pilgrimage to the Gulf of California to seek the ocean wind that brings the rain.

ALLAN HOUSER (HAOZOUS)

"Human dignity is very important to me. I feel that way towards all people, not just Indians....In my work, this is what I strive for—this dignity, this goodness that is in man. I hope I am getting it across. If I am, then I am doing what I have always wanted."

—*Apache Allan Houser*

When Allan Houser died in 1994, the world lost the man who was often called "the master sculptor of North America" and "the patriarch of contemporary Indian art." When rain began to fall during a posthumous ceremony honoring Allan Houser, painter Dan Namingha said, "Among the Pueblo and Tewa-Hopi people, our belief is that when the clouds accumulate and come together and you hear the thunder, and then you feel the raindrops start to fall, we say the spirit of that person who has left us has been accepted into the spirit world and will begin his journey to meet his parents, to meet his grandparents, to meet his aunts and uncles, to meet his ancestors."

Nourished by the stories, songs, and myths his father told and sang to him when he was a child, Allan Houser used his art to bridge the spirit of Apache culture and modern American life. His father, Sam Haozous, was a grandson of Mangas Coloradas and a nephew of Geronimo. He had trained as a warrior and was taken prisoner by U.S. troops when the Chiricahua Apache were deported from Arizona. Blossom White, Allan's mother, was born in captivity at a military post in Alabama. Born in Fort Sill, Oklahoma, in 1914, Allyn Capron Haozous, named after a kind army captain, was one of the first children born after the Chiricahua were released from captivity. He grew up hearing his father's stories about the days when their people wandered freely across the beautiful Apache homeland.

In 1936, Houser studied at Painting Studio at the Santa Fe Indian School. In 1939, he married Anna Marie Gallegos and moved to Oklahoma, where he studied under muralist Olle Nordmark. Houser quickly mastered the muralist's art and painted two murals for the Department of the Interior in Washington, D.C. During World War II, he worked as a pipefitter's assistant in Los Angeles, while he painted and carved at night and audited classes at the Otis Art Institute.

By 1949, Houser had found his medium, creating his first monumental work in stone, *Comrade in Mourning*, a seven-and-a-half-foot (2.3m) figure honoring Indian servicemen who had given their lives in World War II. His biographer, Barbara Perlman, described the "astonishing sensitivity that directed his hands and his tools in an art he had never really learned, but had somehow absorbed only by means of observation, minuscule experiments, and the overwhelming impulse to work large, ever larger."

Guggenheim fellowships followed; in 1951, he became artist-in-residence at Inter-Mountain School in Brigham City, Utah, teaching young Indians and producing his own paintings and carvings.

In 1962, Houser joined the art faculty of the Institute of American Indian Arts, the successor to the Santa Fe Indian School. During his thirteen years at the school, Hauser encouraged Indian students: "Learn to be proud of what you are and what you can make of yourself. In my work, I'm saying here we are: this is the way we look. A beautiful way. If you see ugliness around you, try to find the beauty too. Find the strength in peoples' faces."

During his lifetime, his work was acquired by the Pompidou Museum in Paris, the United States Mission to the United Nations, the British Royal Collection, and the National Portrait Gallery, Smithsonian Institution. Houser also received many international awards for his work, including the Palmes Academique Award from the French government and the American Indian Lifetime Distinguished Achievement Award from the American Indian Resource Institute in Washington, D.C.

In spring 1993, the National Museum of the American Indian/Smithsonian Institution acquired his sculpture *May We Have Peace*, an eleven-foot (3.4m) bronze figure of a warrior holding a peace pipe. Allan Houser addressed the gathering at the dedication, saying, "All my life I've worked to emphasize the values that Indians have had for centuries. Especially ideas or concepts of living in harmony with nature. These ideas can benefit all people, if we just give them a chance."

They honored the ocean with gifts, hoping that the monsoon moisture would accompany them northward as they returned home. If they were successful, great dust storms and dramatic displays of lightning would herald life-giving downpours that soaked the earth.

Of the three O'odham groups, the Pima or Akimel O'odham—the River People—were the only ones able to live in permanent villages. They took their name from the Gila River and its tributaries, which supplied year-round drinking water as well as water for their crops. Sixty percent of their food came from their fields, some of which they gave to their cousins, the Tohono O'odham, in exchange for helping with the harvest.

In addition to corn, beans, and squash, they also grew cotton from which they wove cloth on horizontal looms for blankets and clothing. The high-quality cloth known as pima cotton bears their name.

The Spanish brought the gift of winter wheat, which Pima farmers planted when the November rains brought the Gila River to life after the dry month of October. Wheat provided a heavier yield of grain, doubling the capacity of a unit of irrigated land to support human life and leading some Pimas to think of the new year as beginning not with the saguaro harvest but with the wheat harvest in May. Pima farmers produced such bountiful supplies of wheat that they fed twenty thousand settlers passing through their country in the 1850s as well as all the Civil War troops west of the Mississippi; by 1870, they were selling or trading more than 3 million pounds of wheat annually.

However, such prosperity was not destined to last. The fertile Gila River attracted Anglos and Mexican settlers, who diverted the Pima's water for themselves. In addition to the farmers' irrigation ditches, the settlers built a large canal near Florence, Arizona, in 1887.

A White Mountain Apache girl celebrates her coming-of-age ceremony. The abalone shell token on her forehead symbolizes that for the duration of the ceremony she is White Painted Woman (also known as White Shell Woman), a beloved Apache Holy Being.

NAVAJO PEACEMAKER COURT

Two basic principles, hózhó and nitsés-kees, lie at the heart of Navajo Peacemaker Court. Hózhó is the essence of harmonious relations with the human, holy, and natural worlds; this principle is the very foundation of the Navajo way of life. Nitséskees means "right thinking" and is based on the creative power of thought and intention; the spirit in which any endeavor is undertaken is inseparable from the outcome. Hatred begets hatred; harmonious results come only from undertaking an endeavor in a spirit of love and mutual respect.

The purpose of Peacemaker Court is the resolution of conflict in a peaceful way that restores harmony. Rather than punishment and retribution, Native American law is based on the principle of fair compensation. Recognizing that nothing can undo a wrong, the parties involved in peacemaking instead seek to acknowledge the pain inflicted and to reach a mutually acceptable resolution based on fair compensation for that suffering.

Not only does Peacemaker Court save thousands of dollars in legal fees and years of lengthy battles in court, it also incorporates traditional values into the modern legal process. The peacemaker guides, advises, and mediates, often from a traditional perspective. For example, if a child is involved, the peace-

maker can advise the parents about the mother's and father's traditional roles in child rearing. Elders can also be brought into the courtroom to offer their wisdom and advice.

The Navajo Nation Council approved the peacemaker concept in 1982, but the idea was not implemented until 1990. Today there are three hundred peacemakers in seven court divisions across the reservation. Peacemaker Court handles any case involving land, property, vehicle, and marriage disputes; this includes such issues as domestic violence, bigamy, failure to file a death certificate, and substance abuse. Peacemaker Court also handles certain criminal cases so that those convicted can work out a solution with their victims and avoid prison time. In criminal cases, the parties must first agree that they will no longer physically harm each other.

A session in Peacemaker Court begins with a blessing prayer that asks for assistance and acknowledges that everyone involved is acting with "good heart," meaning that they are open to other peoples' points of view and are willing to work out a mutually satisfying agreement. The session is then conducted in a tone of nitséskees and good will.

Less confrontational than District Court, Peacemaker Court allows everyone the opportunity to speak and to be heard while others listen in respectful silence. This is especially important in cases involving young people, who may not otherwise have a voice. In one case, the children of alcoholics were able to describe how deeply their parents' behavior frightened and hurt them. In another case, the mother of a nineteen-year-old substance abuser took her son to court to let him know how much emotional pain he was inflicting on her.

Peacemaker Court seeks to address the nature of underlying relationships rather than simply the immediate problems. Based on shared belief, Peacemaker Court does not polarize those involved but rather unites them as they try together to reach a mutually acceptable solution. In giving people a voice, sometimes for the first time in their lives; in allowing them to see and hear the impact their behavior has on their loved ones; and in empowering everyone involved to reach their own solution, Peacemaker Court is a powerful tool for the restoration of hózhó.

The Pima, longtime allies of the European settlers, were so impoverished by the people they had befriended that by 1895 the government had to issue them rations. Their entire way of life had been based upon successful farming; in despair, with no fields to tend, Pima men went out to the edge of the dry river and drank. Piman George Webb chronicled the loss: "The green of those Pima fields spread along the river for many miles in the old days when there was plenty of water. Now the river is an empty bed of sand....The dead trees stand there like white bones.... Mesquite and brush and tumbleweeds have begun to turn those fields back into desert."

Today, all three groups of O'odham are united by a resurgence in O'odham Himdag, "the way of life."

Essentially a shared worldview, Himdag involves all things, all people, and all actions. It even encompasses European-derived concepts of religion, history, tradition, language, and belief; Himdag is "a way of being in the world" based on values of family, community, generosity, and respect for the earth.

The River Yumans

"We are still together....Things will be good again. Learn from your elders. Go in a good direction. This knowledge will go on from generation to generation. It will help you go in your life's direction....It will always go on and on.

—*Maricopa elder Ralph Cameron in the book* Spirit Mountain

Just west of the Colorado River in southernmost Nevada lies the emergence place of the Yuman-speaking peoples. They know it as Spirit Mountain; non-Indians call it Newberry Mountain. According to Yuman belief, all the peoples of the world spread out upon the earth from this starting point, each group choosing its own place.

The Yuman-speaking Mohave, Quechan (Yuma), and Cocopah still live on the Colorado River, along the present-day boundary of California and Arizona. Other River Yumans once lived there—the Maricopa, Halchidoma, Kavelchadom, Kahwan, and Halyikwamai—who were weary of being battered by the aggressive Mohave-Quechan alliance and migrated eastward. By 1846, these groups had coalesced with the Maricopa and settled near their Pima allies along the middle Gila River near present-day Phoenix. In 1857, several hundred Mohave, Quechan, and Yavapai warriors crossed 160 miles (257.5km) of desert to attack their old enemies, who, with their Pima neighbors, rallied in a counterattack on horseback to kill over a hundred of the invaders. This was the River Yumans' last major battle.

The River Yuman peoples lived in an oasis in the desert. Before the river was dammed, the annual flooding of the Colorado River supported dense populations in the lush oases of the river valley. Each spring, swollen with the

A Navajo man on horseback herds sheep in Monument Valley. Introduced by the Spaniards, sheep led the Navajo to adopt a pastoral lifestyle based on transhumance. Today, Navajos still herd sheep, but depend much more on a wage economy.

NAVAJO WEAVING SYMPOSIUM

"Navajo rug weaving isn't just visual art, but rather the feelings and wisdom that go into it."

—*Gloria Begay, a third-generation Navajo weaver*

A Navajo Weaving Symposium was part of the eighth annual Navajo Studies Conference held in March 1995 at San Juan College in Farmington, New Mexico. Among the participants were some of the weavers whose work was in the 1994 Museum of Northern Arizona exhibition "Hanoolchaadí: Historic Textiles Selected by Four Navajo Weavers." Navajo Davina R. Two Bears described the exhibition in *Native Peoples* magazine with "Nizhóníyeé," a word that expresses much deeper feeling than its English translation of describing a beautiful creation: "The translation to me is not just that the final exhibit is beautiful, admirable, and a source of pride, but so are the initial concept, the total process, and the people involved."

Weavers and co-curators of the exhibit—grandmother Grace Henderson Nez (b. 1913), mother Mary Lee Begay (b. 1941), and daughters Lena Begay (b. 1969) and Gloria Begay (b. 1970)—searched the museum's extensive rug collection for rarely seen examples of Navajo weaving. Their choices dated from the 1860s to the early 1900s. Anthropology professor Dr. Ann Lane Hedlund, who organized both the Navajo Studies Conference weaving symposium and the MNA exhibition, explained, "The co-curators' decisions were guided by visual and technical appeal, but also by what they felt best represented Navajo heritage and lifeways, historically and today."

Wesley Thomas, a weaver from Mariano Lake, New Mexico, remembers, as a child, hearing the thumping sounds of his mother's weaving fork which she called "the heart beat of the loom." A weaver's rug was her child; when she sold a rug, she was finding a good home for her child. A woman sometimes cried if she recognized one of her weavings, because she was being reunited with her child.

The spirit a weaver brings to the process, beginning with her first inspiration to gathering the materials and stringing her loom, is woven into her rug; all her thoughts become a part of the finished product. This was why a weaver sang prayers—traditional weaving songs—for each step of the process. She sanctified her weaving space with prayers and had to keep her weaving tools together so that her thoughts would not be scattered. In getting the wool off the back of a living being, she brought a sense of wholeness to her weaving; she personified the sheep and had a dialogue with the weaving tools while she wove.

In Navajo belief, it is not the woman who creates the rug; the rug already exists upon the loom. The energy in the weaving fork projects the design into the weaver, who then brings it into manifestation so that it can be seen by others. As she finishes her rug, a woman sings an ending song to acknowledge the coming separation. She also says a prayer before the rug leaves the sacred space where her loom is erected. The rug's physical beauty is the outer manifestation of the inner, spiritual beauty the weaver has brought to the process of creation.

---

melting snows of the Rockies, the Colorado River overflowed its banks, gently spreading silt-laden floodwater over the bottomlands for distances as great as two miles (3.2km) from the river.

By the end of June, the river had receded, leaving its rich deposits of silt behind. In this fertile bottomland, Mohave men planted maize, tepary beans, pumpkins, and melons. These crops ripened rapidly in the intense summer heat and were ready for the women to harvest in late September and October.

While the men were planting, the women gathered wild plants in the bottomlands after the recession of the floods. The mesquite tree provided drink, food, fuel, clothing, and tools; Mohave elders called it "our tree of life." From its roots, they carved cradles and tools. Its sap made glue, and its bark became clothing and shoes. Women ground its bean-like pods into pith that their families ate as mush or baked into cakes. Fresh mesquite beans provided a nutritious juice. Women fired their pots in fires burning mesquite wood.

Finally, mesquite fueled the fire in which an individual was cremated along with his or her belongings. The Mohave honored the deceased person in an elaborate mourning ceremony that transported the soul to the land of the dead. In these powerful ceremonies, orators proclaimed the good deeds of the dead individual while mourners sang thirty cycles of song—each cycle contained two hundred songs. When a prominent warrior or chief died, the Mohave held even more elaborate ceremonies, which included a ritual enactment of warfare.

Known for being great warriors, the Mohave believed that their god, Mastamho, instituted warfare among the peoples he created. At the time of creation, he linked the Mohave and Quechan as military allies, decreeing that in each generation, some men would be given great power in war through their dreams. Such warriors had talents that included the ability to determine the location of an enemy and to foresee the outcome of a war. Despite living in sprawling settlements scattered throughout the valleys and being divided into bands and local groups, the Mohave thought of themselves as a single people. They were a cohesive nation with a well-defined territory and presented a united front against all enemies.

Dreaming was of primary importance in Mohave spiritual life and permeated almost every aspect of thought and behavior. Proper dreaming determined success in all endeavors: warfare, lovemaking, gambling, healing, and leadership. Great dreams conferred power in battle, which was then validated through successful warfare. Mohave leaders established their authority through great dreams, prowess in war, and care for their people; such men inspired trust and solidarity among their followers.

Anasazi pictographs cover a rock face in Canyon de Chelly. The Navajo considered the vanished Anasazi to be a gifted people gone astray; Anasazi sites and artifacts serve as mnemonic devices that remind the Navajo of the importance of living according to spiritual values.

HUNTING AND GATHERING BANDS

Without access to sufficient water to practice agriculture on a permanent basis, the seminomadic Upland Yuman groups developed a hunting and gathering lifestyle. They were able to do some limited farming during part of the year; however, they relied on hunting game and gathering wild plants to sustain them.

The Upland Yumans

"We were taught to pray to the land....if we drink of it we ask it to be blessed so that we can get strength from the Mother Earth. We really meant it from our hearts when we prayed."
—*Walapai councilwoman Sylvia Querta speaking to author Stephen Trimble*

The Upland Yumans, linguistic cousins to the River Yumans, lived a much more nomadic lifestyle to take advantage of the sequence of ripening plants across the landscape. Only the Havasupai, who spent half the year at the bottom of the Grand Canyon, practiced rancheria farming. The Walapai and Yavapai, whose homelands lacked enough water to sustain permanent settlements supported by farming, spent much more time moving through a wider territory in central and northern Arizona.

The three groups of Upland Yumans speak related dialects of the same language. Although the Walapai and the Havasupai are politically and geographically separate groups, they think of themselves as the Pai, the Pa'a, or the People; they speak the same language. The third group, the Yavapai, divided themselves into four subtribes and were the traditional enemies of their fellow Upland Yumans.

The Havasupai had a wider range of elevation than any other group in the Southwest, traveling from eighteen hundred feet (549m) along the Colorado River to twelve thousand feet (3,658m) on the upper slopes of the San Francisco Peaks, the Havasupai "Center of the World."

By the middle of October, families emerged from their summer homes in a side branch of the Grand Canyon to live in semipermanent camps scattered over the surrounding plateau. There, on the Coconino Plateau, they spent the winter hunting deer, antelope, and rabbit, and gathering wild plant foods, such as piñon nuts and mescal.

In the early spring, Havasupai families began moving back into the Cataract Creek Canyon beside the tributary of the Colorado River, where they kept their summer

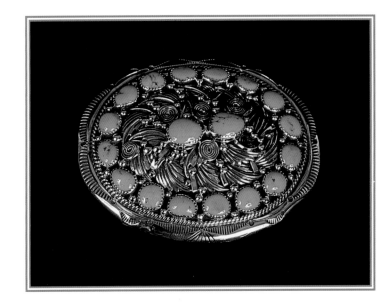

Navajo craftsmen are well known for their beautiful work in turquoise and silver. This belt buckle was made by Navajo Art Begay.

homes and fields. They began planting in mid-April, with corn harvesting beginning in June and continuing until early autumn. They also raised beans, squash, sunflowers, apricots, figs, and peaches. The Havasupai continue to celebrate their traditional harvest Peach Festival, a time when they are joined by Walapais, Hopis, and Navajos; through the years, they have moved the date up to August so that children can participate before they leave for school.

The Walapai moved across the landscape, following the sequence of ripening wild plants. They practiced a fairly regular annual pattern of movement to take advantage of seasonally available wild resources. In the spring, the Walapai gathered and processed the wild mescal or agave they found in the canyons and foothills. They baked mescal stalks in earth ovens for several days so that they could eat the delicious inner core. The women then crushed the outer layers into a pulp, formed them into slabs, and dried them in the sun. The slabs could then be boiled for food, mixed with water to drink, or stored for later use.

In midsummer, women collected the fruits of several cactus species. In late summer and early autumn, they collected ripened piñon cones and juniper and sumac berries.

During the winter the people encamped in larger, more sedentary groups. Men hunted antelope, mule deer, and bighorn sheep. This meat was supplemented with the nutritious vegetables and fruit the women had stored.

In 1865, the Walapai War erupted when drunken Anglos murdered a Pai leader. The Pais (the Walapai and Havasupai) retaliated

by killing miners, which led to the U.S. cavalry setting fire to Pai rancherias. By the end of 1868, U.S. soldiers had wiped out a quarter of the tribe by destroying at least sixty-eight rancherias and killing 175 Pais.

Yavapai bands practiced a similar nomadic hunter-gatherer lifestyle, which ranged across 10 million acres (4 million ha) in central and western Arizona—more territory than any other Yuman people. Today, Yavapai elders still identify themselves as descendants of one of four sub-tribes: the Western, Southeastern, Northeastern, and Central Yavapai. Each group had access to Sonoran desert, mountain, and transition zone environments, which provided a steady food supply of many different plants and animals. They also practiced agriculture by planting corn, beans, and squash in nearby washes, streams, and springs. They returned intermittently, in between hunting and gathering trips, to check on the progress of their crops. When the plants had ripened, they came back to harvest them.

Protected by their rugged environment, which settlers found unsuitable for farming, the Yavapai were able to continue their foraging lifestyle until the 1850s. However, in 1863, gold was discovered near Prescott, and in 1865, farmers began to settle in the Verde Valley. The Yavapai Wars followed. This decade-long conflict left central Arizona with a legacy of morbid place names such as

This Anasazi Kiva mural, dating from around A.D. 1500, is in Kuaua Pueblo, New Mexico.

A Pueblo woman grinds corn into flour. She wears the embroidered woolen dress—the manta—made of cloth woven and embroidered by men (only at Acoma Pueblo do women embroider).

Bloody Basin and Skull Valley. The Indians' hunting weapons were no match for the sophisticated guns and ammunition of the U.S. Army. During a single encounter in Skeleton Cave in the Salt River Canyon, soldiers killed seventy-six Yavapais. Defeat finally came when the army systematically destroyed the winter food supplies of the Yavapai. Today, the Yavapai live on three reservation communities: Fort McDowell, Camp Verde, and Prescott.

THE AGRICULTURAL BANDS

The Athabascan-speaking Apacheans were the last major Native American group to come to the Southwest, arriving as small bands of undifferentiated migrating peoples. They left their linguistic cousins in northwest Canada and Alaska during the 1300s and reached the Southwest sometime before the arrival of the Spaniards.

These adaptive hunter-gatherers learned quickly from their Plains and Puebloan neighbors. The Kiowa Apaches even joined the Plains-dwelling Kiowas. In contrast, the

Above: A little boy in a Head Start class from Laguna Pueblo in New Mexico learns the Buffalo Dance.

Navajo quickly developed an economy and way of life based on herding and agriculture, borrowing many Pueblo traits that they reworked into what became a distinctly Navajo culture.

The Apache

"Leadership that we had a long time ago took spirituality. It took understanding for the mountain...getting up in the morning and the addressing of the Sun, towards family, towards sacred places where the clans came from."

—*San Carlos artist Delmar Boni*
to writer Stephen Trimble

The Apache are the most misunderstood and romanticized group of Native Americans. "The movie industry has really destroyed our image. Even the word 'Apache' means 'enemies'...so everybody's scared of us....we call ourselves Ndee, the People," said the late San Carlos medicine man Philip Cassadore.

White Mountain Apache Edgar Perry described the Ndee as "Nomads—always going and going. They're a very knowledgeable people; they don't get lost."

The Apaches lived in small autonomous familial groups. Several small local groups formed bands, and the bands joined together in subtribal groups. Contrary to their Hollywood image, the Apache were not a single people undifferentiated by language, culture, and geographical location; nor were they a single political entity. There are seven Apachean-speaking tribes that refer to themselves as nations. Some Apachean groups, such as the Lipan, Jicarilla, and Mescalero Apache, ranged onto the Plains; like their Plains neighbors, they practiced little agriculture and lived in tipis rather than brush-covered wickiups like other Apaches. The Chiricahua lived in southern Arizona; the Western Apacheans lived in east-central Arizona and include the White Mountain, Cibicue, San Carlos, and Northern and Southern Tonto. The Navajo are also Apacheans.

The highly mobile local groups controlled their own hunting and farming areas and carried out nearly all important activities. Men hunted deer and antelope, while women gathered and processed wild plants. Families moved frequently within the territory of their local group to take advantage of plants that grew at different elevations and matured in different seasons. The most important plant was the agave or century plant, whose shoot they roasted and whose crown they baked and then dried in the sun and stored. Women also gathered mesquite beans, sumac berries, juniper berries, piñon nuts, and many wild greens.

The Apache considered raiding to be another subsistence activity, one that became increasingly important to their survival as they lost access to their traditional food-gathering locations. Raiding involved five to fifteen men, who rode to their nearest neighbor to take food and horses. Raiding, which in Western Apache is "to search out enemy property," is quite different from warfare, "to take death from an enemy." The relative of a slain individual avenged his death by leading a war party. Raiding was a means of group survival.

Mounted nomads have always preyed on their agricultural neighbors, trading in times of abundance, raiding in times of scarcity. Each Apache group raided the nearest settlements: the Western Apaches raided the Maricopa, O'odham, and Navajo; the Tonto Apache raided the Pai; the Chiricahua raided Mexican ranches; the Lipan raided Texas ranches; and the Jicarilla and Mescalero raided the Spanish and Pueblo villages of the Rio Grande area.

The raiding relationship was well established long before the United States assumed control of the Southwest. The

America. By 1835, the neighboring states of Sonora and Chihuahua had placed a bounty of one hundred dollars on every male Apache scalp.

During the Chichimec wars of the 1500s, the Spanish drew on old animosities to pit one Indian group against another. Years later, New Mexico governor Juan Bautista de Anza used Navajos as auxiliaries in his campaigns against Apache groups. He also persuaded Utes and Comanches to stop fighting the Spaniards and to fight the Apache instead. The U.S. Army also used this divide-and-conquer strategy successfully against various Apache groups.

Apache raided the Spaniards for horses, and the soldiers retaliated by selling Apaches into slavery. The Mescalero Apache killed so many travelers on the Camino Real north from El Paso to Santa Fe that the Spanish called it "La Journada del Muerto," the Journey of Death.

Through the 1700s, the Apache continued to hone their skills by raiding ranches in New Mexico. General George Crook called the Apache the finest light cavalry in North

Sacred sandpaintings continue to be an important part of many Navajo healing ceremonies. All designs are handed down from teacher to apprentice as part of a much larger ceremonial; made from memory, the images are dictated by tradition and require precise replication for success in healing.

In the 1850s, some Apache groups—the Jicarillas, some Mescaleros, and some Chiricahuas—signed treaties in good faith and planted fields on reservations. However, when the government failed to provide the promised rations, the people resumed raiding rather than starve. The story was repeated many times with slight variations. Tucson citizens formed the Committee of Public Safety, blaming every depredation on the peaceful Camp Grant Apaches. Eventually they worked up the fervor to massacre more than a hundred peaceful Aravaipa and Pinal Apache encamped there. By the 1880s, all surviving Apaches were herded onto reservations.

Today, the Fort Apache Timber Company employs about three hundred Apaches and grosses $30 million annually. The tribal Recreation Enterprise became Sunrise Ski area and summer resort, generating $9 million each year. The Apache realize that education is the key to progress; public schools at both Fort Apache and San Carlos have bilingual/bicultural programs.

The Navajo

"We were created from Changing Woman who represents the seasons and the earth....We were created with the assistance of the wind....It is in our fingerprints that we see evidence of the wind."

—*Navajo/Oneida Conrad House*

Changing Woman, the benevolent Holy Person who created the Navajo, also embodies the adaptable, ever-changing nature of Navajo culture. Through time, the Navajo have incorporated technology and beliefs from many other cultures into their own, remaking them in the process into distinctly Navajo products.

The Navajo sense of identity draws from their profound sense of connection to their land. Within generations of their arrival in the Southwest, the Diné—the People—had infused their surroundings with mythic significance, weaving their creation story from the land around them. They emerged through a series of previous worlds to a world bordered by the four Sacred Mountains: Sisnaajiní, Blanca Peak in Colorado, the mountain of the East; Tsoodzil, Mount Taylor in New Mexico, the mountain of the South; Dook'o'oosłíid, San Francisco Peaks, the mountain of the West; and Dibé nitsaa, Hesperus Peak in Colorado, the mountain of the North.

The Navajo ability to adapt served them well on their migration southward from their Athabascan homeland in Canada through varied terrains and climates. Soon after their entry into the Southwest, they adopted agriculture by

Navajo Head Start students smile from the back of their school bus. The vast distances of the Navajo reservation often require long bus trips to and from school each day.

raising corn, beans, squash, wheat, melons, and peaches. Tewa-speaking Pueblo peoples called them "Navahuu" in reference to their ability to cultivate fields in arroyos, or streambeds. By the 1630s, farming had become such a defining characteristic of their culture that the Spaniards in New Mexico referred to them as "Apaches de Nabaju" to distinguish them from other Apache groups.

In 1680, the Pueblo Indians revolted against the Spanish and took over much of New Mexico. In 1696, the Spanish reconquered the land, causing thousands of Pueblo to seek refuge among their Navajo neighbors. It was during this time that the connection between the Pueblo and the Navajo deepened. The Pueblo taught their hosts weaving, pottery-making, agriculture, and animal husbandry, and they shared their ritual concepts and practices—altars, sandpaintings, prayer sticks, and ceremonial masks. Inspired by the

Western Pueblos, the Navajo organized themselves into matrilineal clans. (Among other Apacheans, only the Western Apache adopted matrilineal clans.) The Navajo wove these practices and beliefs into their Athabascan worldview, creating a new system that became the distinctive Navajo culture.

The Navajo, like their Apache cousins, raided Spanish and Pueblo settlements from Zuni to Santa Fe for sheep, goat, horses, and livestock. Unlike the other groups, however, they used the stolen animals to replenish their own herds. Pastoralism became the Navajo way of life. Instead of the nomadic Apachean lifestyle, the Navajo practiced transhumance, moving between two homes: a summer

thousand head of horned cattle, 500,000 sheep, and ten thousand head of horses, mules, and asses, it not being a rare instance for one individual to possess five thousand to ten thousand sheep and four hundred to five hundred head of other stock."

The Navajo relationship with the New Mexicans was complex. Navajo women wove highly prized blankets of such "rare beauty and excellence" that New Mexicans eagerly paid for them with livestock and material items. At other times, New Mexicans captured Navajo women, forcing them to weave what became known as "slave blankets" as part of their duties. It is estimated that at one time there were six thousand Navajo slaves in New Mexico.

Dramatic spires, buttes, and mesas dot the landscape in Monument Valley. Much more than a series of dramatically poised topographic features, each rock formation is a place of power wherein spirits reside and is a living, breathing entity in an animate universe.

home beside their fields and a winter home where better pasturage would see their flocks through the colder months. Charles Bent, the first American governor of New Mexico, claimed that the Navajo tribe possessed "thirty

When the army withdrew most of its troops from the Southwest to fight in the Civil War, Apaches, Navajos, Utes, Zunis, Spanish-Americans, and Anglo-Americans seized the opportunity to wreak vengeance on their enemies. The situation became so chaotic that in 1862 the newly appointed military commander for New Mexico, General James Carleton, retaliated with one of the most violent military campaigns ever waged against any group of Native Americans.

Taos Pueblo, located seventy miles (112.5km) north of Santa Fe, New Mexico, is the northernmost of the Eastern Pueblos. The people of Taos have been in more continuous contact with Plains peoples than most of the other Pueblos; Plains influence can be seen in their dress styles, secular dances and music, and Peyotism.

Carleton's plan centered around the forced relocation of Mescalero Apaches and Navajos to Fort Sumner in east-central New Mexico. Although a military board had recommended another location because of poor water, an inadequate supply of wood, and threat of floods, Carleton insisted on Fort Sumner, also known as Bosque Redondo, as the new home for the Mescalero and the Navajo—who were traditional enemies.

General Carleton appointed Colonel Kit Carson as commander of the troops in the field. Carson was a reluctant campaigner who believed the Indians would eventually agree to terms without the need for war. Nevertheless, Carson led his troops against the Mescalero and subdued them in five months. Carleton told the commander of Fort Wingate to order the peaceful Navajo leaders to surrender; he made no attempt to communicate or negotiate directly with the general Navajo population.

On July 22, 1863, Kit Carson began his campaign, leading more than seven hundred New Mexico militiamen against the Navajo. Using the "scorched earth" strategy later employed by General William Sherman in his "March to the Sea" across Georgia, Carson's troops destroyed any hogans, cornfields, peach trees, water holes, animals, and people in their path. Carleton paid a bounty to each soldier for the capture of horses, mules, and sheep. To make matters worse, the Utes, Mexicans, and Pueblos, longtime enemies of the Navajo, increased the frequency and ferocity of their raids.

Heavy snow covered the ground when Carson and his men invaded Canyon de Chelly in January 1864. By that time, most Navajos were already starving. Sixteen days later, Carson returned to Fort Defiance with more than two hundred Navajos. More Navajos surrendered at the fort during the rest of the bitterly cold winter.

In February troops marched two convoys of Navajos to Fort Sumner. Hundreds died along the way. Soldiers shot stragglers and slavers stole children. Without wagons, nearly everyone had to walk.

Carleton had vastly underestimated the number of Navajos who would surrender. By March 1865, 9,022 Navajos were imprisoned at Fort Sumner, but there were food, blankets, and shelter for only half that number. Droughts, poor agricultural land, epidemics, and raids by other tribes led to the death of many Navajos. Despite an enormous cost to the government, internment at Fort Sumner was a disaster.

After four desperate years, the government sent General William Sherman to review the situation. He wrote, "Last year the crop was an utter failure....The scarcity of wood, the foul character of the water, which is salty and full of alkali, their utter despair...." After signing a peace treaty, the Navajos were finally allowed to return from Fort Sumner to their homeland.

The Navajo relied on resilience, determination, and adaptability to rebuild their culture. Trading posts soon dotted the reservation as women began weaving rugs for eastern markets. Navajo weaver D.Y. Begay believes that the trading posts led to greater creativity among Navajo artisans. The process of studying foreign designs "inspired creative exploration and self-expression."

Navajo livestock herds grew so quickly that by the 1930s overgrazing became a severe problem, and the federal gov-

THE HOPI: CARETAKERS OF ALL LIFE

"The things that were created and given to us are all very precious. We are to protect and use all these precious things wisely, and to share them in order to keep harmony among all people. But we are forgetting these things, making the search for peace extremely difficult. We fear that mankind has gone too far and forgotten too much to find this peace.

"During the ages of life the ancient Hopi have seen and experienced many things, such as changing of an old world order to a new order because of some dreadful disaster [caused] by [the] mindless action of man forgetting the Creator's divine laws. This kind of mindless action has happened in three previous world orders which have then been destroyed. It is very sad indeed that mankind will never learn from our past history. Once again, mankind has failed to live by the divine laws which we promised with our Creator to live by, and so, gradually, the land and nature are getting out-of-balance. Technology is rapidly eroding our ancient culture and tradition. The wildlife and forest are diminishing rapidly, the precious water and air are becoming unhealthy to drink and breathe. Changing climate also is important to consider seriously for it symbolizes a grave warning to man.

"How can we correct the faults? Would retracing our steps back to divine laws be a solution? This will be a difficult step because we are tempted on all sides into material values. The moral values we once followed have now become make-believe living like playthings we use. If we correct our ways we could turn the course of the future. Our prophecy foretold that the time might come that a man with a very clever mind will seek out the secret of Nature and defy its laws. Much of what is discovered will benefit man in good ways, but most of it also has a dangerous side. Because Nature has its own mysterious protection, man will eventually harvest misfortune. It

has become clear now that the products of modern science and technology such as medicine, drugs and weapons are what was prophesied.

"While this is going on, the Hopi who turn against their original vows will unbalance the earthly cycles that control the seasons. This will be done in Hopi land because that is a spiritual center of the earth. This change will affect the entire earth. Hopi land will be the first to feel the effect. We will know the imbalance is coming about when our planting month is delayed by cold weather or when frost comes before our crops are mature for harvest. This happened this very year so our harvest will be less. With trained eyes, we see some wild life begin to disappear. Most summer insects did not return in accordance with seasonal cycles. Perhaps they have gone in search of their natural environment. We look at all these events as signs of some great change or new turn of events coming soon, but only the Great Spirit knows exactly when. Perhaps this is fulfilling Hopi prophecy of a great purification of the present world order. No one knows what form this will take. It can come in peaceful ways or in the form of terrible catastrophe because we are not above the laws of Creation. We Hopi are ready for the outcome. Whatever it may be we all deserve what will be given....

"The way one treats another serves either to strengthen or destroy the spiritual basis of peace in the world. Serious wars are bound to result throughout the world, as long as America continues to oppose the spiritual way of life we call the Hopi way. Contrary to the opinion of many, the greater the military force of a nation, the greater the danger to that nation. Peace can come to the world only through an honest, non-violent relationship with the indigenous people, who are the caretakers of life."

—Carolyn Tawangyowma, Sovereign Hopi Independent Nation

Traditional Native Americans live spiritually, both individually and collectively. Prayer permeates every facet of their daily lives as they live with reverence for all living beings. All things, including those considered by some to be inanimate, possess a spiritual life force or sacred power.

Francisco and Los Angeles. In 1971, the Navajo Nation opened Navajo Community College, the first locally controlled Indian college of its kind. The college is guided by the Diné philosophy of learning, and the curriculum is based on Navajo principles of honoring and maintaining balance in the universe. At least thirty Indian nations were inspired by the Navajo example and have built similar colleges.

In facing the future, the Navajo will have to call upon their ability to integrate and adapt, traits that have repeatedly enabled them to bring order out of chaos. Navajo teacher Rex Lee Jim expressed this well: "Our adaptability is our tradition."

Navajo D.Y. Begay embodies the Diné ability to incorporate the new without loss of identity. She explained that "a belief that is very strong in my heart is that being a Navajo woman means knowing how to weave and how to deal with the process of weaving itself....This belief is a central part of my life." Today she lives in two worlds—"in a traditional one, at home with my family, who speak only Navajo, and with my husband, who is Anglo."

The Diné story has been one of continual evolution and growth. Out of disruption and chaos came order. Conrad House likened Navajo growth to cycles that "always continue on and on, forever and forever, like the seasons. There will be a time of disruption and chaos, and out of that comes order." The Navajo ceremonial basket, he said, "holds our world view. It has the opening to the east and the rainbow band encircling. Designs of clouds, mountain, red evening sunset, night sky, white dawn, and the seasons are indicated on that band. It suggests the ups and downs of life spiraling around—cycles."

"Sa'a naghaí bik'e hózhó" is a phrase heard again and again in Navajo prayers. The concept of hózhó embraces many things: balance, order, harmony, and happiness. When illness or misfortune occur, it is because hózhó—state of goodness—has been disrupted. Balance and harmony are restored through ceremony.

This phrase reflects the Diné recognition that everything is in a constant state of becoming. The Navajo continue to weave the beneficial aspects of other cultures into the fabric of their cultural identity. Within the words "sa'a naghai bik'e hózhó" lie the energy and strength to renew their culture.

ernment ordered forced stock reduction. For the Navajo, who considered their animals to be gifts from the Holy People, the thinning of their herds was traumatic in itself, but the methods the Bureau of Indian Affairs used created great bitterness. Goats and sheep were shot and left to rot or captured and left to starve in holding pens.

Today the major problem that faces the Navajo is overpopulation of their land base; nearly half the population is unemployed. Economic necessity has led many Navajos to live and work in southwestern cities as well as San

CHAPTER 4

California

"The baskets feel very much alive. When I look at the Pomo baskets and hold them, I feel a real connection to the past, to all the grandmothers who have gone before me. And I get a sense of calm, a sense of perfect balance."

—*Pomo basketweaver Susan Billy,*
in All Roads Are Good

California native cultures have miraculously survived the onslaught of Spanish missionaries, European diseases, gold miners, and land-hungry immigrants. In fact, these native peoples are currently undergoing a cultural renewal as new generations learn traditional dances, arts, and languages.

One of the first encounters between natives and outsiders was a clash of two profoundly different worldviews. Maria Copa Frias, a Coast Miwok, summarized her peoples' beliefs about the afterlife: the dead leap into the ocean at Point Reyes and follow a "kind of string leading west through the surf" to a road behind the breakers. The dead then go farther west, to where the sun sets. There they live with Coyote in Ute-yomigo, the Home of the Dead.

In 1579, when the Coast Miwok, who lived north of San Francisco, saw the crew of Sir Francis Drake arriving from the west, they assumed that they were coming from Ute-yomigo. Furthermore, Drake and his men established their encampment directly on the path to Ute-yomigo. With their sparse beards (like native men) and deep tans from years of exposure on the open seas, these invaders could only be departed ancestors. In a fury of mourning behavior, the women tore at their breasts and heads, shrieking and throwing themselves on the ground. Coast Miwok men displayed reverence toward the strangers but refused their gifts because of strict sanctions about bringing anything back from the Home of the Dead. Instead, they gave the British ritual gifts: skins, arrow quivers, baskets, food, feathers, and tobacco.

Opposite: A Hupa woman from northwestern California wears shell necklaces, a buckskin dress elaborately decorated with bead and shell strings, and a fine basketry hat.

Left: This unusual basket is decorated with a pattern of feathers.

The British, baffled by such behavior, concluded that the Coast Miwok perceived them as gods. They described the Indians as a tall, striking, and strong people who were ruled by a king. The British misinterpreted the limited authority of the headman of the local group of Coast Miwok, attributing to him Europeanlike powers of centralized authority. Drake left, convinced that the Indian "king" had surrendered his vast territories to the British Crown.

In reality, the approximately 340,000 Indians in California were divided into at least sixty-four different groups that shared no sense of identification with any large tribal organization. Most groups lived in villages of families related through the male line and loosely associated with other villages in a "tribelet." Often these villages were arranged in a cluster around a large, central village where a local headman resided.

The headman took care of his people by offering them advice, haranguing them daily with a declaration of the right way to live their lives. Only with the support of various councils of lineage elders could the headman galvanize community action. Other important village leaders included family lineage

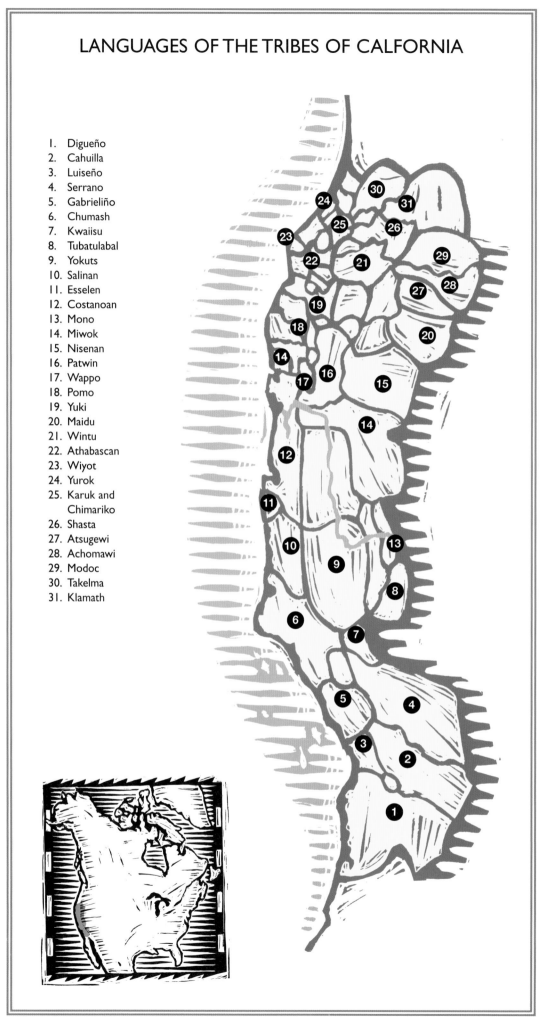

LANGUAGES OF THE TRIBES OF CALFORNIA

1. Digueño
2. Cahuilla
3. Luiseño
4. Serrano
5. Gabrieliño
6. Chumash
7. Kwaiisu
8. Tubatulabal
9. Yokuts
10. Salinan
11. Esselen
12. Costanoan
13. Mono
14. Miwok
15. Nisenan
16. Patwin
17. Wappo
18. Pomo
19. Yuki
20. Maidu
21. Wintu
22. Athabascan
23. Wiyot
24. Yurok
25. Karuk and Chimariko
26. Shasta
27. Atsugewi
28. Achomawi
29. Modoc
30. Takelma
31. Klamath

Spanish soldiers forced California Indians into missions, where the Spanish padres forced the Indians to work in the fields. Rather than being holy places, churches were considered by Native Americans to be "fortresses where they were housed."

heads and shamans, who were spiritual leaders, herbalists, physicians, and psychologists.

California had the greatest diversity of Indian languages of any culture area, with between sixty-four and eighty different languages and several hundred dialects spoken.

These languages can be grouped into Penutian, the Hokan, stock, Yukian, Algic, Athabascan, and Uto-Aztecan language stocks whose speakers were spread out in pockets from Oregon to Mexico.

The mild climate and abundance of wild foods more than adequately supported the most densely populated culture area in North America. This abundance meant that California peoples could live a relatively sedentary lifestyle without agriculture. Furthermore, it made it possible for them to develop complex trade networks and well-defined art forms such as basketry.

Native peoples adapted to the many ecological zones in California by developing regional economic strategies. This area encompasses half a dozen life zones, each with its own flora and fauna.

CALIFORNIA LIFE: THE CHUMASH

With nearly twenty-two thousand people, the Chumash nation was one of California's largest tribes. However, they lived in many separate communities, had no overall tribal organization, and spoke at least six related languages: Ventureño, Barbareño, Ynezeño, Purisimeño, Obispeño, and the Island language. The Chumash lived in the region from San Luis Obispo to Malibu Canyon on the coast and inland as far as the western edge of the San Joaquin valley. They also occupied the Santa Barbara Channel Islands.

The Chumash were the first major group of California Indians to encounter Europeans when Juan Rodriguez Cabrillo landed near Ventura in 1542. Because their culture disappeared before it could be documented, our only glimpse of the Chumash comes from the diaries and journals of Spanish explorers.

Chumash villages were unusually large for California Indians, sometimes numbering more than thousand inhabitants. The Chumash lived in round, thatched dwellings, which were as large as fifty feet (15m) in diameter. Their rancheria settlements also included semisubterranean sweathouses, storage huts, cleared playing fields, and ceremonial grounds. Some Chumash were specialists in curing,

The English explorer and pirate Sir Francis Drake had no idea what sort of civilization he had stumbled upon when he was showered with gifts from the Miwok of northern California.

basketmaking, steatite carving, woodworking, canoe making, and rock painting.

Most Chumash lived inland, but six to seven thousand Chumash lived on the coast and on the Channel Islands.

Fishing from twenty-five-foot (7.5m) planked canoes, or tomol, Chumash crews of three or four paddled far out to sea in fair weather. They reached San Nicolas, some sixty-five miles (104.5km) from the mainland. In their encounter with the Chumash, the Spanish were most impressed by these unique, seagoing boats "composed of some twenty long and narrow pieces" that the Spanish described as "very carefully made of several planks which they work with no other tools than their shells and flints. They join them at the seams by sewing with very strong thread… and fit the joints with pitch."

The best fishing was from late spring to late summer, when sea mammals gathered and fish schooled in the great beds of kelp that grow along the coast. With tridents, toggle harpoons, and woven nets, Chumash fishermen caught many different species of fish—yellowtail, halibut, black sea bass, bonito—and sea mammals—seals, whales, and dolphins. They also collected many kinds of mollusks, which they ate year-round.

As with most California Indians, the acorn was their most important single food source. Gathered in the autumn, acorns were stored for year-round use. Processing the acorn, however, was very time-consuming; women dried, hulled, and pulverized acorns into flour, then leached them in hot water to remove the tannin, a bitter-tasting substance that causes indigestion. They boiled the acorn meal into mush and then molded and baked it into cakes for their families.

Women also collected a variety of other foods: pine nuts, berries, mushrooms, cress, and wild cherries. They ground the roots of the cattail for pinole, which they served as a gruel or paste. Chumash men hunted California mule deer and fox with the bow and arrow, snared smaller animals, and killed rabbits during communal rabbit drives. On lagoons, they harvested migratory ducks and geese.

The Chumash wove a wide variety of outstanding baskets: basketry bottles ingeniously waterproofed on the inside, basin-shaped baskets for food preparation, olla-shaped baskets for seed storage, large burden baskets, and flat circular trays for winnowing and parching. Women lavished the highest level of workmanship on trinket baskets that contained small possessions.

When Juan Bautista de Anza encountered the Chumash in 1775, he was impressed by their finely finished steatite carvings. The Chumash cooked in heavy heat-resistant steatite ollas and on comals, flat skilletlike slabs of steatite. They also carved and polished small bowls to hold beads and other possessions, often decorating the rims with tiny

This reproduction of an etching by H. Chapman Ford shows Mission Santa Cruz when the founding padres resided there.

flat shell beads that they inlaid on asphaltum. Chumash carvers also used steatite to produce carved beads, medicine tubes, smoking pipes, and whale effigies.

The Chumash created the most spectacular polychrome rock paintings in North America. These magnificent red, black, and white pictographs have been designated the Santa Barbara style, taking their name from their location in Santa Barbara and Ventura counties. Specialists have dated these paintings to A.D. 1000 by using radiocarbon dating, erosion rate, and other evidence. Most paintings are abstract, with angular and curvilinear elements in the shape of large "suns." They also feature highly stylized and imaginative human figures and animals, especially centipedes

Pomo weavers created baskets that were unsurpassed for their diversity of forms, excellence of technique, and variety of decoration. Pomo Susan Billy continues this tradition today.

and marine animals. Some of the paintings may have been made by girls during their puberty rites, as was done among the Luiseño Indians.

Shamans probably made or directed most of the Chumash paintings. Deriving his power from a guardian spirit, the shaman's primary function was to cure disease. To accomplish this, he used singing, herbs, and a medicine tube for sucking out the objects presumed to be causing the sickness. Chumash shamans specialized in specific feats: weather shamans controlled the weather; grizzly bear shamans could transform themselves into bears and kill enemies; and rattlesnake shamans handled rattlesnakes.

The mainland Chumash were also great traders who supplied their Salinan neighbors with steatite, wooden vessels, and beads. From the Yokuts, they got black pigment, antelope and elk skins, obsidian, salt, steatite, beads, seeds,

THE SUFFERING OF THE EARTH THROUGH WINTU EYES

"When the Indians all die, then God will let the water come down from the north. Everyone will drown. That is because the White people never cared for land or deer or bear.

"When we Indians kill meat, we eat it all up. When we dig roots, we make little holes. When we build houses, we make little holes. When we burn grass for grasshoppers, we don't ruin things. We shake down acorns and pine nuts. We don't chop down the trees. We only use dead wood.

"But the White people plow up the ground, pull up the trees, kill everything.

"The tree says, 'Don't. I am sore. Don't hurt me.' But they chop it down and cut it up.

"The spirit of the land hates them.

"They blast out trees and stir it up to its depths. They saw up the trees. That hurts them.

"The Indians never hurt anything, but the White people destroy all. They blast rocks and scatter them on the ground.

"The rock says, 'Don't! You are hurting me.' But the White people pay no attention.

"When the Indians use rocks, they take little round ones for their cooking. The White people dig deep long tunnels. They make roads. They dig as much as they wish. They don't care how much the ground cries out.

"How can the spirit of the earth like the White man? That is why God will upset the world—because it is sore all over. Everywhere the White man has touched it, it is sore."

—*Wintu shaman Kate Luckie speaking to ethnographer Cora Du Bois in the early decades of the twentieth century*

and herbs in exchange for white pigment, shell beads, clam, abalone, olivella, limpet and cowrie shells, and dried sea urchin and starfish. They also traded with the Tubatulabal, the Island Chumash, the Kitanemuk, and the Gabrieliño.

EUROPEAN CONTACT

The peaceful world of the Chumash changed abruptly with the arrival of Spanish missionaries who founded the mission San Luis Obispo in 1772. Father Junipero Serra's impression of the Chumash illustrates how profoundly the native and European worldviews clashed. Although Father Serra noted "their general behavior, their pleasing ways and engaging manners," he failed to understand that Chumash society and

the behavior he so admired were based on a complex spiritual system that had provided meaning for thousands of years. Father Serra continued his observations by writing, "My heart was broken to think that they were still deprived of the light of the Holy Gospel."

For these native peoples, the arrival of the Spaniards was devastating. Chumash Tony Romero compared his people's existence before and after the coming of the Spaniards: "Life was just a paradise here, and when they had to change from paradise to...I call it incarceration...You speak of the churches, all Indian people will tell you there weren't no churches, they were better understood as fortresses where they were housed."

Spanish soldiers had to force the people into the missions; few came of their own free will. In 1878, a Kamia Indian named Janitin remembered the brutality of his capture: "I and two of my relatives went down to the beach to catch clams. We saw two men on horseback coming rapidly towards us; they overtook me and lassoed and dragged me for a long distance, their horses running." Once they arrived at the mission, they locked Janitin in a room for a week, baptized him, and took him to work in the fields with the other Indians. "Every day they lashed me" until he found a way to escape. But they tracked him and lashed him until he lost consciousness. "For several days I could not raise myself from the floor where they had laid me, and I still have on my shoulders the marks of the lashes."

By 1804, the Spaniards had founded four more missions and had brought the entire Chumash population—except for those who had fled into the mountains and inland valleys—into the mission system. Exposure to European diseases such as smallpox, syphilis, and the common cold rapidly decimated the Chumash people who were housed inside the mission compounds.

By 1831, there were only 2,788 Chumash registered at the five missions, one-seventh of their original number.

The Mexican government won its independence from Spain in 1821 and secularized the missions in 1834. From then on, the padres were forbidden to compel labor from the Indians. Their hope was that the missions could be transformed into towns populated by Indians who would become Mexican citizens.

When they were freed, the Indians saw this as an end to their enslavement. But by this time, missionization had all but destroyed their native culture. There was no way of returning to the ancient ways of living in peace and

harmony with the land, because the land had been taken over by the Mexican missions, presidios, pueblos, and estates. Corrupt officials kept developed lands from being distributed to surviving ex-mission Indians, whites harassed any Chumash who tried to farm for themselves, and administrators enslaved the few who remained at the missions. Many eventually found work as peons, or feudal serfs, on the Mexican ranch estates.

Profound changes to the landscape also left California Indians bewildered. European-introduced horses, mules, sheep, pigs, and goats had destroyed the delicate native grasses and other plant foods that had provided sustenance for native peoples. Mission agricultural practices had squeezed out native vegetation. The native peoples had no access to their previous hunting and gathering territories because of numerous European settlements. Some tribes had almost completely disappeared.

The despair felt by many Indians is evident in the words of an Indian who had recently been freed from the Dolores Mission at San Francisco: "I am very old. My people were once around me like the sands of the shore. They died like the grass. I am a Christian Indian. I am all that is left of my people. I am alone."

THE DEVASTATION OF THE GOLD RUSH

Even more devastating were the catastrophic conditions that followed the U.S. takeover of California after the Treaty of Guadalupe Hidalgo in 1848. That same year, J.A. Sutter discovered gold in California, which led to an influx of more than 100,000 miners. Incredibly violent hoards of gold-seekers swarmed over northern California, overrunning the tribal hunting and gathering territories of Indian groups who had managed to avoid enslavement in the Spanish mission system.

Whites killed Indians for sport, wiping out entire camps. They contemptuously called all Indians "diggers" in reference to the sticks native peoples used to gather roots. Newspaper headlines reflected the prevalent attitude of the time: "Good Haul of Diggers," "Thirty-eight Bucks Killed," "Forty Squaws and Children Taken."

Indian agent Adam Johnston reported in 1850 that most tribes "are kept in constant fear on account of the indiscrimi-

This picture, taken in 1933, shows Lucy Tellis with a large hand-woven basket that she spent four years making.

nate and inhumane massacre of their people. The immense flood of immigration which spread over their country...was quite incomprehensible to them."

In 1851, the federal government was forced to take action on behalf of the bewildered Indians and established reservations on military reserves, where soldiers were supposed to protect them from white citizens. This was ineffective because in their mistrust of the whites, most Indians chose to withdraw further into remote areas.

With hostilities between whites and Indians raging all over the state, the national government was again forced to take action. After the Senate approved California's admission to the Union in 1850, Senate members debated about how the federal government could remove the Indians from contact with gold miners. They authorized three commissioners, who arranged eighteen treaties during 1851 and 1852.

Fearing that treaty lands might contain gold, whites vehemently protested the proposed treaties, which would have set aside 7.5 million acres (3 million ha) of land for California Indians. In 1852, the Senate failed to ratify the eighteen treaties. With no protected land to live on, the California tribes were quickly decimated. Between 1850 and 1870, the native population of California declined from 100,000 to between thirty and fifty thousand.

In 1864, the federal government finally established the first executive order reservation in the state in Hoopa Valley in Humboldt County. Local opposition continued to block the creation of three authorized reservations until the 1873 Tule River Reservation in Tulare County.

TOWARD THE FUTURE

Even today, many California Indian peoples, such as the Gabrieliño and Juaneño of southern California, have yet to be recognized by the federal government. Other groups, such as the Guidiville band of Pomo Indians, have been terminated and are aggressively seeking reinstatement or recognition. Edward Castillo of Sonoma State University estimated that about 200,000 California Indians live in the state, with as many as sixty thousand living on reservations. Many California Indian tribes that anthropologists consider to be extinct still have descendants.

Given the violent history of white-Indian relations in California, it seems miraculous that any cultures survived. The civil rights era that began in the 1960s provided an opportunity for a resurgence of Native American rights.

Among the Pomo Indians, basket making is more than a craft; it is an expression of the weaver's inner balance and peace. In Creation's Journey, *basket-making teacher Mrs. Matt is quoted explaining to her students that "a basket is a song made visible."*

tribally controlled museum. Also unique to California is the annual California Indian Confer-ence, which was first held in 1984. Here experts at state and federal levels meet to share their knowledge of history, cul-ture, language, and legal matters.

Two individuals who are a vital part of this cul-tural resurgence are Cahuilla Richard Milanovich and Pomo Susan Billy. Both these activists helped to select examples of their peoples' work for display in the National Museum of the American Indian and both contributed articles to one of the museum's first pub-lications, *All Roads Are Good: Native Voices on Life and Culture.*

Richard Milanovich is a member of the Agua Caliente Band of Cahuilla Indians in Palm Springs. He has held a seat on the tribal council since 1977 and has served as its chair-man since 1984. "Cahuilla

San Francisco State University was the first to establish a Native American studies program. The University of California at Berkeley and the University of California at Los Angeles soon followed in creating similar programs, as well as important scholarly journals: *The American Indian Quarterly* and *The American Indian Culture and Research Journal.* These programs not only provided a multidiscipli-nary study of traditional Native American cultures but also addressed the future by training a new generation of Indian leaders who could shape federal Indian policy.

In 1964, Cahuilla traditionalists on the Morongo Indian Reservation established the Malki Museum, the first

means 'powerful ones,'" he explained. "Our nation is comprised of seven bands. The Agua Caliente Reservation consists of thirty-two acres (13ha). We have a unique rela-tionship with Palm Springs. Regarding development on the reservation, final appeal rights rest with the tribal council.

"Indian people are more than feathers, they're more than paint. They are a deeply humanistic group of people who learned to live within their environment in a way that allowed an understanding of their environment and, therefore, of themselves."

The Cahuilla had an innovative and resilient spirit that characterized their ability to survive in a harsh desert environment. They adapted fully to local foods—such as, according to Milanovich, "mesquite and cactus. There are over fifteen types of edible cactus. There are over 150 different types of plants, in an area about one-half by one-quarter of a mile [804.5 by 402m]. We also had beans, including a very sweet-tasting mesquite bean that we called our candy. We made use of the palm seed, the seeds in the gourds, and the beans from the Palo Verde tree."

Milanovich grew up at a time "when it wasn't good to be Indian," but the people of his generation "are attempting to bestow upon our younger people the knowledge that we did not have, but which is so important to Indian people. Let us discover who we are."

An essential aspect of California Indian identity comes from the weaving of their distinctive baskets. Although the California Indian basket makers of the late nineteenth and early twentieth centuries produced what were considered to be the finest baskets in the world, the number of basket makers has declined in the last sixty years. But a new generation of basket makers is emerging; they now hold an annual gathering at Ya-Ka-Ama.

Susan Billy, a Pomo basket weaver from northern California, regards her people's baskets as a primal connection to traditional Pomo values. "There are only a handful of women and a few men making baskets. But I get very upset when I hear people say that weaving is a dying art….I'm doing it…there are others also weaving…there is always somebody who is going to carry on that wisdom and that knowledge…our songs…are just waiting for the right person to bring them out again." she said.

She spoke from experience. Although she was raised in Virginia, away from her people and their traditions, she and her family always revered their Pomo baskets. Eventually, she moved to California and sought out her great-aunt Elsie Allen, whom she did not know. Her great-aunt had always hoped that some of the younger Indian people would want to learn the art of basket making, but until Susan Billy's appearance, none had been interested. When her great-aunt gave Billy weaving tools that had belonged to Billy's grandmother, Billy said, "It was a very emotional experience,

This exquisite example of Pomo basketry is decorated with a pattern of abalone-shell beads.

quite overwhelming. I had these tools and I could just feel that I was where I was supposed to be. And I began to sit with her and learn from her for the next sixteen years."

As she learned how to weave baskets, she also learned about her people's culture. Renowned basket makers, the Pomo were actually more than seventy different tribes. Billy discovered that "Both men and women were basket makers. Our lives were bound the way the baskets were bound together. Generally, our women made the coiled, twined, and feathered baskets, while men made all the fishing weirs, bird traps, and baby baskets." She continued, "Traditionally, a basket was not made before a child was born. The materials would already be prepared. The uncle would show up the day the child was born and work on that basket and nothing else for three days."

Susan Billy compares the process of basket making with "a very long journey, calling for much patience." It begins by gathering the "materials at just the right time and in the right season" and curing them "for one year before we use them. The actual weaving is really at the end of the process."

The sixteen years she spent weaving with her great-aunt gave her a deep understanding of what other Pomo weavers feel when they make baskets; the maker weaves his or her spirit and thoughts into the basket. This is why "these baskets are still alive. They all have an energy to them. One of the most powerful things about these baskets is the great respect that was paid to ancestors, materials, and spirits."

Susan Billy spoke of weaving as being "very repetitious, but the true difficulty lies in the discipline required—having the desire and discipline." The Pomo and Cahuilla cultures are alive today because they had the desire and discipline to weave together a new future. With respect for traditional values and an understanding of the new challenges, Native Americans are blending the old and the new to create strong, viable, and enduring cultures.

CHAPTER 5

The Northwest Coast

"As the dancers danced around...their blankets gently twirled, and you could see the striking images of their family crests outlined in mother-of-pearl buttons against dark blue, black, or bright red backgrounds....To see people wearing these 'robes of power' was something I will never forget. The older dancers swung their shoulders to make their blankets open. Eagles appeared to soar; the Raven mimicked their actions. Bears stood proud....the animal spirits would be proud of their people, for surely the dancers showed their thankfulness to those spirits."

—*Richard Hill, Sr., in* Creation's Journey

*T*his contemporary description of a centuries-old Haida ceremony conveys how the spiritual and natural worlds are related in Northwest Coast native art. Heraldic crests such as those displayed on button blankets evoke a primordial time when spirits easily changed from animal to human form—a time when animals and humans miraculously merged. Such experiences gave a family the right to display the lineage crest of an animal spirit as well as to perform certain dances, sing specific songs, even gather plants in a particular area. Art made visible the mythic, the social, and the sacred.

The distinctive art of the Northwest Coast came out of a rainy, mist-shrouded land, isolated by mountain ranges with peaks that sometimes rose to almost twenty thousand feet (6,096m). Deeply wooded mountains rose almost directly from the sea along the coastal fjords. Heavy rainfall caused mudslides; severe winds sometimes destroyed houses. More like western Europe than eastern North America in climate, the Northwest Coast had (and still has) wet, windy winters; some islands in southeastern Alaska received an average of more than three hundred inches (762cm) of rain each year.

Left: This wooden Kwakiutl feast bowl is carved and painted with the mythological serpent Sisiutl.

Opposite: A Kwakiutl chief wears a Chilkat blanket and a fine carved and painted headpiece made from cedar wood; he had traveled from his home in British Columbia to London for the 1953 coronation of Queen Elizabeth. The Kwakiutl are known for their sculptural style of carving, and they adorned their masks and hats with beaks, fins, wings, and other protuberances.

Because the peoples of this region recognized no large political units outside their individual villages—they had no sense of nation—tribes were essentially language groupings.

Farthest north, the Tlingit, Haida, and Tsimshian lived in the harshest environment. Tlingit country—the panhandle of southeast Alaska and inland British Columbia—is especially rugged, with towering mountains of raw, naked rock. Deep fjords cut the southeastern Alaska coast; rain and snow fall as many as 260 days a year, sometimes totaling 220 inches (559cm) of precipitation annually. The Haida lived on the Queen Charlotte Islands and depended on their large, seaworthy canoes for contact with the mainland; wealthy Tlingit headmen often purchased the 60-foot (18m)-long canoes from the Haida. The coastline and the lower Nass and Skeena Rivers to the north were home to Tsimshian villages. The Kwakiutl (known today as Kwakwaka'wakw) and Salish also lived on the mainland. Other major tribes include the Nootkans (now known as Nuu-chah-nulth) on Vancouver Island and the Chinook along the lower Columbia River. The peoples of the Northwest Coast spoke more than forty separate languages from a dozen different language families.

The peoples of the Northwest Coast region share a similar art tradition in terms of style and materials, even though this narrow arc of land stretches from the top of the Alaskan panhandle, through coastal British Columbia, south to the Columbia River. The formidable mountain barrier kept the peoples from venturing outside this area; instead, they traveled by sea and river to other villages up and down the coast. In the few places where major rivers penetrated the rugged mountain ranges, the coastal peoples influenced, and were influenced by, the interior peoples.

The coastal groups had the freedom to develop rich and complex ceremonial cultures with highly stratified societies, because they lived in the midst of plentiful resources from the ocean, rivers, and land. Through time, the native peoples learned how to make the most efficient use of their surroundings. Their highly specialized knowledge and efficient tools allowed them to harvest enough food in the summer to see them through the rainy winter—the time of ceremonies and storytelling.

The natural abundance of the region enabled the native peoples to live the settled village lifestyle usually enjoyed only by agriculturalists. Before 1774, as many as 200,000 people lived in the Northwest Coast, making it one of the

LANGUAGES OF THE TRIBES OF THE NORTHWEST COAST

1. Athabascan
2. Takelma
3. Coos
4. Kalapuyan
5. Siuslawan
6. Alsean
7. Tillamook
8. Clatskanie
9. Chinook
10. Kwalhioqua
11. Salish
12. Quileute
13. Makah
14. Nootka
15. Kwakiutl
16. Oowekeeno
17. Bella Coola
18. Bella
19. Haisla
20. Tsimshian
21. Gitksan
22. Nishga
23. Haida
24. Tlingit
25. Eyak

most densely populated nonagricultural areas of the world. Strengthened by their rich spiritual life and a well-established social hierarchy—and the fact that, at first, Europeans found little to compel them to stay in the area—Northwest Coast societies withstood the European onslaught until the late 1800s.

THE WEALTHY OF THE NORTHWEST COAST

When a nineteenth-century trader invited a Northwest Coast chief to sail home to England with him, the chief declined, saying, "I have slaves who hunt for me—paddle me in my canoes—and my wives to attend upon me. Why should I wish to leave?" The natural abundance of the area provided ease of life; in their freedom from economic activity, the peoples of this region developed a concept of wealth and aristocracy. The wealthy were those who were born to wealth and could then validate their positions by distributing their

Members of the Kwakiutl Shamans' Society posed in their traditional dress for Edward Curtis' 1914 film, In the Land of the Head-Hunters, *the first full-length ethnographic motion picture of Native Americans. Despite his sensationalistic title, Curtis took great care to present an accurate portrayal; he was helped by Tlingit George Hunt, who had grown up in a Kwakiutl village.*

wealth. Wealth in the form of family crests—heraldic heirlooms that embodied myriad privileges—provided the impetus for the artistic splendor of the Northwest Coast.

Such crests were carved and painted on virtually all the property of the man who was entitled to use them: on house posts, canoes, boxes, horn spoons, dishes, coppers, Chilkat blankets, and hats. A large, splendid house was a sign of wealth; average houses were forty feet by thirty feet (12 by 9m), but larger houses existed.

Home to six families and a total of forty to fifty persons, each rectangular cedar-plank house had hierarchically arranged living spaces and its own name and identity that reflected the owner's relationship with natural and supernatural beings. The house was filled with visible manifestations

of spiritual forces: large-mouthed killer whales, huge hook-nosed thunderbirds, fierce bears with protruding tongues and glittering eyes. The house, like the lineage it sheltered, belonged to the mythical past and future.

Everywhere were visual reminders of the family's place in the social hierarchy and its relationship to ancestral spirit. Families were located according to their social order, with the highest-ranking families living closest to the chief's family; slaves and poor relations lived near the door.

The wealthy house owner and his family lived in the place of highest honor, toward the rear and in the middle of the house. For privacy, the house chief's living area was partitioned by an immense heraldic screen some twenty feet (6m) in length. Inside the Kluckwan Whale House of the Tlingit Raven clan stood the carved and painted Rain Screen or Raven Screen, flanked by houseposts carved to represent the figures of Wood-worm and Raven.

The Tlingit word for family treasure, at.oow, embodies not only a physical object but also the ancestral spirit it depicts and the speeches that accompany its display. The greatest treasure among the Tlingit was the crest hat that symbolized the history of the clan from its time of creation.

Top: Her relatives deliver a Kwakiutl bride (standing, center) to her groom's village. As in many societies, the major purpose of marriage was to create an alliance between two families. Thus, families of equal rank arranged the marriage; presentations of expensive gifts bound the two families together.

Above: A Haida craftsman carved this tobacco mortar from stone.

Similar to a European royal crown, the crest hat was worn by the reigning head of the family on important ceremonial occasions.

The totem pole was a compound coat of arms, depicting the guardian-spirit experiences of the clan ancestor. Not all Northwest Coast peoples carved totem poles; the Tlingit, Haida, Tsimshian, and Kwakiutl peoples were the primary groups who displayed these heraldic monuments. The figures on the pole were not actually totems because there was no sense of avoidance of the depicted animals or prohibitions against killing or eating them. Instead, they were special helping spirits from the animal world who had become heraldic crests.

Totem poles varied in size, depending on their function. Relatives raised a memorial pole to honor a high-ranking person who had just died, placing the pole along the beach in front of the village. Mortuary poles were either set up by the grave of a chief or used to support the grave box itself. Shorter than either of these were interior house posts, which supported the beams of the house.

Among the Haida, frontal house poles stood against the front of a house and combined the crests of the owner and his wife. A houseowner commissioned a skilled artist to carve a totem pole to proclaim his rank through the depiction of the mythical experiences

Tattooing was widely practiced on the Northwest Coast. Men and women had crest designs tattooed on their chests, arms, and legs. The tattoos on the body of this Haida man represent events and crest figures from his family history.

of his lineage ancestors. Because the boundaries between humans, spirits, and animals were once fluid, the sculptural figures appeared to blend into one another as they rose into an elaborately carved monument that could rise as high as forty-eight feet (15m). Such interlocking figures—some grasping a fin, others squatting between the ears or biting one another—were unique to the Haida. Other groups simply stacked the different figures, keeping their forms separate and discrete.

The Northwest Coast is probably the only area in the world where a nonagricultural society had slavery. Obtained through war, slaves formed a distinct social

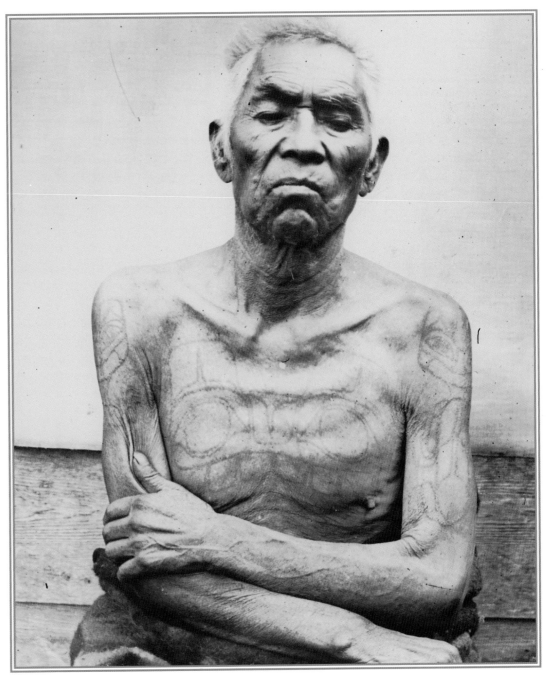

A Kwakiutl craftsman carved this wooden bowl to represent a sea otter.

THE LEGACY OF THE *EXXON VALDEZ* OIL SPILL

"Never in the millennium of our tradition have we thought it possible for the water to die. But it is true."

—Former Alutiiq Village Chief Walter Meganack to Beth Tornes, a reporter for News from Indian Country

On March 24, 1989, 11 million gallons (42 million l) of crude oil leaked from the *Exxon Valdez* tanker, spreading quickly over Prince William Sound and beyond to reach a total of fifteen hundred miles (2,413.5km) of Alaskan coastline. The beaches were coated with oil and "mousse," a frothy, sticky mixture of oil and water whipped up by the wind. And they were littered with more than sixteen thousand dead and dying birds, shellfish, seals, and otters.

Tornes describes the impact that the oil spill continues to have on the native peoples of Prince William Sound. She quoted Helmer Olson, president of the Valdez Native Tribe and member of the Chugach Nation: "We don't have any herring. The herring's all gone, it's dead. There's no more clams. Crabs are null and void.

"Our seal population has been on the decline since '89. That's the bad one. We eat seals. Use the skins for ponchos, eat the meat, render the blubber out for seal oil. It's a traditional food. We used to have a lot of seals in Prince William Sound, but not since the oil spill.

"This sound, our ecosystem, was in great shape until the spill. They [the native fishermen in Chenaga, across the sound] got hurt really bad financially. Some of the fishermen got a few thousand [from the lawsuit], but it doesn't compensate them for what they lost.

"We don't have any '89 herring. They didn't spawn. When they had some kind of disease created by the oil—there were spots on them—we had to shut the fishery down.

"The stress factor was a major upheaval for the native people. There were many broken homes, kids weren't taken care of. Both natives and non-natives were affected.

"Our cultural heritage was damaged. A lot of stress was involved, and the village was pulled apart. We had a lot of alcohol-related incidents as a result of the stress of the oil spill. People moved away from the traditional ways, but now we're going back. I think we'll make it. It seems like all we do is fight the damages to our way of life."

Violet Yeaton, a tribal member from Port Graham, farther down the coast from Valdez, said that the spill has irreparably damaged her people's culture and their way of life and that they can no longer eat traditional foods. "People are afraid of eating a lot of the shellfish. We eat them at our own risk. There isn't that many and you have to travel a long way to do harvesting. Clams, seals, ducks aren't as abundant. The bedarke [a type of fish]...we have to travel farther to find those. All of these are our traditional foods we've eaten for years, for generations.

"It's very disturbing...the disruption it's caused in our community. Our life is encompassed around harvesting. It's like a timeclock—we know when to harvest things. It's like a cycle. The *Exxon Valdez* broke that cycle.

"We're just starting to get back into the cycle of doing traditional harvesting...but at the same time we don't know how safe it is. They say the oil is gone. Where did it disappear? We know it's still there in the ground.

"There's no way they could compensate us for all the destruction that's come from the spill. All the damage done to people, all the humiliation. There's no way they can restore these people's beliefs."

In 1994, seven native corporations in the region—Cordova, Eyak, Seward, Tatitlak, Chenaga, Port Graham, and Nanawalik—along with commercial fishermen—were awarded a $5 billion jury award against Exxon. But Exxon is appealing, and it will be years before anyone receives a settlement. Although the natives of Valdez now have tribal status, because they were not officially recognized as a tribe at the time of the oil spill, they are not included in the settlement. Furthermore, Judge Russel Holland, the U.S. District Court judge who ruled on the case, did not grant the tribes any of the $165 million they asked for to compensate the loss of their subsistence, claiming, "It did not deprive Alaska natives of their culture."

Far from being an isolated incident, this event could be repeated in Exxon's proposed Crandon mine, severely damaging the wild rice beds and other wild foods of the Mole Lake Sokoagon Chippewa. Tribal Judge Fred Ackley said, "If they go ahead with their mine, our tribe is going to be devastated."

Left: *This massive heraldic (totem) pole depicts a thunderbird with spread wings and an elaborately curving beak. Craftsmen carved such poles from cedar to symbolize the heraldic crest of the owner and his family or incidents in their history.*

Above: *This Haida ceremonial robe was made of caribou and decorated with designs similar to those of Chilkat weaving.*

class with no rights whatsoever. They brought prestige to their owner because they indicated success at war or possession of wealth. Enslavement of a relative was considered to be a disgrace to his entire lineage, so the family of a captured slave would make every effort to pay a ransom and secure his freedom. Many war captives were freed and, after purification ceremonies, resumed their normal status in society.

The emphasis on wealth in this culture affected both trade and war. The purpose of trade went beyond the exchange of commodities. Even more importantly, tribes conducted formalized trade to preserve good relations and thus enhance the prestige of high-ranking men.

Wearing visored wooden helmets, wooden collars across their throats, and body armor fashioned from cedar slats, Tlingit warriors used bows and arrows to defeat their enemies. The Haida and Tsimshians also wore such protective coverings, which all three groups decorated with heraldic designs that served to denote membership in special groups.

Northwest Coast peoples fought war for conquest and plunder. Nearly all Northwest Coast groups conducted feuds in which a raiding party slipped into enemy territory to avenge the death of a kinsman. The northern groups, driven by their strong concepts of property rights in lands and places of economic importance, also conducted wars of conquest. Through warfare, groups such as the Nootkan, Kwakiutl, and Haida tried to drive out or exterminate other lineages to acquire land. These groups also took war captives who became slaves.

SONS OF THE SEA

The sea that surrounded the Northwest Coast peoples affected the social, spiritual, material, political, and economic aspects of their cultures, providing both transportation and sustenance. Although they did not make long voyages over the open sea like the Polynesians, many of the northern groups cruised coastwise on voyages of several hundred miles. In their huge war canoes, the Kwakiutl and Haida raided Puget Sound villages by sailing down Queen Charlotte Sound.

The Haida, who lived thirty to eighty miles (48 to 129km) off the coast of British Columbia on the Queen Charlotte Islands, built red cedar canoes with sterns and

ing among the Nootkans; the whaler was always a chief. He ritually prepared for months by bathing, scouring his body, and praying. He used a fourteen- to sixteen-foot (4 to 5m)-long harpoon with a heavy yew wood shaft and a single toggling harpoon head armed with a mussel-shell blade, two lines forty to sixty fathoms (73 to 110m) long, sealskin floats, and lances. The six paddlers and one steersman who accompanied him also had to prepare themselves with purification and prayer. Relatives with their crews in other canoes completed the whaling expedition.

When a whale was sighted, the canoe approached it from the rear on the left side. The whaler stood in the bow of the lead canoe to thrust his harpoon into the whale behind the left flipper just as it was submerging. As soon as the harpoon struck, every man had to perform his task precisely so that the canoe veered to the left as the line played out, and the floats went overboard. If the hit was successful, men in

Left: The inverted eyes on this Tlingit mask represent the spirit of death; part of a shaman's ritual equipment, this mask portrays a dead man.

Below: A Haida artist carved this portrait mask of wood and later added hair and copper. The same painted designs that were used in facial painting indicates that it is a portrait mask; the flat upper lip and broad nose are characteristic of Haida carving.

projecting bows raised high above the water to facilitate seagoing travel. Mainland groups tried to buy Haida canoes when the tribes gathered at the candlefish fishing grounds on the Nass River every spring. Outstanding canoe makers, the Haida built seven types of canoes.

The Nootkans of Vancouver Island were renowned for their graceful and practical canoes, some of the finest seagoing vessels built by native peoples. The flowing curve from forefoot to prow and the bold sheer of the bows of Nootka canoes may have inspired the New England designers of the American clipper ship.

Nootkans built special types of canoes to harvest marine mammals. Tlingit made heavy-prowed ice-hunting canoes for sealing; the Stikine built small "moon canoes"—named for their upturned ends—for fishing and hunting sea otter.

Although most groups only butchered whales that had beached themselves, the peoples of Vancouver Island and the Olympic Peninsula actively pursued such species as the California gray whale and the humpback whale. The Makah built sturdy eight-man, thirty-two-foot (10m) dugout canoes, from which they harpooned gray and killer whales for food and trade thirty miles (48km) off the Pacific shores of Washington State.

The Quilleute and Nootka also pursued migratory whales for days on end far out to sea. Whaling was the noblest call-

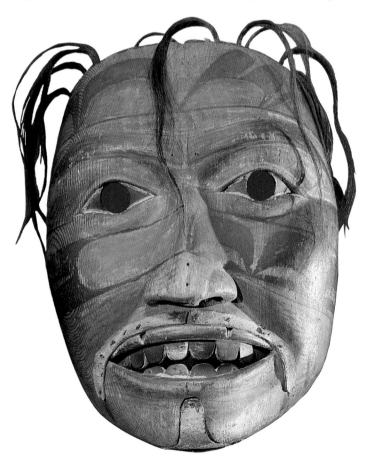

"As we came around the cliff face, the other canoes of our flotilla came into view up ahead. All in time, the paddles of our fifteen-man crew slipped silently into the salt water of Discovery Passage….The sun was just cresting the mountains to the east—this was the best time to be on the water in our great cedar canoe."

—*Kwakuitl David Neel, in an article for* Native Peoples *magazine*

Neel was describing the canoe journey south along the inside passage between Vancouver Island and mainland British Columbia, where the Commonwealth Games were held. The Oweekeno people began the journey from their village at River's Inlet carrying the Queen's Baton and passing it on to the Gwasla' Nakwak'dakw, Namgis, Kwakiutl, and so on, who carried the baton in a canoe through their traditional territory. Three First Nations artists—Art Thompson (Nuu-Chah-Nulth), Richard Hunt (Kwakiutl), and Charles Elliot (Coast Salish)—created the engraved sterling silver version of a relay runner's baton that contained the Queen's message.

Some native peoples were opposed to the idea of participating in the Commonwealth Games because they considered this to be exploitation, given the shameful history of Commonwealth countries in their dealings with aboriginal peoples. Others, such as Coast Salish Danny Henry, who coordinated the Native Participation Committee, called the Tribal Journey a healing journey that would give the First Nations a chance to share their cultures with the world. Neel also had his doubts about supporting Commonwealth countries, but ultimately decided that the most important factor to consider was the resurgence of the oceangoing tradition among coastal First Nations.

The oceangoing canoe was but one of the different types of canoes the people of this region made; they built canoes for whaling, sealing, fishing, freight, river, racing, and war. But by 1900, all but the racing canoes had disappeared. In 1989, the Paddle to Seattle broke new ground in bringing back the great canoes. This event was followed by the Haida Nation's Paddle to Haidaburg, Alaska, and, later, along the Seine River to Paris, France, and the Heiltsuk's Paddle to the 1986 World Expo in Vancouver. In 1993 in Bella Bella, British Columbia, the Heiltsuk Nation hosted the most important canoe revival journey, the Quatuwas Festival ("people coming together"), which inspired a dozen or so villages to build canoes.

Laura Howell of the Comox First Nation explained the Bella Bella journey's significance: "The canoe brings back other parts of the culture as well; the singing, dancing, and feasting. It brings the community together. With the drumming comes the drum making and other parts of the tradition. It's…a tool for the community." Young people, who prior to the journey knew no songs or dances, were now able to lead their groups. The Squamish people are an urban First Nations people whose reserve is in the metropolis of Vancouver, yet they built a canoe, put together a crew, and prepared for the 1993 Bella Bella journey with the traditional sweat lodge, ritual bathing, and songs and dances.

In Duncan, home of the Cowichan people, Neel was part of one of the most impressive sights of the entire journey: two hundred singers, dancers, and drummers of the Niss'ga people of the Nass River Valley, in northern British Columbia. Neel wrote, "They came out led by the chiefs and followed by the young men, each playing a hand drum, each in beat with the other. Three athletic-looking men in their twenties carried out large wooden box drums, which filled the hall with their loud bass sound. They were followed by the many dancers in regalia: women, youths, and children. The most impressive of all was the sound of the drums! I have heard many different drums from many different nations, but the dozens of hand drums playing three separate but coordinated beats, underlined by the bassy box drums, was truly incredible. It is a sound not easily forgotten."

The journey concluded with the Parade of Nations into the Inner Harbor at Victoria, which brought together First Nations from as far west as Hawaii and as far east as New York and Ontario. Three thousand people greeted their friends and relatives in the canoes and watched Chief Sam Sampson (Salish) smudge the baton and offer thanks to the Creator for the safe journey. He then handed the baton to the Premier of British Columbia, Mike Harcourt, and a representative of the Queen's Baton sponsor, BC Hydro, who later took it to the Queen of England that afternoon to open the Commonwealth Games. With the passing of the baton, the journey of the great canoes was completed. But this journey was just one more link in the resurgence of Northwest Coast cultures: Tom Jackson of the Quilleute Nation invited all the canoe nations to gather in 1997 in the Quileute village of La Push, Washington. The First Nations continue their voyage toward the future and the revitalization of their traditions.

other canoes moved in to attach more harpoons and floats. They finally dispatched the weakened whale with a lance.

After towing the whale back to the village beach, the tribe's people butchered it and used all parts of the animal. The meat and skin were eaten, the sinews were braided into rope, the intestines were made into containers, and the blubber provided valuable oil. In honor of his high status, the chief harpooner received the choicest piece of blubber from the whale's back; the townspeople shared the rest of the animal.

As with all Native American groups, the rhythm of life moved with the seasons. In late spring or early summer, the Tlingit, who relied heavily on salmon, moved to the fish camps until autumn to take advantage of the runs of five species of salmon: chinook, sockeye, pink, coho, and chum. Most Northwest Coast peoples followed the taking of the first salmon with a rite of thanksgiving; only after a ceremony honoring the salmon could the men begin to fish.

They captured large numbers of fish by using traps, nets, and weirs. Weirs were barricades placed across streams to divert the runs of fish into traps. Men worked the traps, and women filleted the fish.

Totem poles served as "family crests" for the families who lived in the houses behind them on this street in Alert Bay, British Columbia. Each totem pole was unique; no other clan could use the same combination of animal symbols.

Families ate part of the catch fresh by boiling, baking, or roasting it on spits. Women cut, sun-dried, smoked, and finally bundled the cured salmon. Each woman marked her fish with distinctive cuts and kept her bundles separate in the cache. When they returned to their villages, the women hung some fish in the rafters of longhouses to dry in the smoke of slow-burning fires. Each year, they preserved as much as five hundred pounds (227kg) of fish per person. Women among the Tlingit gained their high status from their control over this staple food; they put much more labor into preserving the salmon, the mainstay of their diet, than the men did in catching it.

Other groups relied more on shellfish, such as mussels, clams, and oysters, which they usually gathered in the spring, when the lowest tides of the year occurred in daylight. They dried shellfish to eat during the winter months or to trade with inland groups.

MAKAH WHALE HARVESTING TODAY

Makah elder Charlie Peterson told *News from Indian Country* that whale harvesting "gave me a sense of identity. It will give our people a chance....You had to have your body in perfect shape and be mentally sharp—a lot of praying. Everything was silent, to not frighten the whale away in the ocean current. All of your equipment, preparation of the canoes with velvet smooth bottoms, special yew wood paddles for stealth, all this had to be done." Peterson's strongest memory as a young man is preparing for the whale hunt with his grandfather, Chestoqua, who owned one of the last whaling canoes.

The Makah Tribe of Neah Bay, Washington, seeks to harvest up to five whales for ceremonial and subsistence purposes starting in 1996. The Makah were forced to stop whaling when European and American commercial whalers hunted the northern gray whale nearly to extinction through the first few decades of this century. After international protection, the gray whale population began to rise, and in January 1994, it was removed from the list of endangered species.

The 1855 Treaty of Neah Bay is the only treaty in the United States written specifically for whaling; this treaty reserves to the tribe forever the right to hunt whales in their traditional hunting areas off the Pacific Coast. Archaeologists have confirmed that the Makah people have hunted whales for at least two thousand years.

Makah Fisheries Director Dan Greene underscored the importance of restoring tribal whale hunting: "For the survival of our culture, our children today need to experience what our traditions are all about as far as whaling is concerned....We intend to fulfill our responsibilities for the management of whale resources as well," he added, referring to their successful management of the salmon, halibut, groundfish, shellfish stocks, and marine mammal resources within their usual and accustomed fishing areas.

"It is really an issue of balance that was understood by our elders with their knowledge of the whales, their life cycles, migration patterns and habitat needs—not harvesting more than they needed to not impact populations. The tribe was part of that balance and understood and participated in that balance," said Dave Sones, Makah Fisheries Enhancement Manager. He concluded, "The tribe was forced to suspend whaling. Now there is an opportunity to sustain balance, exercise our treaty rights and revitalize part of our culture as well."

Another important fish was the eulachon, a species of smelt that runs in larger streams in early spring. The Kwakiutl and groups farther north especially valued the eulachon as a source of oil. Also called the candlefish, the eulachon is so oily that a string threaded through it burns like the wick of a candle. Other Northwest Coast groups fished for sturgeon, halibut, herring, and cod.

Inland groups, such as the Nishga and Gitksan, relied more on deer, elk, bear, and other land mammals, which men hunted either communally or alone. They also hunted the mountain goat, prized for its horns, which they shaped into spoons, and for its wool, which women wove into garments. For northern groups such as the Tlingit, hunting and fishing were not only means of subsistence, but also moral and spiritual activities. They never killed animals needlessly or wasted any part of the bodies. Before the hunt, men purified themselves by bathing, fasting, and continence. After a successful hunt, hunters prayed to the dead animal and to their totemic spirits to ask forgiveness. They thanked the dead animal in song, even honoring it with eagle down, as they would an honored guest, and by burying essential parts.

Women gathered plants most extensively in late summer and early autumn, but also as early as spring. Ferns with edible roots, lilies with edible bulbs such as rice-root, and starchy tubers such as camas were the most important. In some areas more than forty kinds of berries and fruits were available. Women dried those that their families did not eat fresh.

After the harvest, those who had been living in summer fishing camps moved back into their permanent villages of great cedar-plank houses, where each family had its own small interior house with semiprivate bedroom spaces. For large ceremonies, people removed the temporary partitions that sectioned off family sleeping areas so that the house and its benches became an amphitheater. The long, dark winter nights were the time when dancers, drummers, singers, and speakers brought ancient stories to life.

NORTHWEST COAST ART

Art in the Northwest Coast went beyond aesthetics to express the social and spiritual meaning of life. From the embellishment of everyday utensils to the elaboration of ceremonial objects, art permeated nearly every aspect of peoples' lives. Artists brought the supernatural to life through the masks they created. Other pieces commemorated mythical ancestors or events in a family's history. They used sophisticated, highly stylized forms characterized by calligraphic lines of varying width, splitting of the image, and U-form and ovoid motifs to mark joints and fill space.

Women in the Northwest Coast wove twined basketry hats and fringed Chilkat dancing blankets. They made "robes of power," as Gitksan artist Doreen Jensen calls the button blankets that proclaimed their family crests. The men built monumental houses and immense seagoing canoes, and carved intricately decorated boxes, bowls, and masks. Most adults developed the ability to make articles for their family's everyday use, but specialists created ceremonial and monumental art. Master carvers taught apprentices how to carve totem poles and masks. Each Haida house owner commissioned renowned artists to carve a monumental totem pole to proclaim his or his wife's rank and social affiliation.

Among the Tsimshians, art was considered to be such a powerful force that a group of professional artists—the gitsontk—occupied an important social class. Despite the similarity of all Northwest Coast art, three regional substyles developed based on stylistic and cultural differences. Rank and inherited privilege were more important in the northern and central regions, which led to greater creativity. In the northern region, Tlingit artists expressed the nobility of chiefs and the power of shamans by bringing to life the powerful forces that permeated the world. The Kwakiutl, in the central area, were renowned for their development of elaborate, theatrical rituals in conjunction with the potlatch (see pg. 119). Farther south, women devoted more time to basketry; men carved or painted representations of supernatural beings in stone, bone, antler, and on wood and hide.

A major purpose of art was to reinforce status. During elaborate ceremonies, the lineage head of the Chilkat clan of the Tlingit wore the bear crest hat when he danced. The bear's gleaming abalone inlay eyes, ears, and teeth glittered in the firelight. Atop the hat, eight rings of spruce root swayed back and forth with his movement; the bear's movable copper tongue gleamed in the light.

OIL DRILLING IN THE ARCTIC NATIONAL WILDLIFE REFUGE

The Alaska Federation of Natives Board voted 19–9, during their June 1995 meeting, to back oil drilling in the Arctic National Wildlife Refuge (ANWR). It was a split and painful decision. Oil companies claim that the last great U.S. oil field lies beneath the refuge's coastal plain, and environmentalists are trying to protect the land which supports caribou and other wildlife.

Jacob Adams, president of Arctic Slope Regional Corporation, pushed for drilling because he said such a move would benefit the state's ailing economy. U.S. Senator Ted Stevens, a Republican from Alaska, also favored opening the refuge for drilling. Oil industry supporters at the ANWR lobbying group Arctic Power have enlisted Roger Herrera to work full-time in Washington, D.C.

Sarah James, a leader of Alaska's Gwich'in Indians, said that the Arctic Slope Regional Corporation should respect her people's right to protect the caribou they hunt for food on the refuge. Ada Deer, President Clinton's top official on native issues, supported a "no" vote to protect the caribou and the untouched wilderness.

Kim Fararo, in an article published in *News from Indian Country*, points out, "It's hard to argue ANWR's oil is necessary for the nation's security while asking to export Alaska oil."

After the ceremony, the lineage head stored the crest hat in an elaborately carved cedar trunk. The Tsimshian were particularly renowned for their carving of such trunks; Tlingit nobility often commissioned work from Tsimshian master woodworkers. Sometimes the artist constructed the trunk as a double chest, one that contained an inner box that shared the same bottom. Using a single plank of cedar, he carefully grooved, steamed, and bent it at the corners to make the sides. He carved designs on the front, side, and

back panels in low relief and inlaid small faces with opercula shells on the lid.

THE POTLATCH

"Now, he gave away the four sea otter blankets, ten marten blankets, seven black-bear blankets, thirty-five mink blankets, and fifty deerskin blankets. As soon as he finished the potlatch, he told the [guests], 'You will call me Lalelit. Therefore I am full of names and privileges.'"

—Franz Boas

These words from a Kwakiutl chief describe the impressive display and exchange of Northwest Coast art that took place at lavish ceremonies known as potlatches. The word "potlatch" comes from Chinook trade jargon meaning "to give."

The potlatch was a way of establishing and maintaining relationships between different local segments of a more extended tribe; people never potlatched members of one's own group or family. Potlatches were extremely important for validating rank and leadership. By accepting the food and gifts from the host, the guests confirmed the host's right to the privileges he claimed.

Potlatches were also a vital means of circulating material wealth. The host could be bereft of material possessions at the end of the gathering, but he had gained honor and prestige. High-ranking guests then reciprocated with their own potlatches, sometimes exceeding the gifts of their former host.

In addition to its social and economic roles, the potlatch was extremely important for passing on a rich cultural heritage. Children saw the dances, songs, and artwork that symbolized the history and legends of their family and their people. This oral tradition functioned as a cultural text, recording centuries of heritage through communal memory.

WINTER CEREMONIALS

When darkness lingered longer in the morning and came earlier each evening, the time for the great ceremonies drew near. By then everyone had returned to their permanent villages from their summer fish camps. Gone were the long summer days of outdoor activity; the final few weeks of feverish activity—catching, filleting, smoke-drying, and storing the early autumn run of salmon—had freed the people of any serious search for food during the wet, stormy months ahead. Their focus turned inward as the long succession of rainy days forced them to stay inside.

The world outside their immense cedar houses took on a forbidding quality. The salmon were no longer running, and in the early twilights, the impenetrable forests on the mountains above their villages seemed menacing. The cold, wet winter months were the time when supernatural spirits were most active and most dangerous; this was when monstrous man-eating birds swooped from the sky in search of victims.

It was a time when the mythic past seemed especially near, when boundaries blurred like the mist so that men and animals were once more kindred spirits who mingled, trading bodies and souls. Dances brought these spirits to life: the Tseyka, the Kwakiutl Cedar Bark Dance, roughly translates as "making manifest the powers of the spirits." Transformation masks showed the shifting soul of one being into another. Although their form varied, guardian-spirit power dances were a part of cultures up and down the coast.

In one version of the dance, a young man from a noble family mysteriously disappears into the forest, kidnapped by an immense bird with the taste for human flesh. He is later found in the woods running wild, possessed by the spirit of the man-eating bird. Snapping at his would-be rescuers, he hops about crying, "Eat, eat!" until they seize him and carry

This Tlingit house blends a Euro-American house style with traditional monumental art. The figures on the heraldic (totem) pole, as well as the killer whales painted on the house, represent the ancestral crest figures of the family that resides there.

"To survive in this world and help your people, you have to be multifaceted. I see us living in a technical world today, using products like gasoline and getting fish or harvesting whatever we need, to eat from fisheries and farms. I always felt it was hypocritical of people who are against that sort of thing [modern technologies using nature's resources]. It's necessary to do it in a correct manner as far as not polluting and not destroying land unnecessarily."

—*Tlingit photographer and professor Larry McNeil, in* Winds of Change *(spring 1994, vol. VIII, no. 2)*

A professor of photography at the Institute of American Indian Arts in Santa Fe, Larry McNeil teaches his students to balance the corporate world's needs and their own heritage and personal visions. He emphasizes hard work and the achievement of excellence in technical skills. At the same time, he uses technology to express imagery from the heart.

His own body of work embraces a wide spectrum from corporate assignments to numerous art gallery and museum exhibitions. Major museums (such as the Heard Museum), universities (such as Princeton University and the University of Alaska in Fairbanks), and the (Tlingit Nation) Sealaska Heritage Foundation display his work. Since 1982, he has covered many of the biennial indigenous coastal cultural celebrations. His efforts are sponsored by the nonprofit Sealaska Corporation, which asked him to visually document the speakers and events for future generations.

McNeil became a photographer because, as he says, "Where I'm from in Alaska, the Alaska Indians are not represented accurately or fairly in the media as to who they are and what they're all about. I thought that I would try to fill that need."

He inspires his students to raise questions through their imagery. When Sky Felix, one of his students, complained about the stereotyping of Native Americans in the media, McNeil encouraged him to address this issue in his work. Felix created a series that includes such images as "The Rez. 1993," which shows hands bound by barbed wire and gently cradling a feather. The sharp, bright foreground contrasts with a dark and mottled background, which contains a dictionary-style typeface with a definition of "Rez." The type is deliberately readable in places and unreadable in others to emphasize how most people perceive the issues: "sometimes seen in the light of day and much of the time, hidden in its shadows," according to McNeil.

A turning point in Native American imagery came in 1985 when Princeton University sponsored "The Photograph of the American Indian Symposium," which allowed scholars to meet indigenous individuals who used the camera to continue the ancient tradition of storytelling. Also in 1985, native photographers organized their first conference in Hamilton, Ontario, and founded the Native Indian/Inuit Photographers' Association, whose mandate is the promotion of "a positive, realistic and contemporary image of Native Indian/Inuit people through the medium of photography."

McNeil's work certainly furthers this mandate. In "response to photos I had seen of Native dancers which seemed static or dead," he used a blurred technique to capture the fluidity and graceful movement of a Tlingit dancer. Another unique image he created is called "Jesse and the Killer Whale on the Loose in the Big Apple." It depicts Jesse Tooday, a Tlingit photographer who belongs to McNeil's clan, the Killer Whale Clan. Tooday has lived in New York for many years; the photograph shows him exiting a subway protectively accompanied by a hand-drawn, spiritlike, visual mirage of a killer whale.

Through his camera lens and his teaching, Larry McNeil continues to reshape the portrayal of contemporary Native Americans. Although remaining true to his own vision, he has achieved commercial success, becoming a role model for Native Americans who are "living in both worlds."

---

him to the dance house. The members of the Hamatsa society must tame and purify him to return him to the world.

Feeling the thrill of the drama about to unfold, the audience sits spellbound in the great room of the big-house. Seen only in the light from the central fire, monstrous figures of giant man-eating birds cast monumental shadows on the walls. They dance and sway to chanted songs and the rhythm of drumbeats. Cedar bark strands obscure the dancers' hands and bodies as their great beaks snap open and shut. To initiate the novice dancer, they reenact his kidnapping, possession, taming, purification, and return to the human world. Dancers douse the man-eating bird with sea water or fish oil and feed him bites of meat from a specially prepared human "corpse" in an effort to calm his craving for flesh. After dancing quietly, his frenzy recurs, and he escapes from his attendants to run into the audience. His great mouth opens as he lunges for someone's arm, biting off a piece of flesh. After a long series of dramatic dances, the initiate was sufficiently pacified to return to normal life.

A tender salmon steak baked on a spit over hot coals is a favorite dish of the Indians of Puget Sound. Here a young boy (in a Plains Indian headdress) begins his feast with gusto.

The masked figures had taken the members of the audience to the boundary of everyday life, letting them touch the world of the sacred and supernatural. Gradually, they reestablished the boundaries between initiate and ancestor, human being and spirit.

Unsurpassed at creating sensational stage effects, the Kwakiutl were masters of illusion. Many of their masks had movable parts so that they could change form. Their houses had trap doors and tunnels so that the actors appeared and disappeared miraculously; hollow kelp stems concealed under the floor helped them to project their voices from under the fireplace. They suspended wooden puppets and monsters from ropes that were invisible in the shadows; figures appeared to fly across the room. The Kwakiutl alternated the pace so that quiet dances and periods of clowning were interspersed between the most frightening scenes in an effort to heighten their effect.

THE VITALITY OF NORTHWEST COAST CULTURE

The Hudson's Bay Company controlled much of the Northwest Coast area until the 1840s, when American settlers began moving in. The Treaty of Oregon signed in 1846, established the 49th parallel between the United States and Canada; through the late 1800s, non-native settlement of the Northwest progressed at a staggering rate. During the nineteenth century, native peoples suffered devastating population losses from smallpox and other European diseases.

By 1900, most of the totem poles and great beamed communal houses had fallen into ruin. During the last quarter of the nineteenth century, museum officials collected Northwest Coast art and commissioned many carvers to produce models of houses, totem poles, and canoes.

Since the 1960s, Haida artists have led a cultural revitalization movement. In 1969, Robert Davidson carved the first totem pole to be erected in nearly a century, at the Haida village of Masset. In 1978, a carved and painted house was built and dedicated in memory of Davidson and his great-grandfather, chief Charles Edenshaw. Another house and pole were later built at Skidegate.

By 1985, the seagoing tribes had nearly lost the art of canoe making, but a seventy-five-year-old Quinault, Emmett Oliver, led his people and the members of some twenty other tribes in the construction of forty canoes. On July 20, 1989, some seven hundred people gathered for feasting and traditional dances. The next morning the canoes sailed across Puget Sound to Seattle. Five thousand people greeted the paddlers with tribal dances, stories, songs, and feasting.

In the early 1990s, a group of native Hawaiians traveled to Alaska to ask Tlingit and Haida people for the gift of red cedar trees. The Hawaiians had already sailed the Hoku'lea, a fiberglass canoe, across the Pacific; they hoped to build their second seagoing canoe of natural materials. Because there were no longer koa trees of sufficient size on their islands, they sought out Northwest Coast peoples for the gift of their traditional canoe-building materials. The Hawaiians recounted that their ancestors had told them of the great cedar logs that sometimes found their way to Hawaii. They considered them to be a gift of the gods. The Tlingit and Haida responded warmly to the Hawaiians' request and, with proper ceremonies, supervised the cutting of several large trees from which the Hawaiians then made their traditional canoes. This is just one example of native

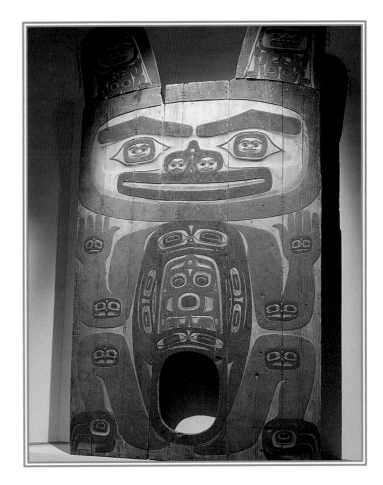

This house partition screen is painted with a squatting bear to represent the Brown Bear clan crest of Chief Shakes. The oval opening at the base of the screen provides access to the sacred room at the rear of Chief Shakes's house in Wrangell, Alaska.

peoples joining forces to renew and revitalize their cultures. Such efforts, including the preservation of everything from native plants to intellectual property rights, are occurring all over the world.

The Tlingit were renowned for their finely woven blankets. These were usually made from a combination of pounded cedar bark and wool from the coats of specially bred dogs.

CHAPTER 6

The Great Plains

"The old people...are gone, but their wisdom is still followed.... Great flexibility and pragmatism were the keys to the culture's survival, as they are today. This way of being is something you wrap around yourself and wear like a blanket. When you are away from home, the identity given to you by your people protects and comforts you, for you always know who you are."

—*Osage Diane Fraher in* Creation's Journey

Guy Dull Knife, Sr., one of the oldest living Oglala Sioux, told biographer Joe Starita that the one thing he remembered above all else in his nearly ninety-five years of life was his constant struggle to remain Lakota (Sioux). Starita wrote, "When they cut off his hair for the first time, he wept, then grew it back. When they outlawed his language, he spoke it anyway, in the old log house above Red Water Creek. When they forbade his sacred Sun Dance, he retreated to the far end of Yellow Bear Camp to fast for four days and nights, as his people had done for generations before him."

In World War I, Guy Dull Knife, Sr., wore his sacred medicine bundle around his neck when he went to France with "Black Jack" Pershing; his brother wore a similar bundle when he fought with Patton in World War II; his son wore one in Vietnam with Westmoreland; and his grandnephew wore one in Desert Storm with Schwarzkopf.

The late Abe Conklin, a Ponca-Osage dancer and storyteller, advised young people that the spirits "will help you" and "give you the understanding and wisdom of your people." He described his personal history in *All Roads Are Good*: "I received good teaching from the descendants of three chiefs: Big Elk, Standing Buffalo, and Big Snake. They would sit and talk to me for hours about Ponca culture and

Left: A Shawnee powder horn and pouch. The pipe tomahawk on the right is said to have belonged to Tecumseh, who formed a great Pan-Indian alliance based on spiritual renewal.

Opposite: George Catlin's painting The Scalp Dance *depicts celebrating Teton Dakota (Sioux) warriors. Nearly all Plains tribes had military societies, which not only took a foremost role in war and guarded the camps during periods of intertribal raiding, but also preserved order during the tribal bison hunt.*

ways. A lot of the things I learned from these people apply to my life today."

The vitality of Plains traditions today comes from the strong sense of cultural identity described by Osage Diane Fraher, Lakota Guy Dull Knife, Sr., and Ponca-Osage Abe Conklin. The cultural survival of their peoples is a testimony to their resilience and spiritual strength.

Some of the most powerful Native American voices today come from the Great Plains. They echo the voices of their ancestors—Crazy Horse, Sitting Bull, Red Cloud, American Horse, Gall, Dull Knife—who fought long and hard for their sacred lands and had to deal with the worst onslaught of settlers, military, and gold seekers. Fierce warriors, the Indian nations of the Plains were subdued only when buffalo hunters slaughtered the bison on which the Indians depended for food, shelter, clothing, fuel, and the implements of life. Of all native nations in North America, few were less suited to the sedentary farming existence of reservation life than the nomadic bison-hunting peoples of the Great Plains.

The Great Plains stretch from the North Saskatchewan River in Canada to the Rio Grande in Mexico and from the Mississippi-Missouri valleys to the foothills of the Rocky Mountains. This immense swath of land was mostly made up of rolling grasslands, stretching from horizon to horizon.

In some areas of the Plains, the annual rainfall was less than ten inches (25.5cm), resulting in the so-called badlands. In the eastern part of the region, however, enough rain fell— at least twenty inches (51cm) annually—to produce green prairies with tall and luxuriant grass. Farther west, in what is now Kansas, Nebraska, North and South Dakota, and Montana, "buffalo grass" covered the rolling hills. Yet even this western land of buffalo grass had groves of trees—cottonwood, oak, elm, and willow—along the riverbanks.

Bear, deer, rabbit, waterfowl, and game birds lived in the riverbank woodlands and surrounding grasslands. The prong-horned antelope roamed the Plains in vast herds, surviving by its swiftness and acute vision. Throughout the centuries, the antelope provided an important resource for Plains peoples. Prehistorically, they stampeded antelope into deep pits. In the late 1700s, when groups such as the Cheyenne moved onto the Plains, they repaired the ancient pit remains to capture antelope for food, clothing, and ceremonial headdresses.

The vast sea of grass also provided a vital food source for the bison (as the American buffalo is more correctly

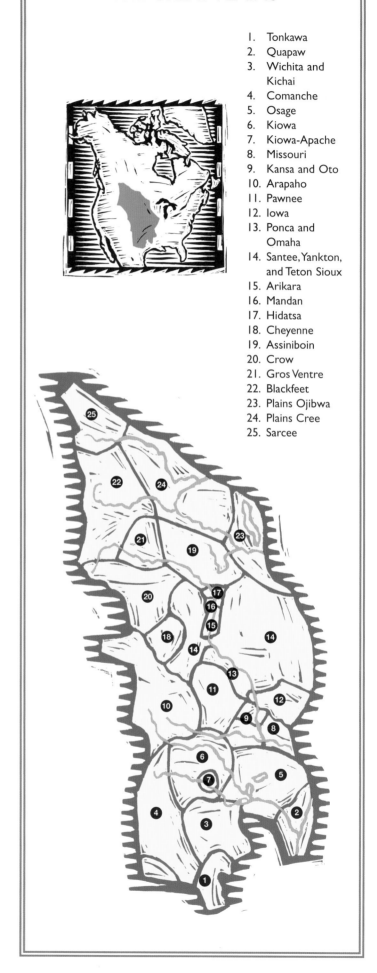

LANGUAGES OF THE TRIBES OF THE GREAT PLAINS

1. Tonkawa
2. Quapaw
3. Wichita and Kichai
4. Comanche
5. Osage
6. Kiowa
7. Kiowa-Apache
8. Missouri
9. Kansa and Oto
10. Arapaho
11. Pawnee
12. Iowa
13. Ponca and Omaha
14. Santee, Yankton, and Teton Sioux
15. Arikara
16. Mandan
17. Hidatsa
18. Cheyenne
19. Assiniboin
20. Crow
21. Gros Ventre
22. Blackfeet
23. Plains Ojibwa
24. Plains Cree
25. Sarcee

Bison graze by the Firehole River in what is now Yellowstone National Park, Wyoming. Plains peoples used nearly all parts of the bison for food, clothing, shelter, and tools.

called), whose total population reached at least 60 million. A bull bison weighed a ton (907kg) and stood nearly six feet (1.8m) high at the shoulder. In contrast to the antelope, however, the bison's vision was poor, which made them much easier to hunt.

For hundreds of years, Plains nations hunted the bison on foot and drove them over cliff edges known as "buffalo jumps." The Blackfeet called such places Estipah-Sikikini-Kots, meaning "Where he got-his-head-smashed-in." These were ritual places because only with spiritual assistance could the people trap the bison; they evoked the spirits of the winds, the mountains, and the raven, the wisest bird of all.

Old Fool Bull recalled the importance of "buffalo callers," who were "specialists who knew the beasts so well that they had almost become buffalo themselves. They dressed themselves in buffalo skins, and when they spotted a herd they positioned themselves at its head, walking before the chief bulls to lead them. Like the buffalo, they snorted and rolled in the dust, luring the herd ever onward."

The prehistoric native horses of North America, called *Eohippus*, disappeared eight to ten thousand years ago. Although Columbus brought the first European horses from Spain to the West Indies on his second voyage in 1493, it was not until the 1680 Pueblo Revolt in the Southwest that Indians acquired great numbers of horses. The Spaniards fled for their lives, abandoning both horses and land; although they returned to reclaim their settlements, by then their horses had been widely dispersed northward through trade and warfare.

PEOPLES OF THE PLAINS

"My grandmother told me that when she was young...the people themselves had to walk... [and] they did not travel far nor often. But when they got horses, they could move easily from place to place. Then they could kill more of the buffalo and other animals, and so they got more meat for food and gathered more skins for lodges and clothing."

—*Iron Teeth, a Cheyenne woman*

Although the hard-riding Plains warrior bedecked in flowing feathered war bonnet provides the most common image non-Indians have of Indian people, this form of Plains culture only began in the later 1700s and existed for about two centuries. The Plains was also home to sedentary farming peoples who lived in the timbered Missouri River Valley and its tributaries. Although they also had horses and hunted the bison, they lived in permanent villages for most of the year and relied much more on foods they raised by farming.

One of these village peoples were the Siouan-speaking Mandan, who have one of the longest documented archaeological traditions of any American Indian group—dating back to the 1200s. The Mandan were part of the vanguard of peoples who worked their way westward onto the Great Plains because of increasing population in the Woodlands.

Early inhabitants of the northern Plains also included the Blackfeet, Plains Cree, Plains Ojibwa, and Gros Ventre, all of whom spoke Algonquian languages. The Sarcee, allies of the Blackfeet, spoke an Athabascan language.

Other semisedentary Plains peoples were the Siouan-speaking Hidatsa and the Caddoan-speaking Arikara of the central Plains. The agricultural Wichita and Pawnee of the southern Plains also spoke Caddoan languages.

The Europeans traded guns for furs with the Algonquian groups in Canada and the Iroquois, which gave these groups superior strength over peoples who had no firearms. During the 1650s and early 1700s, the Iroquois in upstate New York, motivated by European trade, expanded their territory to control access to lands with fur-bearing animals. The Siouan-speaking Osage, Omaha, Kansa, and Missouri, who originally lived in the Ohio Valley, fled westward to escape the well-armed Iroquois. These groups quickly adapted to their new homeland, integrating a farming and gathering existence with bison-hunting.

Other groups, such as the Sioux and Siouan-speaking Crow—who called themselves Absaroke, or Children of the Large-Beaked Bird—took a longer and more indirect route west. By the late 1700s, Iroquois expansion pushed many Algonquian-speaking nations such as the Ojibwa west; in turn, the Ojibwa displaced some Siouan groups onto the Plains.

These Cheyenne powwow dancers perform in Gallup, New Mexico. From the Algonquian word for "conjurer," powwows today are intertribal festivals held by Indians for themselves, but they are open to the public.

On their upper arms, Sioux dancers wore armbands such as these, adorned with porcupine quillwork and feathers that float and trail beside the dancers, heightening the sense of movement.

The Sioux divided themselves into three main groups. The Santee or eastern Dakota (made up of the Sisseton, Wahpeton, Wakpekute, and Mdewakanton) were woodland hunters, farmers, and gatherers of wild rice on the lakes of Minnesota. West of them lived the Nakota—the Yankton, Yanktonai, and the Assiniboine—on the tallgrass prairies of eastern North and South Dakota. Farthest west lived the Teton, who called themselves Lakota ("Alliance of Friends") on the semiarid plains of Kansas, Nebraska, western North and South Dakota, Wyoming, and Montana. Seven autonomous groups made up the Lakota: the Oglala, Brule, Hunkpapa, Miniconjou, Sans Arcs, Two Kettles, and Blackfeet. These three main groups of Sioux never acted as a single political unit or confederacy. In fact, the Assiniboine frequently fought with the Cree against the Yanktonai.

In about 1750, when the horse first appeared in the northern Plains, the Lakota crossed the Missouri River to the western high Plains. The Oglala, the most populous of the Lakota bands, came to live in southwestern South Dakota, western Nebraska, and southeastern Wyoming. Before this time, they had hunted on the eastern banks of the Missouri River, the James River basin in present-day South Dakota, and the upper Minnesota River Valley in Minnesota.

The Lakota were not directly drawn into the northern fur trade as were their eastern relatives. The horse drew

Men and women had their own artistic domains: women embellished clothing and household objects, and men painted spiritual symbols on the outside of tipis and made objects for war, hunting, and ceremonies. Both men and women painted robes to protect the wearer, to use in a ritual, or to express personal spirituality. Their designs, however, differed. Men used a realistic style; women decorated their robes with abstract designs such as the feathered circle, box and border, horizontal stripes, bilateral symmetry, or border and hourglass. A woman often painted a robe for her husband with a geometric design made up of hundreds of triangular feather motifs arranged in concentric circles—symbolizing a war bonnet. Through proper songs, stories, and dances, these designs came alive with power.

People known as paint-gatherers collected and prepared minerals and other pigment sources. Color was vitally important to their expression. Bernalda Wheeler, a present-day Cree writer and broadcaster, said that the mother, aunts, grandmothers, and female friends of a newborn baby not only gave the baby a name and guardian spirit but also chose a color to influence or reflect the child's character. This was the major color used in making the child's clothes.

These Crow leggings were fringed with tassles of scalp hair. Warriors rarely wore them in combat, but used them for ceremonial purposes.

Women made the clothing, except for Ghost Dance shirts. Before they acquired trade beads, women decorated clothing with quill embroidery. The smooth, shiny quills of the porcupine grew up to five inches (13cm) in length. Women soaked the quills in water to make them flexible.

Although the peoples of the Northwest and Northeast also produced quillwork, Plains quillwork had its own distinctive techniques and bold geometric style. The Sioux, Cheyenne, and Arapaho were known for their fine sewn quillwork. Plains women used a variety of techniques. Typically, they made two-thread quillwork by plaiting two or more flattened porcupine or bird quills to produce broad stripes on leggings or shirts. They also made one-quill wrapping to produce a pattern of parallel rectangles for breastplates and

moccasins. To achieve a pattern of interlocking triangles, women used a one-quill folded technique, but to cover broad sections, such as cradle covers or clothing, they folded quills between two lines of stitches. They used two parallel threads to make the thin ribbons of quillwork wrapped around pipe stems and other objects.

The Crow, Blackfeet, and other Northern Plains tribes also made quillwork. Crow women in particular used a distinctive technique of wrapping quills around a core or filler of horsehair to decorate clothes. Quill-wrapped horsehair embellished shirts on over-shoulder and over-sleeve strips. Often bordered with beads, quill-wrapped horsehair resembled fine beadwork.

Some tribes had guilds and societies to create sacred objects. Women had to be sponsored and tutored by other members to join. These tribes emphasized technical perfection of quillwork using the sacred stripe style.

A woman could also undertake sacred quillwork or beadwork on an individual basis to fulfill a vow. She might promise to quill a tipi liner or robe as a form of prayer for the well-being of a relative or close friend. Although the process of creation was sacred—she had to follow prescribed behavior and carefully put away her work until it was completed—the finished product was not considered sacred because the vow had been fulfilled.

Women also decorated dresses with elk teeth. Such dresses were prestige items, prized for their scarcity because each elk has only two teeth of the type used for adornment. Oku'te Lakota Elk Dreamer said, "Two teeth remain after everything else has crumbled to dust...and for that reason the elk tooth has become an emblem of long life....When a child is born...an elk tooth is given to the child." In 1852, a Swiss collector recorded that among the Crow, one hundred elk teeth were worth a horse. Among the Crow, the dresses were symbols of formal exchange, used to celebrate marriage, to settle conflicts, or to transfer ceremonial titles.

these groups onto the Plains as well in the seventeenth and early eighteenth centuries, but they functioned as middlemen in trade by distributing guns, ammunition, and other goods to Northern Plains peoples in exchange for horses, bison robes, dried meat, and other products. The Lakota acted as middlemen for the Yankton of the Nakota, who controlled the catlinite quarry in southwestern Minnesota. Through the Lakota, the Yankton supplied most of the Northern Plains tribes with this precious material, also known as red pipestone.

The Algonquian-speaking Cheyenne had also lived in the upper Minnesota River Valley and in present-day southern Canada, where they supplemented their hunting and gathering of wild foods with some agriculture. By the late 1700s, the Cheyenne were living in eastern North Dakota. Although they still grew corn, they, too, became increasingly dependent on the horse and the bison.

The Arapaho, close allies of the Cheyenne, were the greatest trading people on the Great Plains. Arapaho comes from the Pawnee word "tirapihu" meaning "He Trades"; they call themselves Invna-ina, or People of Our Own Kind.

The Arapaho, the Comanche, and the Kiowa spoke distantly related languages in the Aztec-Tanoan phylum. The Kiowa-Apache of the Colorado and Oklahoma plains had a linguistic and cultural relationship with the Apache of the Southwest, but politically and geographically, they were closer to the Kiowa and Pawnee.

This Oglala (Sioux) bison robe decorated with painted designs was bought in 1890 from the wife of Crazy Horse at the Rosebud Reservation, South Dakota.

THE NOMADIC PEOPLES OF THE PLAINS: THE LAKOTA

"The Black Hills are known to the Lakota as the 'Heart of Everything That Is.' We say it is the Heart of our home and the home of our Heart."
—*Lakota Charlotte A. Black Elk*

The Lakota mirrored the movements of the stars—which they called The Holy Breath of the Great Spirit—in their annual migration. Several of the major constellations represented specific sites in their sacred Black Hills. When the sun moved, it directed the Lakota to specific places where they were to conduct certain ceremonies. At the same time, the same ceremonies were being performed in the spirit world above them.

By mirroring these ceremonies on earth, the Lakota believed that they became attuned to the will of Wakan Tanka and were thus able to draw down sacred power to help them in achieving and maintaining tribal well-being. As with all Native Americans, such observances are an intensification of daily activities conducted in a sacred manner. Lakol Wicoh'an—the Lakota Way of Life—is their religion.

The Lakota leader Red Cloud referred to his people's spiritual need to move freely on the Great Plains when he spoke to his people in 1903: "We told them [government officials] that the supernatural powers, Taku Wakan, had given to the Lakota, the buffalo for food and clothing....We told them that the country of the buffalo was the country of the Lakota. We told them that the buffalo must have their country and the Lakota must have the buffalo."

Some time between 1832 and 1837, George Catlin painted these Sioux leaders in council as they deliberated on a crucial issue regarding their people.

By performing their ritual responsibilities, of which their annual migrations were an important part, the Lakota kept a sacred balance in their world. In turn, Wakan Tanka provided them with all they needed—especially the bison, whose body contained practically everything the people needed.

Bison meat was the center of the Lakota diet; the meat from a mature bull fed an entire family from late autumn to early spring. Everyone filled up on roasted meat and raw bits after a kill; women dried the rest of the meat on racks and made it into jerky or pemmican, a concentrated, high-protein food made of meat, fat, and berries.

The bison provided nearly all the materials needed for a lifetime: a Lakota began his life swaddled in the soft skin of a bison calf; at the end of his life, he was wrapped in a buffalo hide shroud. Summer hides were used to make tipi covers and inner curtains to keep drafts out of the lodge. Softened skins, tanned with brain grease, became moccasins, shirts, dresses, leggings, and gloves. The bison also provided tallow for candles, tendons for bow strings, intestines for canteens, and sinew for sewing. The Lakota glued arrows together with boiled hooves. The bison's neck pelt became a warrior's shield; other parts of the hide were made into rattles and drums. Bison hair grew thick and long in the autumn and winter, making it ideal for cold-weather robes and blankets. Tails became fly whisks. Rawhide had many uses, such as lassos and strings for lashing stone heads to war clubs and arrow points to shafts.

The Lakota wove bison hair into strong rope; rolled it into balls for games; loosely padded cradleboards and pillows with it; and used it as insulation in gloves and moccasins. They carved bison horns into ladles and drinking cups. Large bison bones became tools for fleshing and tanning; small bones became knives and awls. In the winter,

The maker of this Sioux warbonnet fastened the eagle feathers with rawhide straps to make the feathers flow as they would on an eagle; an enemy would target its wearer for attack because of the honor to be gained by striking such an outstanding warrior.

The skin of the bison provided the tipi, an essential element of the nomadic Plains lifestyle. These large semicircular covers were pulled over conical frameworks of straight poles. Smokeflaps at the top of the tipis could be adjusted to regulate the draught of smoke from the central fire. Early tipis were no larger than eight feet (2.4m) in diameter because they had to be pulled by dogs, who could only carry about seventy-five pounds (34kg). After the arrival of the horse, women were able to use more skins to make lodges; dogs could only carry a six- to eight-bison-skin tipi, but horses could easily manage a tipi made from twelve or more hides.

children played on bison-rib sleds. The bison's skull played a major ritual role.

The bison's paunch made a perfect cooking pot. Women prepared a delicious stew by suspending the large, leathery paunch from four sticks and dropping hot rocks into a mixture of water, meat, and vegetables.

The women pitched the tipis with their backs toward the direction of the prevailing westerly wind; the tipi's design, with its wide base and sloping sides, was ideally suited to the strong and sudden winds that swept across the Great Plains. Such winds determined how many poles were used

TSA-LA-GI: THE OKLAHOMA CHEROKEE HERITAGE CENTER

Today more tribes and nations are telling their own stories and celebrating their history through tribal visitor centers and museums. One of the most renowned is Tsa-La-Gi, the Cherokee Heritage Center near Tahlequah, Oklahoma. The Cherokee are the largest of Oklahoma's Indian tribes; more than sixty thousand of the Cherokee Nation's ninety-five thousand members live in Oklahoma. The Cherokees are leaders in Oklahoma in the areas of education, health care, housing, vocational training, and economic development, programs that they administer from a modern complex south of Tahlequah.

Each summer, a guided tour takes visitors through the Ancient Village at Tsa-La-Gi, where thirty to thirty-five villagers recreate the lifeways of a sixteenth-century Cherokee settlement. Also during the summer, on every night except Saturday, seventy Cherokee bring the story of their people to life in a live drama about the Trail of Tears.

Near Tsa-La-Gi is the Murrell Home, which affluent George Murrell and his Cherokee wife, Minerva Ross, built in 1845. The white two-story antebellum-style mansion was a center for social activity in the area, where young women from the Cherokee National Female Seminary and soldiers from Fort Gibson met for social events.

Exhibits at the Cherokee Nation Museum document the history of the Cherokee Nation, whose sixteen thousand members were forced to embark on the Nunna da-ul-tsun-ji, "Trail Where They Cried" (The Trail of Tears). After they reestablished themselves in Oklahoma, the Cherokee reinstated their democratic form of government, churches, schools, newspapers, and businesses, and built higher-education institutions for their young adults.

Sequoyah's creation of the Cherokee syllabary paved the way for the first Indian newspaper, *Tsa la gi Tsu lehisanunhi*—The Cherokee Phoenix—which appeared on February 21, 1828. Wilma Mankiller explained why the name was appropriate: "The power of that mythical bird—which was swallowed by flames but rose from its ashes—reminds us of the Cherokees' eternal flame. It has come through broken treaties, neglected promises, wars, land grabs, epidemics, and tribal splits. According to our legend, as long as that fire burns, our people will survive."

Tsa-La-Gi and the tribal headquarters in Tahlequah are a tribute to the resilience and strength of the Cherokee Nation. The spirit of the people continues to flourish in their many tribally run enterprises.

CROW SHIELDS

An essential piece of a warrior's equipment was his shield. The Crow were renowned as the best shield makers in their area. Crow shields usually had an outer cover of undecorated buckskin, an elaborately decorated inner cover, and a circular rawhide base about twenty-four inches (61cm) in diameter and a quarter inch (6mm) thick. Joseph Medicine Crow, a World War II veteran and teacher with a master's degree in anthropology, said in *All Roads Are Good* that baxbe (sacred power) is represented on a shield or in a medicine bundle. He said that baxbe comes from the Creator and is given to a person by the Supreme Being through an animal emissary, like an owl, eagle, butterfly, bear, wolf, or other animal; power is attained by going on a vision questing experience or by fasting. Sometimes the shield depicted bullets, which might mean that the owner has a medicine that repels enemy bullets. Only the shield's maker knows what these symbols represent, so that the shield, according to Joseph Crow, "is a personal insignia or stamp—kind of like the old European standards. Whenever the camp was on the move, a wife would proudly display that symbol on the side of her saddle."

as the tipi's foundation. The Blackfeet, who lived in the more sheltered northwestern Plains, used four poles; the Assiniboine of the windswept plains of present-day Saskatchewan and Manitoba used a three-pole foundation for greater stability.

The nomadic peoples of the Plains followed Wakan Tanka's gift—the bison. In the Lakota Moon of Making Fat (June) until after the end of The Moon When the Geese Shed Their Feathers (August), bison congregated in herds of thousands to graze upon the vast tableland of luxuriant native grasses watered by spring and summer rains. From June until late summer, the many bands of the Oglala Lakota lived in a single camp from which the men communally hunted bison herds.

As the summer wore on and the rains ended, the grass grew patchier on the dry land; the Lakota called September "The Moon of Drying Grass." The Lakota, following the movements of the bison, which dispersed into smaller herds, split up into many small camps from late summer until the following June. Such dispersal also ensured that there would be adequate winter pasturage for their horses

and a better supply of dried bison dung, which was the Indians' major source of much-needed fuel for winter fires on the nearly treeless Plains.

Winter camps sometimes stretched for miles along timbered river valleys, which protected the people from the bitter cold. December, "The Moon of Popping Trees," was so cold that the sap and moisture within the trees froze and cracked.

If a band had many horses, the group had to move several times during the winter to find fresh forage for their animals. In deep snow, however, men had to hunt on foot because horses floundered in the drifts. When they could not find sufficient deer, elk, and bison, the people subsisted on dried meat.

The severe winters of the Great Plains seemed to last forever, but eventually the geese flew north, and the ice cracked on the rivers. March ensured the continuation of the bison herds; the Lakota honored this month by naming it "The Moon When the Buffalo Cows Drop Their Calves."

The summer encampment was the high point of the Oglala year. Each incoming band took its own definite position within a huge circle opened to the east. Summer was a joyous time. The people replenished food supplies; friends and relatives, who had not seen each other since the previous summer, renewed their ties; people relaxed by gossiping and gaming; parents made matches for their children; young men and women took new notice of each other; and men made speeches and debated important issues. Older men recounted their glories in warfare and discussed serious problems that affected the well-being of the entire Oglala group, and younger men raced horses and planned war parties for later in the year.

Even more important than these activities was the Sun Dance, the greatest and most important tribal ceremony of the Plains peoples. According to Oglala tradition, the Sun Dance was held at the time when the bison were fat, when the new sprouts of sage were one span (23cm) long, when the chokeberries were ripening, and when the moon rose as the sun set.

Although the rites varied, the Sun Dance was usually initiated by an individual who had vowed to hold the dance in return for supernatural assistance. This could have been

Opposite: Painted bison tracks decorate the shield on the left. Shields embodied sacred power and their designs were inspired by a spiritual experience; only the maker of a shield knew its full meaning.

Above: In the eighteenth century, the horse transformed the lives of Plains peoples: suddenly, now that they could ride like the wind, settled village life seemed dull. No longer on foot, men were now able to ride among herds of bison, and women could sew larger lodges because horses could haul four times the load that dogs could carry.

a request for supernatural aid in curing himself or a kinsman, or in response to a vision. Usually, several individuals pledged to hold the dance. Each of these men then approached an older shaman to act as his instructor. The shaman appointed two akcita, or messengers, to travel with a message stick inviting other bands to assemble.

This twelve-day ritual was not only a shared tribal experience, but also a testimony to individual courage in the name of the Great Spirit. The individual participants were blessed by taking part in this ceremony, which ensured the well-being of the entire tribe.

The first four days were a time of festivity as the people came together to renew ties with their friends and relatives after the long winter separation. During the next four days, rhe participants were isolated and received instruction from the shamans.

Most sacred were the final four days. They began with a warrior's search for the proper cottonwood tree, which a special group of virtuous women brought back to camp in a ceremonial procession the next day. The cottonwood was a special tree for the Lakota because its leaves, which resembled tipis, were thought to have been the source of their dwellings. The people prepared the cottonwood by painting its trunk with the colors of the four sacred directions. They placed sacred objects in the fork of the tree before raising it. The ceremonial climax came on the final day as dancers, some with skewers implanted in their skin, hung from the central cottonwood pole. Through visions, each experienced personal communion with the Great Spirit. Not only did they find individual rewards, but their sacrificial suffering ensured blessings for all their people, including a plentiful supply of bison for the coming year.

Among the Red Cloud band of the Oglala Lakota, the chiefs' society elected seven of its own members to govern the people. Rather than govern themselves, they appointed four younger men to carry out the daily government of their people. These four men, the real power in the government, were called "owners of the tribe" or "shirt wearers," in reference to the special form of hair-fringed shirt they were given. Both Crazy Horse of the Oglala Lakota and Chief

RECONCILIATION CEREMONIES AT THE LITTLE BIGHORN

"When we smoke the Pipe, we will put the past in the past. Those who smoke the Pipe have a responsibility to forgive. They have a responsibility to go home and tell the people it's time to heal, time for unity. The leaders smoking have a big responsibility beyond just the ceremony here. We will take the Pipe and use it for God's blessing. He'll be there to smoke with us. In the future good will come from it."

—*Crow spiritual leader Burton Pretty On Top, quoted by Candy Hamilton in* News From Indian Country

From the time the Crow and the Lakota became major forces on the Plains, they fought each other over horses and control of the Northern Plains. The animosity between them grew when the Crow served as scouts for the Lakota's longtime enemy, General George A. Custer—a man who had led troops in the Cheyenne massacre at the Washita and gold-seeking expeditions into their sacred Black Hills. After two centuries of animosity, representatives of the Crow and Lakota shared the reconciliation pipe to mark the beginning of their new, peaceful relationship.

Lakota Phillip Under Baggage said, "Congress is eroding our treaty rights. It's time to bury the hatchet and unite as Indian nations for sovereignty and treaty rights."

This landmark ceremony was part of an even bigger celebration of reconciliation at the Little Bighorn that brought together scout tribes, such as the Crow (who hosted the celebration because the battlefield is within their reservation); warrior tribes including the Lakota, Northern Cheyenne, and Arapaho; and representatives of the 7th Cavalry. During five days in July 1995, these groups gathered for the first time to commemorate the 119th anniversary of the Battle of the Little Bighorn.

The monument has a new area designated for a marker that honors the Lakota, Northern Cheyenne, and Arapaho, who defeated Custer on June 25, 1876. On this site, the tribes told their own stories and presented exhibits. Mandan Hidatsa Gerard Baker, the superintendent of the Little Bighorn Monument, described the site as "a very controversial area. I want to turn it around from controversial to educational and balance the interpretive story." He added that the celebration is "not a political day; it's an Indian day."

The celebration and commemoration began on June 24—designated Scouts' Day—at 8 A.M. when all the tribes and the 7th Cavalry raised the flag and conducted Sacred Pipe ceremonies. Afterward, descendants of the Crow scouts made presentations on the battle, treaties with the United States, and Crow values. Ed Daily, a retired member of the 7th Cavalry, spoke about the 7th Cavalry today, and in the afternoon, the Arikara Tribe concluded the presentations.

Don Many Bad Horses said an early morning annual prayer for peace on June 25—the anniversary of the actual battle. This was the day that the Northern Cheyenne Societies led a victory march and dance, closing the day with gourd dancing.

The next day the Lakota, Nakota, and Dakota conducted the Lakota Charge Ceremony dawn attack. They also presented special honoring ceremonies, including one for Crazy Horse. They ended the day with dancing and traditional Lakota horse games. Arapaho day was June 27, and 7th Cavalry day was June 28, which included portrayals of Elizabeth Custer and General Phil Sheridan talking about the battle.

Northern Ute Barbara Sutteer (formerly Barbara Booher) said, "I think this observance is great. It can make people realize there really is another side to that story besides the U.S. military's." The celebration was particularly meaningful to her because during her tenure as park superintendent there, she had engineered the changing of the site's name from the Custer Battlefield National Monument to its present title, the Little Bighorn National Monument. The name change took a long, hard fight begun by the Assiniboine Sioux at grassroots meetings in Poplar, Montana, in 1972. It took passage through two Congresses and four Congressional hearings as well as President George Bush's signature for the bill to become law on December 10, 1991.

On July 21, 1989, the Northern Plains tribes officially requested that the name of the monument be changed to one that did not honor the perpetrator of a crime against their people. As Richard Simonelli put it in *Winds of Change*, "From the point of view of the descendants of the people camped on the Little Bighorn that day, it was a drive-by shooting by the Seventh Cavalry." The tribes also asked that the ethnically one-sided presentation of history be balanced out by placing a memorial at the site for the Indian warriors involved in the battle.

Barbara Booher Sutteer reflected on the lengthy battle to change the name of the monument: "The Elders helped me to keep a good outlook. Two Moons prayed for me a lot to do a good job, and he always asked me to have an open heart and an open mind so that I could understand the issues and be able to deal with those issues. He always helped me to level out and calm down and to look for whatever good there might be in any kind of confrontation. The Elders helped me to realize that whatever kind of situation you're in, somewhere in that situation there's going to be a lesson for you." These thoughts express not only the fight to change the monument's name but also the healing that occurred at the 119th anniversary of the Battle of the Little Bighorn.

A military, spiritual, and political leader of the Hunkpapa Sioux, Sitting Bull was a major figure in the war for the Black Hills and helped to engineer the victory at Little Bighorn. In 1890, fearing a new Sioux uprising, government officials had Indian police kill Sitting Bull during a Ghost Dance ceremony at Standing Rock.

Spotted Tail of the Brule Lakota were "shirt wearers" or councillors; today, their shirts are preserved in the National Museum of the American Indian.

Lakota men gained high status through success in warfare and their ability to capture many enemy horses. Warriors appealed to higher powers for assistance in attempting to evoke spiritual forces. Although the peoples of the Plains could easily have annihilated each other once they received guns in the 1700s, their ritualized style of warfare kept such large-scale killing from occurring. Touching an enemy—counting coup—brought far more honor than killing him, because of the danger involved. Through such exploits, a warrior displayed his courage and gained distinction and glory.

Young Lakota men were encouraged to join one of the five or more warrior societies. Although they did not fight as units in battle—men always fought as individuals— each group did plan and lead attacks on their enemies. Each society also had its own style of dress, dances, songs, and set of four leaders. The only time a warrior society operated as a group was when it policed the camps. Its duties included camp protection by scouting for the presence of enemy raiding parties, correcting mischievous young boys, and intervening in village disputes.

Horses were indispensable not only for hunting bison, but also for warfare. Before battle, warriors often dismounted and spoke directly to their horses. Siyaka, a Lakota warrior, said to his horse, "We are in danger. Obey me promptly that we may conquer. If you have to, run for your life and mine. Do your best and if we reach home, I will give you the best eagle feather I can get and the finest cloth offering, and you shall be painted with the best paint."

Lakota men recorded their war exploits in a number of ways. Warriors wrapped themselves in robes made of the whole skin of a bison. If his wife had not decorated the robe with geometric designs, the owner, a gifted artist, painted an action scene of men and horses to depict the winning of war honors.

When bison hides became scarce in the early 1880s, men relied on muslin sheeting to record war exploits and winter counts. Noted Yanktonai spiritual leader Black Chicken portrayed the Sun Dance on muslin at the turn of the century. His paintings of the medicine lodge—a circular arbor with a center pole and an entrance to the east—are unusual because native artists seldom depicted major ceremonials.

A MODERN CHEYENNE WEDDING

"My wedding is a testimonial to the adaptability of Native Americans—encompassing our traditional elements with those of mainstream America. A culture that cannot adapt, ultimately cannot` survive. We are redefining and creating a new tradition every day."
—Nico Strange Owl-Raben to Brenda Himelfarb in Native Peoples *magazine*

Two hundred guests attended the Northern Cheyenne wedding of Nico Strange Owl-Raben and Harry Hunt in Piney Lake at the base of the Gore Range in Colorado. Traditional clothing, the honor song, the tipis, and Southern Cheyenne elder Richard Tall Bull's blessing in the Cheyenne language took the guests back in time, while Judge Stanley legally bound the couple in marriage.

Nico wore a hand-beaded buckskin dress that Elaine Strange Owl and her sisters spent three winters designing and making for Nico's graduation from college. Nico elaborated on her clothing and that of her attendants: "We are each wearing a scalp tie—a beaded feather—which is attached to a piece of braided hair. I have mink tails attached to my braids. To the neckline of the back of my dress, my mother has attached a small bundle which contains my Hististah, umbilical cord. My grandmother beaded a case for it soon after I was born. I am to keep it with me throughout my life, for it is believed that it ties me to the earth, my tribe and culture. With it, I will never be lost or in search of something. It was vital that this be with me for my wedding."

Artist and friend Bob Blazek spent six years constructing Nico's parents' wedding gift—a traditional Cheyenne lodge. Blazek explained, "Although the materials I used are modernized, for instance the tipi is canvas and not buckskin—the general color pattern and other materials such as the buffalo tails and deer toes are traditional. The interior floor is covered with a buffalo hide. The liner, blankets, pillows, backrests and rawhide suitcases are either beaded or painted in the traditional Cheyenne line design—a block of color within a line representing a Cheyenne historical event."

Nico responded with tears in her eyes, "It was extremely touching to have someone whom I had never met spend six years preserving my culture through his art. To have this person love and respect my mother to the degree that he would give her this incredible gift so that she could give it to Harry and me makes me very honored. He knows of the love and respect I have within my family and tribe. He understands the Cheyenne Way."

The Pawnee lived in earth lodges made of heavy posts, cross-beams, brush, and earth. In 1702, when the government began to move them to present-day Oklahoma, such villages disappeared under the plow. The word "Pawnee" comes from pariki, *meaning "horn," in reference to their scalp-lock hairstyle, which curved like a horn over their heads; their name for themselves is Chahiksichahiks, "Men of Men."*

VINE DELORIA, JR.

"Sacred places are the foundation of all other beliefs and practices because they represent the presence of the sacred in our lives. They properly inform us that we are not larger than nature and that we have responsibilities to the rest of the natural world that transcend our own personal desires and wishes."

—*Vine Deloria, Jr., in* God Is Red: A Native View of Religion

Vine Deloria, Jr., recognized as one of today's leading Native American spokesmen, is a prominent author, scholar, lawyer, and philosopher. He comes from a distinguished Standing Rock Sioux family with scholar, churchman, and warrior-chief ancestors. He has been executive director of the National Congress of American Indians and a member of the National Office for Rights of the Indigent. He is a practicing lawyer and is currently a professor at the University of Colorado, Boulder, at the center for Native American Studies. He has written numerous books, including *Behind the Trail of Broken Treaties* and *Custer Died for Your Sins.*

As with the novels of N. Scott Momaday, Deloria's books carry a universal message for Indians and non-Indians alike. When *God Is Red* was published in 1972, it was in the vanguard in the recognition of sacred places. Today, as environmental awareness continues to grow, his message has reached even more people. In the two decades since *God Is Red* was first published, many writers have contributed to a deeper understanding of the sacredness of the earth. Deloria, pleased at this outpouring of books and articles, said, "It will take a continuing protest from an increasingly large chorus to reprogram the psychology of American society so that we will not irreversibly destroy the land we live on. Today our society is still at a primitive aesthetic stage of appreciating the personality of our lands, but we have the potential to move beyond mere aesthetics and come to some deep religious realizations of the role of sacred places in human life."

Another way in which men honored ancestral warriors was through ledger art. In the late 1800s, Lakota Red Dog sketched his own experiences in war in a ledger book. Plains artists painted realistic images of battle on shirts, tipis, tipi liners, and ledger books.

Such ways of honoring native veterans continue today: dances continue to be held in their honor, and the people still sing old-time traditional honoring songs at powwows. The songs tell of ancient battles as well as the First and Second World Wars, Korea, Vietnam, and the Gulf War. Researchers have found that Native American Vietnam veterans suffered fewer and less severe cases of post-traumatic stress syndrome when their native communities honored them with dances and the bestowal of feathers for their heroism.

FARMERS OF THE PLAINS: THE PAWNEE

Ruwerera, ruwerera,	*Star of Evening, Star of Evening,*
Operit ruwereara,	*Look, where yonder she cometh,*
Operit ruwereara.	*Look, where yonder she cometh.*
Rerawha-a, rerawha-a,	*Stars of heaven, stars of heaven,*
Operit rerawha-a,	*Lo, the many are coming,*
Operit rerawha-a.	*Lo, the many are coming...*

—*Translated by Pawnee Lesa-Kipiliru*

Not all Plains peoples were nomads who followed the bison. Sedentary farming peoples like the Mandan, Hidatsa, Omaha, Kansa, and Missouri lived in the timbered Missouri River Valley and its major tributaries on the eastern Plains.

SHARING THE SACRED CIRCLE THROUGH EDU-TOURISM

Blackfeet guide Curly Bear Wagner believes it is important to avoid swearing and hubristic travel, because they "have an effect on the outcome of any trip. There's no cussing, especially when you're on the water. If you do these things you're going to get punished. It's the law of the land that was handed down generations ago. It's all based on respect. To carry bad thoughts is not healthy. That's why you go into the mountains, to relieve yourself from pressure from the outside.'"

More Native Americans have been opening their reservations to outsiders through Indian or tribally owned and operated tourist facilities across the country. In *Winds of Change* (spring 1995, vol. X, no. 2), writer Dick Pierce defines "edu-tourism" as "tourism that provides the dual benefits of economic development, and a sharing of…history, culture and beauty with outsiders."

Some Indians oppose opening reservations to non-Indians because, after sacred sites have been identified, they are often looted or overrun by those drawn to their inherent power. The Bighorn Medicine Wheel is "perhaps the most famous spiritual magnet in the Plains Indian world. Eighty feet [24.5m] in diameter with a fourteen-foot [4m]-wide hub, the medicine wheel in Wyoming's Bighorn National Recreation Area is revered by nearly a dozen tribes as a nexus to the Creator," said *Winds of Change* writer Todd Wilkinson. Unlike Britain's most exploited outdoor tourist attraction, Stonehenge, the medicine wheel, although managed by the United States Forest Service, is actively used by the descendants of those who built it. Shoshone, Northern Cheyenne, Arapaho, Sioux, Blackfeet, and Crow spiritual elders have protested the invasion by thousands of non-Indians who hike to the site's promontory at ten thousand feet (3,048m) above sea level because "for centuries the wheel has been a remote escape where young warriors could retreat in solitude, with nothing but pure thoughts to guide them on their spiritual journeys. Today, however, young Native Americans learning their religion are reluctant to undertake rituals and quests at the site because they don't want to be heckled by white tourists who've created a less than spiritual atmosphere."

But, as Wilkinson points out, secretiveness does not work either because "refusing to divulge specific sites to the government has led some federal land managers to be insensitive to Native Americans' rights of religious freedom—rights supposedly guaranteed under the Native American Religious Freedom Act of 1978 and the United States Constitution. Because the United States Supreme Court has denied legal protection for some highly recognized spiritual sites on public land, development is erasing many of these sacred landscapes from the map."

Curly Bear Wagner sees Native Americans and environmentalists as allies against development. In the late 1980s, petroleum companies proposed oil and gas drilling in the Badger-Two Medicine area, where warriors have fasted, quested, prayed, and hunted since the Ice Age. By escorting non-Indians into the area, Curly Bear teaches them about the land's importance and beauty and about how destructive drilling can be.

Curly Bear and Linda Wagner run Blackfeet Historical Site Tours, which take visitors to centuries-old tipi rings, sweat lodges, hallowed Sun Dance grounds, and, if requested, sacred sites with-

Around the thirteenth century, the Pawnee—probably because of drought and population pressure—moved three hundred miles (483km) from what is now east Texas, where they had been agriculturalists. Their new homeland on the Platte River and its tributaries had fertile soil and tens of thousands of bison on nearby grasslands. By the mid-1700s, Pawnee villages stretched all along the Platte River.

For most of the year, the Pawnee of the Nebraska plains and prairies lived in earth-lodge villages similar to those of the Mandan. Pawnee dome-shaped houses reached ten to fourteen feet (3 to 4m) in height and thirty to fifty feet (9 to 15m) in diameter, and had sleeping compartments lining the inner walls. Each house was home to a middle-aged man, his wife, the couple's married sons and their families, and the owner's parents and unmarried relations. Men often sta-

bled their favorite riding horses in the house at night to protect them from being stolen by a raiding party. Women cooked the food around a central fire.

On pleasant days, old men basked in the sun on the domed roof. Women dried and stored food and aired skins on platforms between houses to keep these items out of the reach of hungry village dogs.

Pawnee sod homes, built of logs and covered with tangle-rooted soil, were so ideal for Plains life that settlers later adopted them. These well-insulated, log-and-dirt lodges provided ideal protection from the intense summer heat and the bitter winter cold.

Women gathered wild plants and cultivated small patches of corn, beans, and squash in the lowlands near the river. They planted in early May, with each family

in the wilderness. When guiding non-Indians into the Badger-Two Medicine area, Curly Bear adheres strictly to tribal etiquette through such rituals as the smudging of hikers with sweetgrass and pine boughs to purify them before they enter the mountains and by leaving tobacco offerings to the trees and animals. Honoring the Creator is a serious thing. Curly Bear insists that people reap what they sow: "The spirit world offers no pardons to those who breach the sanctity of holy places."

Several years ago, before he and several Blackfeet accompanied Bureau of Land Management officials down the upper Missouri River, the Blackfeet smoked their sacred pipe and made a prayer to the water spirits to grant them safe passage. When they offered the pipe to the officials, Curly Bear recounted, "The BLM guy didn't believe in what I was saying and kind of shook his head. At a big bend in the river, his boat turned over and he lost a two-way radio. He was just lucky he didn't lose a lot more."

Dick Pierce listed the four requirements for a successful edu-tourism enterprise: "1, a tribe and tribal council willing to 'seed' and promote Indian tourism; 2, a cultural center or museum to serve as the focal point for activities; 3, a tribal or community college to train guides and provide Indian studies courses; and 4, a group of entrepreneurial individuals willing to provide the various services and tours."

Wilkinson explained the dilemma that faces Native Americans: "While these cultures cherish an ancient and rich bond with the land, their reservations are among the most economically poor outposts on earth. The intricacies and values of their traditions often have been overlooked by lawmakers, government agencies,

and the public; their beliefs and traditions misunderstood and underappreciated." Most of the hiking public, although inspired by the beautiful backcountry, seldom realizes that they "could be stepping into divine Indian sanctuaries and outdoor cathedrals," which Wilkinson compares in importance to "the Vatican, Mt. Sinai, or Mecca."

Most non-Indians do not realize the significance of these sacred places. Acclaimed Lakota author Vine Deloria, Jr., explained, "Buffalo Gap on the southeastern edge of the Black Hills marks the location where the buffalo emerged each spring to begin the ceremonial year of the Plains Indians. It may indeed be the starting point of the Great Race that determined the primacy between the two-leggeds and the four-leggeds at the beginning of this world. Several mountains in New Mexico and Arizona mark the places where the Pueblo [and] Hopi...peoples completed their migrations and were told to settle, or where they first established their spiritual relationships with the bear, deer, eagle, and the other numerous forms of life that participate in ceremonies."

The opening of reservation land can provide non-Indians with a better appreciation of Native American cultures. Pierce sums up the value of edu-tourism, which gives economic benefit directly to the individuals and the tribe. "Jobs are created at or near home, and revenue is generated within the context of one's own culture, and the culture transfer is given under the control, and at the pace, of the individual guide and the tribe. Tourists receive a lesson in history and culture with no translation or filters, and a direct 'culture to culture' connection with people who are incorporating their traditional values into today's world."

tending its own acre. When the first tender corn shoots pushed through the soil, villagers had to guard their crops vigilantly against gophers and rabbits and to weed their family plots carefully.

In a month the corn toughened, becoming less attractive to animals; this enabled the Pawnee to leave on the first of their two annual summer bison hunts. They usually restricted the earlier hunt to tender young bulls and

and deer, but also found time to play games of chance for which they wagered clothing, skins, and food.

Although the scattered Pawnee settlements constituted a tribe through their shared language and culture, each village was autonomous. During his term of office, the village chief kept the village's sacred bundle, from which he derived his power; his home thus became the gathering place for important councils. Priests, schooled in rituals,

The Comanche, who speak a Shoshonean language, were nomadic bison hunters and had a reputation as the finest horsemen of the Plains. Every July in Walters, Oklahoma, they celebrate an annual homecoming powwow in honor of the time that Comanche warriors returned to the home camp. Today, they live in the vicinity of Lawton, Cache, and Apache, Oklahoma.

yearlings who came to drink at streams; the autumn hunt was a time for stampeding a herd over a cliff to ensure sufficient meat to see them through the winter.

The Pawnee celebrated when they returned to their villages. Autumn was a time of great abundance and relaxation. Although some women harvested the corn, beans, and squash, and others tanned skins for clothing and summer tipis, there was also time for leisurely gossip. Men added to their winter meat supply by hunting antelope, elk,

songs, procedures, prayers, and the use of the sacred bundle, formed a special learned class. Shamans cured the ill and foretold the future, taking preventive measures against sickness, drought, food shortages, and enemy raids. Highly respected warriors belonged to men's societies.

The greatness of the Pawnee lay in their rich mythology and poetic interpretations of the heavens and earth. Their profound interest in the heavens led the Pawnee to develop a unique star- and constellation-based religion. Unlike other

N. SCOTT MOMADAY

"Dypaloh. There was a house made of dawn. It was made of pollen and of rain, and the land was very old and ever-lasting. There were many colors on the hills, and the plain was bright with different-colored clays and sands. Red and blue and spotted horses grazed in the plain, and there was a dark wilderness on the mountains beyond."
So begins the Pulitzer prize-winning novel *House Made of Dawn*, by Kiowa novelist, poet, and artist N. Scott Momaday (b. 1934). His writing reflects his people's mystical attachment to their land and spiritual beliefs. At the same time, his work transcends the tribal by focusing on the universal need for healing.

House Made of Dawn focuses on the struggle for survival of Abel, a young Indian who has just returned home from World War II. Caught between his traditional tribal world and modern industrial society, Abel tries to find his place in relation to the land and his home community. As he incorporates traditional stories into his life, he achieves a state of wholeness and spiritual balance.

Momaday's parents were teachers, artists, and authors. The poems he began while teaching on the Jicarilla Apache reservation led to a Creative Fellowship from Stanford University, where he earned master's and doctorate degrees. He taught at the University of California at Santa Barbara and later at the University of California at Berkeley, where he established an Indian literature program. He continues to encourage Native Americans to become writers and to collect traditional stories from previous generations.

James R. Murie, whose mother was Skidi, recorded his people's star knowledge, including the sacrament of the Morning Star ceremony, held to ensure the land's fertility and the replenishment of the bison herds. At one time, this included the sacrifice of a young maiden kidnapped from a neighboring tribe. After months of ritual purification, the girl was given to the Morning Star so that her spirit could renew the earth and she could become another star in the heavens. In 1838, however, Petalasharo, a Skidi Pawnee leader, stopped this practice when he rescued a young Comanche girl and returned her to her people.

THE COMING OF THE WHITES

"We kill buffaloes...for food and clothing...to make our lodges warm. They kill buffaloes for what? See the thousands of carcasses rotting on the Plains....All they take from dead buffalo is his tail, or his head or his horns, perhaps to show they have killed a buffalo....You call us savages. What are they?"
—Sitting Bull, Hunkpapa Lakota

Although whites had brought the horse, which gave Plains peoples the freedom to ride with the wind, the whites ultimately destroyed this unfettered independence. The Plains nations flourished for decades, even after their lands became a crossroads for white travelers in their westward migrations. But conflict inevitably erupted when the discovery of gold brought thousands of fortune hunters to the Colorado Rockies in 1858. This marked the beginning of the end of the bison-based Plains way of life.

Plains Indian populations, however, had begun to decline long before this, with the arrival of smallpox, cholera, and whooping cough. In 1837, a major smallpox epidemic reduced the numbers of Mandan, Arikara, and Hidatsa so dramatically that they had to coalesce by combining clans and family lines, moving to an area near what is now the Fort Berthold Reservation in North Dakota. Contact with whites was especially devastating to the Pawnee because diseases spread rapidly in their compact villages. Besides spreading diseases, European settlers seized Pawnee land and slaughtered the indispensable bison, and other tribes stole Pawnees to sell them into slavery. Of the tens of thousands of Pawnee who had once settled along the Platte River and its tributaries, only six hundred remained by 1900.

groups to whom the sun played a dominant role, the Skidi Pawnee attributed the sun's power to Morning Star or Evening Star. They recited long, poetic prayers to invoke the presence of various stars. The Pawnee also believed in a supreme Creator who never revealed himself to humans but transmitted his power through lesser holy people. The arch of the heavens and the grandeur of the night sky were expressions of the Creator.

Celestial beings directed their lives: women planted during the first new moon after the willow leaves appear; when the eighteen Skidi villages gathered, they arranged themselves in specific positions to mirror the positions of the stars. Each village had a different star guardian, which conferred its powers through a medicine bundle. This sacred bundle, from which Pawnee chiefs derived their status, was assembled under the direction of the star and contained corn, tobacco, a pipe, and other sacred objects.

In the 1851 Fort Laramie Treaty, the U.S. government assigned territorial boundaries for the Plains peoples. However, the government continued to reduce tribal territory by creating smaller and smaller reservations over the next thirty years. Traditional enemies, such as the Arapaho and the Shoshone, were forced to share reservations.

Groups such as the Lakota, whose spiritual life depended on their ability to move to sacred places across the Great Plains, fought fiercely for their freedom. In spring 1868, the Sioux nation agreed to accept present-day South Dakota west of the Missouri River as a reservation; this left the sacred Black Hills in Sioux hands. In exchange for ceding territory, they received the government's promise to abandon the Bozeman Trail forts and to regard the Powder River country as "unceded Indian territory," where groups could roam freely if they did not want to live on the Sioux reservation.

Many Lakota, including Red Cloud himself, settled on this reservation. In accordance with the treaty, others—Crazy Horse, Sitting Bull, Black Moon, American Horse, Gall, and Man-Afraid-of-His-Horses—chose to roam freely.

The Sioux War of 1876 erupted when the Indian Bureau ordered the Indians to abandon the unceded territory. The

Taken in 1910, this photograph shows a man from the Black-feet nation. The Blackfeet Indians of the United States are one of four closely related tribes of Plains Indians known generally as Blackfeet; only the Southern Piegan have a reservation in the United States. The others—the Northern Piegan, the Bloods, and the Blackfeet proper—live on reserves in southern Alberta.

continued encroachment of settlers and miners into tribal territory—including Colonel George Custer's discovery of gold in the Black Hills—and Sioux depredations in Montana, Wyoming, Nebraska, and Dakota led to bloody conflict. In 1876, Sioux and Cheyenne warriors annihilated Custer and about 225 of his men in the Battle of the Little Bighorn. That winter, the army waged a fierce campaign; groups of Sioux and Cheyenne surrendered early the next year with unhealed gunshot and knife wounds, their gaunt faces hollowed out from hunger, their clothes reduced to rags. The Sioux War ended when Crazy Horse surrendered 899 of his Oglala Lakota in May 1877 at Fort Robinson, Nebraska. He was bayoneted and died at Fort Robinson in September of the same year.

Between 1872 and 1876, professional hunters slaughtered more than 6 million bison with newly developed heavy-caliber guns and repeating rifles. Lieutenant General Sheridan applauded their efforts, saying, "The white hide hunters have done more in the last two years to settle the vexing Indian question than the entire regular army has done in the past thirty years....For the sake of lasting peace, let them kill, skin, and sell until the buffalo are exterminated."

Although Sitting Bull had safely led his people to Canada in October 1876, they were starving because few bison remained. People slipped back across the border to give up; with only a handful of followers, Sitting Bull surrendered at Fort Buford, Montana, in July 1881.

Between 1887 and 1934, the government tried to divide and privatize Indian land through a land allotment policy that issued 40- to 640-acre (16 to 256ha) tracts to individual tribal members; the government then sold entire sections of unallotted land, which meant that whites lived in the midst of reservation lands. Allotment failed because the division of semiarid land was ecologically unsound, a lack of access to credit made it virtually impossible for Indians to farm, and the property was divided into minute parcels when an allottee died without a will. Furthermore, when allotees were granted citizenship, local communities refused to accept reservation Indians as social or political equals.

After World War I, Plains peoples were experiencing such a severe agricultural depression that the government extended the 1933 Civilian Conservation Corps to include reservations. The Indian Emergency Conservation Work, known more commonly as the Civilian Conservation Corps Indian Division, provided employment for reservation irrigation, forestry, and grazing projects. This program employed nearly 95 percent of the Rosebud Reservation's working population.

When men and women returned to their respective reservations after World War II, they were determined to improve their peoples' economic, health, and housing conditions. However, because of the reluctance of industrial leaders to build plants near Northern Plains reservations, the government encouraged native families to relocate to cities for employment. Relocation scattered tribal populations across the country.

The international energy crisis led companies to pursue coal and oil contracts with several Plains groups. Some tribal leaders hoped that energy leases would provide jobs and increase tribal government budgets, but many feared the

RUSSELL MEANS

Oglala-Yankton Sioux activist Russell Means (b. 1940) led the American Indian Movement (AIM) in the 1973 armed seizure of Wounded Knee, South Dakota, where, in 1890, 7th Cavalry troops had massacred a group of Sioux. Means, along with Dennis Banks and Leonard Peltier, led the AIM forces that held off hundreds of federal agents for seventy-one days.

A long history of unrest between full-blood traditionals and mixed-blood progressives set the background for events in 1973. The situation became so hostile that in 1972, Raymond Yellow Thunder, an Oglala man, was beaten, publicly humiliated, and locked in a car trunk, where he died. Means led a caravan of AIM supporters to demand the arrest of the two brothers who had committed the crime. In January 1973, a South Dakota businessman killed Wesley Bad Heart Bull, resulting in a riot between AIM followers and police at the Custer, South Dakota, courthouse. The Federal Bureau of Investigation (FBI) sent sixty-five agents to Pine Ridge to enforce security. At the end of February 1973, Means and his supporters went to Wounded Knee demanding recognition for his people as a sovereign nation. Their protest became a prolonged siege when the FBI surrounded them. In the end, two Indians died and a federal marshal was permanently paralyzed. After a lengthy trial, a federal judge threw the case out of court.

Born on the Pine Ridge reservation in South Dakota, Means was raised near Oakland, California. Before returning to work in the Rosebud Agency's tribal office in South Dakota, Means was a rodeo rider, Indian dancer, ballroom dance instructor, and public accountant. He later moved to Ohio, where he became director of the Cleveland Indian Center. He left AIM in 1988. In 1992, he played the role of Chingachgook in the film *The Last of the Mohicans*. Means recently wrote his autobiography, *Where White Men Fear to Tread*.

Means, who participates in today's Sun Dance, interprets its meaning by saying, "We want to get in balance with the female, so we create purification ceremonies for boys and men to bring us to an understanding of what it's like to give birth. We dance the Sun Dance...so we can try to begin to understand the suffering of pregnancy....The ceremony's about coming into balance with the female."

long-term environmental and cultural effects of strip mining. In the late 1970s, when strip mining threatened to destroy nearly half their Tongue River Reservation land base, the Northern Cheyenne voted to reject massive coal sales. The Crow did sign coal-mining contracts; the Blackfeet contracted with oil companies for exploration; and the Fort Peck reservation is now opened to oil exploration.

Some reservations, such as Fort Peck, Montana, and Fort Totten, North Dakota, have built manufacturing plants to fulfill government defense contracts; Turtle Mountain reservation, North Dakota, has manufactured trailers for hauling heavy military equipment for the Department of Defense. Unfortunately, such reservation industries can only employ a small percentage of the population.

Plains reservations today are some of the most impoverished places in the United States; unemployment on the Northern Cheyenne reservation stands at 80 percent. Nevertheless, Plains cultures endure because many tribal peo-

Only five of the sixty-five Indian nations that have lived in Oklahoma are native to the state. Even before the military implemented President Andrew Jackson's Indian Removal Act in the 1830s, the government pressured native peoples to move to Oklahoma, whose name—Okla Homma—means "Home of the Red People."

ple maintain contact with their rural tribal communities, returning home to attend powwows, tribal fairs, Sun Dances, sweat ceremonies, and naming ceremonies. Those who cannot return home participate in tribal social activities at urban Indian centers.

Oglala Lakota Emil Her Many Horses, who lives in Chicago, reflected on this renewal of cultural heritage in *All Roads Are Good*: "There seems to be a great resurgence of interest in the old ways. People are going back to traditional religious practices. Throughout the summer, for example, several Sun Dances are now sponsored at Pine Ridge, Rosebud, and other reservations. Younger people are attending yuwipi ceremonies, purification ceremonies, and learning songs."

OKLAHOMA: HOME OF THE RED PEOPLE

"Indian sensibility...has to do with the idea of a collective history. It's reflected in your upbringing and the remarks that you hear every day from birth and the kind of behavior and emotion you see around you."

—*Caddo-Kiowa T.C. Cannon*

Chief Allen Wright's Choctaw name for this state, Okla Homma, means "Home of the Red People." On nineteenth-century maps, Oklahoma was labeled "Indian Territory"; today this state remains home to the greatest concentration of Indian people within the United States and Canada. Historically, more separate tribal groups have been associated with this state than with any other state.

Yet of the federally recognized native nations within Oklahoma today, only a few lived there before European contact; most of them were forcibly removed from their lands to Oklahoma. The most dramatic separations occurred in the decade following the late 1820s when the Five Civilized Nations—the Choctaw, Chickasaw, Seminole, Creek, and Cherokee—were marched west on the Trail of Tears.

Throughout history, sixty-five Indian nations have lived in Oklahoma. Only five nations are native to Oklahoma: the Wichita and Caddo, who lived in farming villages; the Osage, who hunted there; and the Kiowa-Apache and Comanche, who pursued the bison into Oklahoma.

The government induced native peoples to move to Oklahoma even before President Andrew Jackson's Indian Removal Act, which the military implemented in the 1830s. As they came to recognize the inevitability of relocation, many groups agreed to move to Oklahoma voluntarily to avoid being forcibly marched there under military guard at a later time.

After the Civil War, a new and more determined phase of energetic white expansion engulfed the Indians of Oklahoma. Riding the crest of the Union victory or recovering from the Confederate defeat, land-hungry settlers pushed into Indian land to begin a new life. Fueled by technical advances such as mechanical harvesters, the westward thrust had a more efficient and better organized quality to it. Whites considered the Indian land to be abandoned land because it was not being farmed, mined, or lumbered.

During this time, the number of Indian tribes in Oklahoma dramatically increased, representing nations from nearly all culture areas. In 1865, negotiations produced treaties with the Kiowa, Comanche, Kiowa-Apache, Cheyenne, and Arapaho, nine bands of Sioux, and the Five Civilized Nations. During the next fifteen years, some of the tribes that moved to Oklahoma included the Sauk and Fox, Potawatomi, Osage, Iowa, Pawnee, and Ponca, as well as several smaller groups from Kansas. The assumption behind these treaties was that all Indians would become self-supporting agriculturalists by the time the bison disappeared. However, this did not occur. Unable to feed themselves and denied full rations by a parsimonious Congress, reservation Indians continued to starve into the 1890s.

Government officials considered the reservations to be a temporary expedient. Under continuous pressure from whites to reduce Indian land holdings, the government began a program of 160-acre (64 ha) allotments to Indian heads of families and 80-acre (32ha) allotments to unmarried adults. The surplus land that had previously been held by the tribe was then opened to white settlers.

In 1889, Oklahoma became a microcosm for the previous four hundred years of Indian history. Until this year, all of Oklahoma was Indian-owned, legally, politically, and socially. The only non-Indians there were government or military officials directly involved with Native Americans. However, in 1889, a territorial government was established, and the Oklahoma land rush of April 22, 1889, opened ten thousand 160-acre (64ha) farms to whites.

Unfortunately, not all Native Americans enrolled when tribal lands were shifted to individual members. Some were enrolled against their wishes, and others escaped or refused to enroll because they believed that the United States was violating their treaty rights. Today some tribal rolls have been closed by an act of Congress, resulting in the denial of education and health benefits to which Native Americans are entitled because of their blood quantum.

In Oklahoma today, there exists a great diversity of heritages: descendants of Geronimo's Chiricahua from Arizona; Osceola's Seminoles from Florida swampland; the Sauk and Fox from the prairies of the Midwest; Sequoyah's Cherokees from the Smoky Mountains; and the buffalo-hunting Cheyenne of the Great Plains. Torn from their homelands, they lack the sacred geography vital to most Indian people. Yet they are united by common problems, including a shared history of removal and mistreatment by the U.S. government. Oklahoma's Indian groups also share nearly two centuries of intertribal cooperation. Such a concentration of the Indian population, in proportion to non-Indian numbers, has led to a renewed sense of pride.

Indians have learned to adapt to constantly changing circumstances to survive. Individuals such as the great athlete Jim Thorpe have shown their ability to excel in both white and Indian worlds. Instead of a schizophrenic opposition of conflicting worlds, Oklahoma Indians have learned how to integrate seemingly disparate elements and diverse cultural traditions into a unified whole, drawing strength from each. Native peoples in this state are individuals: a state highway patrolman who dons the feathered bustle of a fancy dancer; a scientist who seeks out a medicine person to heal his daughter; a leader of the Ponca Hethuska Society who fought in World War II; the director of the National Museum of the American Indian, Smithsonian Institution, who is a member of the Cheyenne and Arapaho Tribes of Oklahoma.

Rennard Strickland of the University of Oklahoma expressed the adaptability, resilience, and rootedness of native peoples in this state by saying, "The corn road, the buffalo road, and the peyote road are different from one another, but the spirit with which one follows the road, not the road itself, is the essence of Indianness." Despite variations in material culture, languages, and specific beliefs, Oklahoma's Indians are spiritually united, bonded by a

Above: Photographers were fond of taking formal studio portraits of Native Americans—especially Plains peoples—in traditional finery.

Opposite: A shop sign in Tahlequah, Oklahoma, is written in the Cherokee syllabary—each symbol indicates a combination of consonant plus vowel. The most famous of Native American writing systems, the Cherokee syllabary was invented by Sequoyah in the nineteenth century. Sequoyah borrowed the shapes—but not the sounds—of some letters in the English alphabet, attributing Cherokee sounds to letters.

shared philosophy that recognizes the sacredness of the earth, the primacy of the Creator, and the interrelatedness of all living things.

THE CHEYENNE COUNCIL OF FORTY-FOUR

For the Cheyenne, the Council of Forty-four and the warrior societies provided order and control. The Sweet Medicine chief, who was responsible for keeping the package of sweet grass known as the Sweet Medicine bundle, headed the Council of Forty-four in its political and spiritual duties. Four other sub-chiefs represented specific supernatural beings and were just under the Sweet Medicine chief. Thirty-nine ordinary chiefs provided the next level of power.

Each of these chiefs served for ten years and was expected to display ideal human behavior by taking care of the poor, settling individual disputes with wisdom, and guiding ritual performances that protected the people. The chief was known for his generosity, kindliness, even temper, detached involvement, and constant awareness of the larger good of the 350 people under his care and guidance.

The Cheyenne developed their own tribal court system through the warrior societies and the Council of Forty-four. One of the most important roles of the warrior societies was to restrain eager hunters so that everyone had an equal opportunity to kill game for their families. The welfare of the Cheyenne people through the long, fierce Plains winter depended on the bison they killed during the summer hunts. To maximize the hunters' chances, it was vital that the bison herd not scatter. Leaders told their people to refrain from individual hunting for many days before the hunt. It was up to the policing warrior society to strictly enforce the prohibition against hunting; if they found someone disobeying this order, thus

threatening the well-being of the entire tribe, the warrior society members assumed the role of de facto judges by beating the overeager hunter with whips, shooting his horses, and slashing his tipi.

Responsible for their people's spiritual well-being, the Council of Forty-four acted as a jury to decide when killing was a criminal act, because such an act threatened tribal welfare. The most sacred of Cheyenne tribal medicine bundles contained the sacred arrows, symbolic of Cheyenne hunting and warfare; the sacred arrows were said to be polluted by the murder of one Cheyenne by another. When these arrows were polluted, all the people suffered because the game animals upon which they depended deserted the Cheyenne hunting grounds and the warriors became more vulnerable to their enemies. In the case of murder, the sacred arrows were renewed through ritual purification, thus restoring tribal well-being.

In each case, the leaders considered the unique circumstances to determine the punishment and restoration of tribal well-being. The Cheyenne chiefs based their reasoning on a range of factors: murder included cold-blooded killing as well as acts that compelled another person to commit suicide. Under some circumstances, such as defense from incestuous rape, killing was considered to be justified. In such a case, they did not banish the person, but they did purify the sacred arrows. If the Council of Forty-four decided that an individual had committed murder, the person was banished with his or her family, and friends who chose to accompany him or her, for five to ten years.

CHAPTER 7

The Plateau and the Great Basin

✚

"What is needed [to combat the global environment crisis] is a fundamental shift in consciousness, and this means that the views of indigenous peoples—our laws and rules and relationships to the natural world—have to be brought back into the picture. In fact, these natural laws and rules have to become the focus of humanity."

—Ruby Dunstan, Lytton Indian Band of the Lil'wat

Many great Native Americans leaders came from the Plateau and Great Basin area: Shoshone Sacajawea, who traveled with Lewis and Clarke from St. Louis to the Pacific Ocean; Flathead-Shoshone Washakie, who was instrumental in establishing a Wyoming reservation for his people; Nez Percé Joseph, who led his people on a courageous journey ended by his eloquent surrender speech ("From where I now stand, I will fight no more"); and Paiute Wovoka, who brought a message of spiritual regeneration and healing that spread to the Great Plains and beyond. Their spiritual legacy is carried on today by Ruby

Dunstan and others who are trying to avert global destruction by sharing the native perspective based on the interrelationship and sacredness of all living beings, including Mother Earth.

In their ancestral homelands stretching from inland British Columbia through Washington, Oregon, and Idaho to parts of Montana, the Plateau peoples once enjoyed evergreen forests lush with myriad varieties of roots, berries, game, and salmon-rich rivers. In contrast, the Great Basin peoples of Nevada, Utah, western Colorado, and southeastern Idaho survived as foragers and gatherers in a high desert and intermontane region, protected from intruders by the harshest environment in all of North America.

Left: The Klamath Indians of Oregon used this basket to play the Four Stick Game.

Opposite: The Ute Mountain people celebrated the Bear Dance in early spring to conciliate the bear; the dance was also a festive social occasion when women took the initiative by selecting male partners and directing the elements of the dance.

The Great Basin—about 400,000 square miles (1,036,000 sq km) between the Sierra Nevada and the Rocky Mountains—was the last major frontier of North America to be explored and settled by European-American intruders. The most striking geological feature of this area—from which its name is derived—is the hydrographic basin formed from the interior drainage of rivers and streams into remnant Pleistocene lakes or playas. One of the highest and most rugged mountain ranges in North America, the Sierra Nevada catches and deflects most of the eastbound rain clouds, creating one of the most parched and inhospitable regions known to humanity. Life in the rain shadow of the western mountains was a tribute to survival. Everything that lived in the shimmering air of intense midday heat had to survive with only the barest minimum of water. Yet, by observing and adapting to nature's cycles, native peoples lived and even thrived in this region for more than ten thousand years.

For thousands of years, the wandering peoples of the Great Basin maintained an ancient way of life based on the gathering of wild seeds. Closely linked to the Plateau and California areas by a reliance on wild seed subsistence, the Great Basin was set apart from these two areas because wild seeds provided the bulk of their diet. Although California peoples ate acorns, they also had access to a multitude of other foods, such as game and fish. Plateau peoples, who depended upon camas and other wild root crops, supplemented their food resources with salmon.

The Great Basin—with its buttes, short chains of ridges, mountains, and plains formed by internal drainage—is an area literally turned inward both geographically and culturally. Although some water flows along the Green, Colorado, and Snake Rivers, most of the moisture in this region flows back into the Basin, accumulates in shallow lakes, and evap-

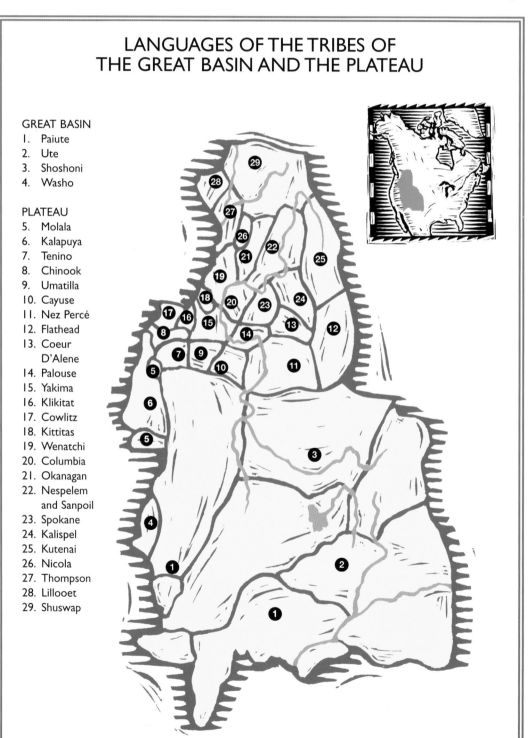

LANGUAGES OF THE TRIBES OF THE GREAT BASIN AND THE PLATEAU

GREAT BASIN
1. Paiute
2. Ute
3. Shoshoni
4. Washo

PLATEAU
5. Molala
6. Kalapuya
7. Tenino
8. Chinook
9. Umatilla
10. Cayuse
11. Nez Percé
12. Flathead
13. Coeur D'Alene
14. Palouse
15. Yakima
16. Klikitat
17. Cowlitz
18. Kittitas
19. Wenatchi
20. Columbia
21. Okanagan
22. Nespelem and Sanpoil
23. Spokane
24. Kalispel
25. Kutenai
26. Nicola
27. Thompson
28. Lillooet
29. Shuswap

grow along the banks of
streams, attracting limited
population concentrations
in areas along the eastern
slopes of the Sierra Nevada
and in Utah's Wasatch
Mountains. Juniper, an
important source of wood,
and piñon, a staple food
in the south, grows most
abundantly at elevations
of eight thousand feet
(2,438m). The peoples of
this region were masters
at utilizing available
resources, harvesting more
than seventy-five species of
wild food plants. Great
Basin peoples also hunted
some antelope, rabbit, and
deer; however, game was
never plentiful. Rather
than large game, native
peoples ate locusts, ants,
ant eggs, fly larvae,
lizards, snakes, rats, mice,
and gophers. Those fortu-
nate enough to live near
the rivers that surrounded
the Basin—the Snake,
Truckee, Carson, John
Day, Walker, and
Humboldt—caught fish,
but their catch was so
minimal that they neither
smoked nor stored any

orates slowly, becoming highly saline. Thus, Utah's Great
Salt Lake and, to a lesser extent, Pyramid Lake and Mono
Lake, are extremely high in salt content. The few streams of
this area usually end in saline marshes or lakes.

In the valleys between the ranges, five to twenty inches
(13 to 51cm) of rain falls annually. The high rate of evapo-
ration limits vegetation to such xerographic plants as sage-
brush and greasewood. Plants with edible seeds and roots

fish. That the peoples of this inhospitable region survived
at all is a tribute to their tenacity and resourcefulness.

In contrast to the intensive dryness of the Great Basin,
the Plateau was a well-watered land of forested mountains
and semidesert. Bordered by the Rocky Mountains to the
east and the Cascades to the west, the Plateau is drained
by two major river systems, the Columbia and the Fraser.
In areas of western drainage, the tributaries of these great

rivers allow the passage of salmon, the major native food resource. Nearly all Plateau tribes depended on salmon to some degree, fishing by a variety of methods during the spawning runs. Deer, elk, mountain sheep, and rabbits were also hunted.

Most of the peoples here spent summers living in lodges made of cottonwood frames and layered with bullrush mats. When they needed warmer winter quarters, many of them moved into semiunderground earth houses, which they entered through a central roof opening on a notched ladder. In the early spring, when the camas plant's sky blue petals had withered, women dug out the starchy bulb with willow digging sticks. The people ate the bulbs raw, roasted, or pulverized into cakes that they boiled. However, as the territory, distribution of water, and vegetation cover varied in the Plateau, so did the peoples' cultures, including their patterns of exploiting their environment.

THE PEOPLES OF THE PLATEAU

Within the Plateau area, the peoples developed great cultural diversity from differences in geographic location and the availability of natural resources, as well as contact from other native peoples. Linked by travel and trade along two great arterial rivers, the Columbia and the Fraser, and their tributaries, Plateau peoples borrowed and adapted much from their neighbors outside this region. Unlike the peoples of the inward-oriented Great Basin, Plateau peoples had the resources, time, and greater receptivity to external influences

More than half the seventeen hundred Ute Mountain Utes are unemployed. The Ute Mountain Casino, a high-stakes gambling casino that opened in 1992, is part of a tribal effort to provide work for the Ute people; other tribal enterprises include a model mineral lease and a park that protects Anasazi ruins.

and historical contacts. Contact with others led to the sharing of political and social structures, dress, customs, and housing, as well as spiritual concepts and practices. Plateau groups who lived east of the Rockies acquired such Plains traits as the tipi, patterned warfare, and the use of the horse. The Northwest Coast institution of slavery and Southwestern patterns, such as pottery and earth paintings, spread to adjacent areas of the Plateau.

Each group within the Plateau area had its own subtle character and identity and spoke a distinct dialect from one of four different linguistic families. The Salishan-speaking Shuswap, Lil'wat, Thompson, and Okanagan lived in the north, in the inland areas of what is now British Columbia. Other Salishan-speaking tribes included the Kalispel, Coeur d'Alene, Spokane, Colville, Sanpoil, Spokane, Columbia, and Flathead, who lived in present-day Washington and Idaho. The Shahaptian-speaking Walla Walla, Yakima, and Klikitat lived in the area where the Columbia River meanders southward, merging with its largest tributary, the Snake. The Nez Percé of Idaho and the Wishram, Umatilla, and Oregon also spoke related dialects. The Kutenai spoke an Algonquian language, and the Nicola spoke an Athabascan language; these two groups lived in present-day southern Alberta and southern British Columbia, respectively.

THE KLAMATH OF SOUTHERN OREGON

"As indigenous peoples we have always tried to convey [a] sense of the sacred[ness of all life] to the newcomers to our traditional territories and homelands. With generosity and compassion, we have attempted to share our ceremonies and our songs with the newcomers to our homelands, because these rituals convey our successful relationship with the lands and seas around us and our necessary knowledge for those who would share our lands with us. But the forces of development have refused to recognize the fact that indigenous peoples around the globe have in place complex systems of obviously sustainable resource management which have been successfully practiced for millennia."

—*Ruby Dunstan, Lytton Indian Band of the Lil'wat*

Ruby Dunstan's words reflect the spiritual relationship that Plateau peoples had with their land and with each feature of the landscape. The Creator carefully placed each river, rock, and cliff, transmitting its origin story to the people so that they would understand its significance and remember its sacredness. Each mountain, lake, and forest emanated its own kind of power, which it could confer upon individual spirit seekers through songs of power. People sought spiritual contact by purifying themselves with prayer, fasting, and sweating in a special lodge. The songs came through dreams and visions to those who sought them with the proper reverence. Living on sacred Klamath soil, the people found a constant sense of connectedness to the universe, of being in the right place.

Klamath women wove durable overlay twined baskets to carry the roots, bulbs, berries, and nuts they gathered. The bulb of the camas, a widely used sweet and nutritious vegetal food, was the major trade item the Klamath bartered when they attended the great Dalles Rendezvous every autumn on the Columbia River to trade with such peoples as the Nez Percé, the Wishram, and the Wasco.

The Klamath are a mountain and forest people, in contrast to other Plateau peoples, such as the Sanpoil, who lived in the desert-plain of the Columbia Basin. The Klamath have lived on their four-thousand-foot (1,219m)-high plateau in central and southern Oregon for tens of centuries; archaeologists have found evidence that indicates that the Klamath have lived in this area for at least ten thousand years.

To the west of their land, on higher ground, lies spectacular Crater Lake. Klamath lands are located in a shallow depression on the high plateau and include a chain of lakes and the headwaters of the river that bears its name. The Klamath call themselves Eukshikni, which means "People of the Lake," in reference to their major settlements on Upper Klamath Lake.

Traditionally, they built their winter settlements on higher ground on the lake shores and on the main streams that connected lakes and marshes. The distinctiveness of their culture comes from their adaptation to a lake and marsh

THE PEOPLE OF WARM SPRINGS BUILD THEIR OWN MUSEUM

"In the old days, baskets were made in the winter months. The winter months were the least busy time of the year, and they [basket makers] could devote entire days—and evenings—toward the completion of a basket."

—Antoinette Pamperien, quoted by Olney Patt, Jr., in Native Peoples *magazine*

Pamperien learned how to make Klikitat baskets from her mother, Irene Queahpama, and she has passed the tradition on through workshops and living history demonstrations at the Museum at Warm Springs. These tribal treasures represent a cultural continuity that spans centuries. By 1968, the people at Warm Springs realized that precious tribal artifacts were rapidly disappearing from the reservation into museum and private collections. In addition, master basket makers, weavers, and beadworkers were dying without passing on their knowledge to young apprentices; knowledge was no longer being transmitted through the traditional learning networks of mother-to-daughter and father-to-son.

In 1974, tribal leaders set aside a $50,000 annual budget to purchase tribal artifacts. They built a museum designed to resemble a streamside encampment into which they incorporated motifs that reflected the cultures of the three tribes of Warm Springs.

The nomadic, hunter-gatherer heritage of the Paiute people is symbolized by angular roof features designed to resemble a travois, an essential device for frequent travel. The Warm Springs people, who were also hunter-gatherers but were able to live longer in one place because of more abundant resources, chose a tulemat dwelling to reflect their culture. A curved ceiling plankhouse represents the Wasco, who lived in more permanent homes because of their reliance on fishing and trading.

One of the guiding forces behind the museum has been Viola Kalama, whose husband, Nick, was the chief of the Paiute in Warm Springs for twenty years. She remains the only person at Warm Springs still actively making willow baskets in the centuries-old style of ancient Paiute nomads. Kalama told Olney Patt, Jr., "Spring is the best time to get willow because the bark is easier to peel off then." Despite lessened mobility, she continues to gather willow branches along the banks of Seekseequa Creek near her home. Kalama says that the most important and most difficult part of basket making is the gathering and processing of materials, something that cannot be taught in the classroom. Without including the gathering, peeling, splitting, and soaking time, Kalama estimates that she devotes at least forty hours to making one basket.

In the 1940s, the Warm Springs people stopped making cornhusk bags, which were used primarily as trade baskets and gift items. Fortunately, they have been able to collect more than two hundred existing cornhusk bags for their museum.

The Klikitat people, who lived on the Washington side of the Columbia River Gorge, invented the basket-making style that bears their name. The demanding process begins with hours of digging up the shallow roots of a red cedar tree to gather about twenty feet (6m) of root material for the first six inches (15cm) of a basket's side; it takes many more hours of cedar-root digging to gather enough material for an entire basket. Before she begins weaving, Pamperien must prepare the root by splitting or drying it. The technique used to make a Klikitat basket is called imbrication, which involves covering the coils with strips of colored grass that are fastened by folding under each stitch when the coils are sewn. A well-made Klikitat basket is very durable, and will survive years of gathering, transporting, and storing berries.

The museum also has exhibits devoted to less tangible aspects of tribal culture, including the languages of the three tribes who live at Warm Springs. Tribal members have worked diligently since 1980 to revive these languages. Maryann Meanus and Caroline Tohet believe that language is the heart and soul of the culture, and have created a four-inch (10cm) -thick dictionary of the Shahaptin language. At one time, this language was the first language a Warm Springs child learned. Today, however, as with many other native languages, Shahaptin has virtually disappeared.

Oral history is another intangible form of culture that community members are striving to save. In a museum exhibit film, community member Wilson Wewa, Jr., speaks of this irretrievable loss: "Each time an elder passes on, they take 50 percent of their knowledge to the grave with them." Although the tangible aspects of culture can be relearned, once oral history and language disappear, they are lost forever.

Established in 1855, the Warm Springs Reservation now houses more than two thousand artifacts and twenty-five hundred archival photos and documents in its museum. Elders continue to pass on their stories, songs, and personal reminiscences—tribal treasures whose value cannot be measured.

Left: During the fleeting summer season, the forested and alpine zones of the high mountains became pastureland for large, widely scattered populations of big game animals such as deer, bighorn sheep, elk, and pronghorn antelope. Hunters said prayers and left offerings whenever they killed game.

Left, below: Ouray (1820–1880) was a Ute leader revered as a great warrior who later, realizing the inevitability of white settlement, stressed conciliation over warfare. He became a skilled negotiator who traveled to Washington, D.C., several times in efforts to protect Ute land. However, nothing seemed to stem the tide of white encroachment, and the Utes were repeatedly forced to cede more and more of their land.

environment. In summer they roamed their territory to gather wild plants, hunt game, and conduct war.

Their winter settlements are best described as hamlets because they were not centralized communities. Usually composed of several semisubterranean earth lodges with roof entrances, hamlets were often spread out over a large area. Several related nuclear families lived in each earth lodge; sometimes a single earth lodge was the sole dwelling in a hamlet.

Several nearby hamlets made a tribelet; although the members of different tribelets might feud with each other, they also intermarried and went out as a war party to raid non-Klamath for booty and slaves. Unlike other Plateau peoples, the Klamath had little use for chiefs; a chief would lead a group in war but had little overall authority. War was the only institution that brought together men from different hamlets and tribal sections. Although different sections of the Klamath occasionally feuded with each other in retaliation for an abducted child or a slain kinsman, they directed concerted warfare only against neighboring tribes for reasons of revenge and the amassing of booty. Men joined a war party voluntarily, usually choosing to follow a proven war leader known for his skillful strategy; a large war party—as many as thirty warriors—was led by several war chiefs. Depending on surprise, warriors rushed into an enemy settlement, whooping, clubbing, and shooting arrows.

A chief was respected for his wealth; indeed, the word for "chief" in the Klamath language meant "rich man." Wealth

proven himself through killing a surplus of game and fish, which he then reluctantly shared with other, less productive members. Klamath women were respected for their industry in gathering wild plants, dressing skins, basket weaving, and cooking. Chiefs gave their surplus goods to the poor without any trace of graciousness; the poor were not particularly grateful to receive such grudgingly given bounty.

was an important aspect of Klamath culture. However, lacking the natural abundance of resources that surrounded their neighbors in the Northwest Coast, the Klamath did not have the leisure time to devote to artistic pursuits or the necessary raw materials. Thus, for the Klamath, wealth took the form of amassing a surplus of any item they could collect in quantity: food, shells, skins, and weapons.

Although the Sanpoil of eastern Washington were known for their generosity and the emphasis they placed on maintaining harmony in all relationships, the Klamath, while stressing harmony, were driven to acquire property. Individual achievement was the major theme in Klamath society. A person gained a good reputation through application and industry; laziness and poverty were synonymous. Each person had a moral responsibility to work, to produce, and to amass a surplus. A respected man had

Women wove a variety of tule items, such as the mats they used to cover their above ground summer dwellings, round basketry hats, and cooking and storage baskets; today, women have revived the art of making baskets from tule. Both sexes wore simple Plains-influenced buckskin clothing, including moccasins. They tattooed themselves and flattened the heads of their children when they were bound in cradleboards by pressing a board against the infant's padded skull. Men wore armor made either of slats or of elkhide; bows and arrows and clubs and spears completed a warrior's outfit.

Both men and women could be shamans because both sexes could experience visions. Besides curing sickness and controlling the weather, shamans had the power to find lost articles and make game return. They also accompanied war parties. The shamans' most stirring activity was the winter seance, when they initiated novice shamans and proved their own power. Before an audience of families from several communities, the shamans swallowed fire and arrows and hurled their power at rival shamans. Chiefs had little power in comparison to feared and respected shamans.

European Contact

Between 1806 and 1809, Meriweather Lewis and William Clark opened what is now Montana, Idaho, Oregon, and Washington to outsiders through their exploration of the Louisiana Purchase region. They were fortunate to be assisted by Shoshone Sacajawea. Chief Kameawaite, overjoyed to be reunited with his sister, who had been stolen years before, led the expedition through Montana to the country of the Flathead Indians, who took them across the Idaho panhandle. The Nez Percé generously provided enough canoes and supplies to see the party to the Pacific and guide them to the Palouse homelands. Tribes such as the Yakima, Walla Walla, and Wanapum sent representatives to meet and trade with Lewis and Clark. Friendly relations continued as the explorers canoed down the Columbia River, visiting the villages of the Skin, Wishram, Tenino, Wasco, Clackamus, Cathlapotle, Wahkiakum, and Cathlamet. After wintering with the Clatsop Indians south

COLUMBIA RIVER TREATY TRIBES PRESENT PLANS FOR SALMON RESTORATION

"Salmon are our responsibility, and we're here to assert our authority to protect and restore the salmon."
—*Alphonse Halfmoon, the chairman of the Umatilla Fish and Wildlife Committee, speaking to members of the House of Representatives in Washington, D.C., on June 22, 1995*

Tribal representatives from the Columbia River Treaty Tribes stressed that their plan to restore salmon in the Columbia Basin goes beyond the federal government's Endangered Species Act plan and the state's Columbia Basin Fish and Wildlife Program. The tribal plan includes greater limits to activities that disturb the land. These limitations are to be determined by water quality and stream channel guidelines. The Columbia River Treaty Tribes also favor using artificial propagation to rebuild badly damaged salmon populations, reintroducing species where they were found historically, and ending the trucking and barging of juvenile salmon in mainstream Snake and Columbia Rivers. Other aspects of the tribal plan include improving river migrating conditions through increased water flows; structural modifications to dams, including drawdowns;

and restrictions on ocean harvests based on salmon and chinook populations, instead of fishing quotas.

Alphonse Halfmoon said that by implementing the Endangered Species Act, government officials have undermined tribal and state sovereignty. "Instead of co-management, unilateral decisions are made by the federal government—by the very agencies that are responsible for managing these salmon to the brink of extinction."

The cost of the tribal plan—$195 to $325 million—is about the same amount as the cost of the Northwest Power Planning Council's Columbia Basin Fish and Wildlife Program and the National Marine Fisheries Service Snake River recovery plan. Tribal representatives emphasized that their plan is based on the need to return the fish to the rivers where they belong and to care for those rivers.

of the Columbia River, Lewis and Clark returned to report the rich resources of the Northwest, including the abundance of fur-bearing animals.

Fort Astoria in Oregon soon became a key trading center for the Americans. In 1824, the Hudson's Bay Company opened Fort Vancouver in Washington. By the 1850s, the vast number of fur-bearing animals had already been depleted.

In the 1830s, Presbyterian missionaries established themselves among the Cayuse and Nez Percé; Catholics followed and established themselves among groups such as the Flathead, Sanpoil, and Yakima. Many Plateau Indian villages were divided into pro- and anti-Christian factions.

Between 1836 and 1843, former fur trappers opened the Oregon Trail, which eased the way for settlers to reach the fertile lands of present-day Oregon and Washington. Diseases such as measles soon spread among the Indians, decimating their populations.

In 1848, with the discovery of gold along the American River in California, huge numbers of miners invaded Indian lands, including the lands of the Klamath. From there miners soon extended their claims north into Oregon and Washington and east into Idaho and Montana. The U.S. government concentrated the Indians onto small reservations, liquidated all Indian title to the land, and created the Oregon and Washington Territories in 1853. However, miners and prospectors continued to invade the remaining Indian lands on the Columbia Plateau, sparking the Plateau Indian War in 1855. The war lasted until 1858, when U.S. troops defeated the Yakima, Flathead, Palouse, and others at the Battle of Four Lake and Spokane Plain.

Unlike their Modoc relatives, the Klamath always lived peacefully with invading whites. In 1864, along with the Modoc, they ceded most of their territories to the U. S. and settled on the Klamath Reservation in southern Oregon, north of Klamath Falls. However, in 1954, the U.S. government "terminated" the Klamath reservation, which meant that the people lost treaty-guaranteed health and education benefits, as well as their land base. In August 1986, after years of work by the people, full federal recognition was restored to the Klamath tribe.

Two of the success stories in the Plateau region are the Warm Springs Indians of Oregon and the Yakima people of Washington, who are particularly active in educational and economic self-development programs. The Warm Springs people own the Warm Spring Forest Products Industries, which includes a plywood plant and a sawmill. They use the income from Kah-Nee-Ta, their resort and convention center, for education and health programs, and encourage their young people to seek university degrees. They also sell wild horses and manage a salmon hatchery. In 1982, the Warm Springs Indians became the first U. S.

TRIBAL ISSUES IN THE GREAT BASIN

In the 1970s and 1980s, tribal issues in the Great Basin centered on treaty and agreement rights, water rights, jurisdiction, economic development, and educational and social needs. The people in this region have signed more than twenty treaties and agreements, which became the basis of Indian rights. In 1980 and 1981, a confederation of Great Basin tribes formed to deal with the establishment of the MX missile system on treaty lands in Nevada and Utah. Off-reservation treaty rights are guaranteed to the Fort Hall Northern Shoshone-Bannock tribes by the Fort Bridger treaty of 1868 and the Agreement of 1898. They cited these rights to National Forest and Bureau of Land Management areas for hunting, fishing, trapping, and gathering of wild plant resources when the state governments and private interests pressed for title to extensive federal lands in the far West in the late 1970s and early 1980s.

In the arid Great Basin, there are many competitors for water. In the 1980s, the federal government endorsed negotia-

tion of Indian water rights rather than seek determination by the courts. However, state and urban interests are pressing for changes to gain control of water resources.

Despite having their own constitutions, Nevada tribes had to decide whether they wanted to be under state or federal jurisdiction in the 1970s, instead of their own. Nearly all tribes chose federal jurisdiction. Many conflicts have developed with state governments over criminal jurisdiction of non-Indians, nuclear waste storage, liquor control, urban growth, and the taxation of non-Indian businesses on reservation land.

Women have been participating more in tribal government. During 1980, several tribal councils, such as the Ute Mountain Utes and Northern Utes, had female chairpersons. Water needs and urban expansion continue to be a threat to tribal resources. The tribes are working to form new or revitalized tribal councils to protect Indian rights and create a better life for Indian people.

By 1840, bison no longer lived west of the Continental Divide; the Northern Shoshone and Bannock then had to risk venturing onto the Great Plains. Snowshoes made winter hunting possible; horses sank up to their bellies in snowdrifts.

SHERMAN ALEXIE

Born in 1966, Sherman Alexie grew up in Wellpinit, Washington, on the Spokane Indian Reservation. He has published more than two hundred poems, stories, and translations in respected literary journals. He won a 1991 Washington State Arts Commission poetry fellowship and a 1992 National Endowment for the Arts poetry fellowship. In 1992, he published his first book of poetry and short stories, *The Business of Fancy Dancing*, which earned a favorable front-page review from the *New York Times Book Review*.

tribe to open their own hydroelectric plant, the Pelton Reregulating Dam; they sell the energy generated by their plant to the Pacific Power and Light Company.

The Yakima have successfully maintained their spiritual beliefs while promoting economic self-determination. They manage their own forest products industry, their own furniture manufacturing plant, and 2.7 million acres (1.1 million ha) of rangeland and 150,000 acres (60,000ha) of farmland. Through the Wapato Project, they control their own water; they have also been highly successful in banking, fishing, and small businesses. The tribe has also generated money for the Yakima Tribal Housing Authority. In 1980, they opened the largest tribal cultural center in the country, which contains a library, museum, theater, restaurant, office space, and gift shop. The Yakima tribe encourages its young people with tribal scholarships and a summer educational program to prepare students for college. They also support their heritage with numerous festivals and powwows.

GREAT BASIN PEOPLES

No major natural barriers separate the Plateau from the Great Basin, but the two great rivers—the Columbia and the Fraser—decline as they flow south. This meant there were few avenues for trade and travel; with no rivers draining to the sea, Basin peoples looked inward for their survival.

The languages of this region reflect this inward geographic cultural orientation. The Great Basin is the only

In the eastern range of Ute territory, the Rocky Mountains of Colorado have peaks that reach fourteen thousand feet (4,267m). There were originally six eastern bands—the Muache, Capote, Weeminuche, Uncompahgre, Parusanuch, and Yampa—which ranged almost as far east as Denver.

region in North America in which a linguistic area and a culture area coincide. Except for the Hokan-speaking Washoe, all the peoples of this area speak Numic, a division of the Uto-Aztecan language family; such a coincidence of language and culture seldom occurs and shows close internal cultural unity.

The lack of precipitation in this area forced Basin peoples to establish an even more delicate balance with their environment than did their neighbors to the north. One of the most resource-poor areas in North America, the Great Basin required reliance on an immense range of plant and animal resources. The peoples of this area depended on a foraging lifestyle that kept them almost constantly on the move so that they did not exhaust the resources of any single location. The central and western Shoshonean groups, who lived in present-day Utah and Nevada, were remarkably adaptable and resourceful as they sustained the traditions of their ancestors for thousands of years.

Archaeologists have found evidence of a lifeway they term the Western Archaic, which extends back at least ten thousand years. Over time, peoples responded to local environmental and demographic conditions by developing different yet related regional traditions. The Great Basin is unique because the peoples of this region maintained their ancient ways of life with relatively few changes.

It is misleading, however, to think that because they were linguistically and culturally uniform, the Basin peoples remained isolated from interchange with peoples of other regions. In the late seventeenth century, the Southern Ute and Eastern Shoshone obtained horses; by the early eighteenth century, most of the Ute, the Northern and Eastern Shoshone, and the Bannock had horses and the equestrian culture of the Plains. Although the major habitat and relations of the Washoe were in close proximity to the Northern Paiute, their range extended westward over the crest of this mountain range, and they shared many cultural traits with California peoples.

The Southern Paiute and Ute peoples share a language but differ in culture because the Ute, especially those east of the Colorado and Green Rivers, were among the first peoples to adopt the horse. They were instrumental in spreading equestrian culture from the Spanish settlements south of them to groups farther north. This led the Ute to become effective bison hunters on the western Plains and to adopt many features of Plains culture. The Northern Shoshone and Bannock also hunted bison until around 1840, when these animals were no longer found west of the Continental Divide. When bison disappeared from this area, the Northern Shoshone and Bannock had to risk venturing onto the Great Plains, where they vied for game with Plains peoples, who had the advantage of firearms.

GREAT BASIN ROCK ART

For the last several thousand years, Great Basin peoples have painted or inscribed images onto rock faces. From eastern California across Nevada to central Utah, they have left hundreds of sites. Petroglyphs are pecked, scratched, abraded, or otherwise cut into the surface of bedrock, boulders, and cliffs, and pictographs are painted onto these same surfaces.

Rock art cannot be read as writing because it does not represent speech; meaning and symbolic content may illuminate culture history as style and content reflect change and continuity through time and between regions. Although it represents ideologies, it is important not to misinterpret imagery from the past.

The Great Basin Abstract tradition, which is present in a limited number of sites on the Colorado Plateau, has a curvilinear (circles, concentric circles, circle chains, sun disks, curvilinear meanders, wavy lines or snakes, and star figures) and a rectilinear (dots, rectangular grids, bird tracks, crosshatching, and rakes) style. An anthropomorphic tradition dominated the northern Plateau and, later, the Basin. This tradition depicts mountain sheep, birds, and stylized human figures. Evidence indicates that Great Basin rock art styles functioned in connection with hunting rituals and in other shamanic contexts.

The Eastern Shoshone

"Being the first people of this land, but the last citizens of the Nation, American Indians have a perspective of America and the United States that is exclusively ours....We cannot change the past, but we must know the past in order to contemplate a better future. Although it may be said of the past century that American Indians have not been the beneficiary of this Nation's strengths, but the victim of its weaknesses, we can direct our energies to the task and challenge that this expression shall bear no truth in the future."
—Northern Paiute Melvin Thom, 1965

The far-reaching perspective envisioned by Melvin Thom, who was chairman of the Walker River Tribal Council, reflects the strong leadership and resilience of Basin peoples. These qualities are evident in the Eastern Shoshone, who lived in western Wyoming and adjoining areas since at least A.D. 1500 and combined Great Basin cultural tradition with the prehorse and horse-period Plains. Through intercultural borrowing, they integrated their culture with aspects of Spanish, Meti, and Anglo-American cultures. Their population dramatically declined in the nineteenth century—from three thousand people in 1840 to eight hundred in 1900. By 1981, however, their numbers had increased to twenty-four hundred.

Like many other peoples, the Eastern Shoshone practiced a pattern of concentration in the summer and then dispersal into three to five bands each winter through the early spring. Effective leadership in the bison hunt, trade, warfare, and winter shelter held the key to Shoshone survival. The tekwahni (chief), a middle-aged or older man who had distinguished himself in war or in shamanism, ordered the tribal march or hunt. In the absence of a tribal council, the tekwahni also counseled important decisions, but not internal disputes. The badges of his office included a broad yellow band painted on his tipi, a special feather headdress, and the eagle standard that marked his place in the battle charge.

The bitter contest for access to bison demanded strong leadership, disciplined control, careful organization, and solidarity. Two military societies controlled the people during the tribal march and before the hunt: the Yellow Brows, with their yellow painted cockscomb hairdos, were the vanguards on the march, and the Logs acted as rear guards. The Yellow Brows enforced discipline so that no one unintentionally alerted the bison, known for their keen hearing. Two or three scouts first located the herd, then signaled the camp by loping back and forth. Hunters, mounted on their fast bison-hunting horses, then charged the herd, shooting and spearing their prey.

The Shoshone hunted the bison for a brief period in the spring and a longer season in the autumn. During the hunts, they consistently ran the risk of attack from hostile Plains tribes. Shoshone women were skilled at rapidly butchering and drying bison meat into strips, which were packed into leather parfleches carried on pack horses. While on the hunts, Shoshone horses quickly consumed available fodder on the short-grass prairies, but they could not be too widely dispersed for fear of theft from raiding parties. The vulnera-

bility of their horses meant that the Shoshone could not rely on the bison for even half their annual food supply.

When other food supplies were low in the spring, they dammed a stream with wattle work and rocks, leaving a gap with a weir to catch fish, such as cutthroat trout, Rocky Mountain whitefish, and Montana grayling. Below the dam, others rode their horses into the stream, lashing at the surface of the water with poles as they moved upstream singing. They ate some fish fresh, preserving the rest by sun-drying or smoking.

WASHAKIE

Believed to have been born in Montana's Bitterroot Mountains in 1804, Washakie later went to live with his mother's Eastern Shoshone family in the Wind River Mountains of Wyoming. As a young man, he fought with great courage against the Blackfeet and Crow. During the 1820s and 1830s, Washakie became friends with mountain men Jim Bridger and Kit Carson.

In the 1840s, Washakie became the principal head of his band, leading them in diplomatic relations with the whites. Washakie even provided regular patrols of his men to assist immigrants along the Oregon Trail. He was friends with Mormon Brigham Young.

Washakie was instrumental in establishing a reservation for his people; his sagacious leadership kept his people unified and helped ensure peaceful relations with the whites. The Shoshone served as scouts for the military against the Cheyenne, Sioux, Arapaho, and Ute. In honor of his assistance to the U.S. military, Camp Brown, in present-day Wyoming, was renamed Fort Washakie in 1878. Washakie was buried there with full military honors in 1900.

The Shoshone found their next most important resources in the upland valleys and forests; elk, mule deer, mountain sheep, antelope, and beaver were also vital to survival, although trappers had virtually eliminated the beaver by the 1830s. They also ate jackrabbit, sage hen, marmot, moose, and wood rat.

Opposite: "My heart is sick and sad. From where the sun now stands I will fight no more forever." With these words, Nez Percé Chief Joseph announced his surrender. His band, cold and hungry, had eluded the army for more than one thousand miles (1,609km), only to be surrounded just thirty miles (48km) short of the Canadian border.

In the late summer and autumn, women gathered currants, rose berries, hawthorns, and gooseberries in the upland forests and high prairies. In September, a variety of roots, camas, and wild onions were available. The people ate berries fresh, in soups, and pounded with bison or elk meat and fat in the high-protein food known as pemmican. In June, women gathered seeds and pods, such as thistles. Greens, pistils, leaves, the sugary honey plant, gilia, cinquefoil, and sunflowers added variety to their diet. Although seldom eaten, prickly pear, gathered in the drier steppe and desert regions, was an important source of glue and paint stock.

After the annual Sun Dance in May or June, the people collected obsidian and pipestone; July was a month of trading, gaming, and gambling, which required cognitive and physical skills. In August, they collected salt and seashells. Autumn was a time of preparing for war and winter. When the men raided for a brief period in October, women prepared hides and pemmican to see their families through the bitterly cold winter.

Shoshone warfare centered around war honors, which provided greater prestige than any other activity; distinguished warriors displayed their honors with black finger marks on either side of their tipi doors, with red finger marks below. Death in battle was not a favored goal, although suicides on the battlefield were respected.

Winter was the hardest time of year because it always brought the possibility of starvation; however, it was also a time of storytelling and winter games. By April, the horses were growing fat, which meant that the warriors could indulge in a brief period of raiding in mid-May.

After 1800, when it was introduced by a former Comanche shaman, Yellow Hand, the Sun Dance unified the people. In the winter, an experienced Sun Dancer and shaman announced a vision requiring him to perform the Sun Dance for his survival. By spring, he had sent invitations summoning various groups for a Sun Dance to be held in May or June. Participants and onlookers shared the sacred ceremonial that brought tribal and personal well-being. For each of them, the Sun Dance symbolized their people's cultural standing, wealth, and alliances with other groups.

The Sun Dance leader, his assistants, and respected warriors prepared for the ritual by building the lodge, making a Sun Dance doll, and practicing for the ceremony. A cere-

Orian Box is a Southern Ute artist as well as a council member. Here, he sits in front of one of his paintings, which depicts markers of Pan-Indian identity. A larger-than-life-size, stylized Plains Indian wears an American flag whose stars echo those of the immense geometric star of a Lakota star quilt.

monial bison had to be killed to provide the head and backhide for the central pole. Men and women then conducted a ritual battle to locate, "hunt," and "kill" the trees for the Sun Dance lodge.

Following ritual preparation and purification, the four days and three nights of the Sun Dance began. Participants fasted and danced around the center pole on which the bison head had been mounted. Afterward, the people celebrated a great, communal feast of bison tongues. Those who were ill symbolically discarded their illnesses by tying old clothes to the center pole, the only part of the lodge not disassembled after the ceremony. Until World War II, such clothes remained there until they had rotted away. Today, the Sun Dance continues, with the integration of Christian and Peyote beliefs.

Before the introduction of Christianity and the Native American Church, Eastern Shoshone ceremonialism included both individualistic spirit-seeking practices and group ceremonies for the welfare of the community. Individuals attained personal success and survival by acquiring supernatural power from the dangerous world of spirits. Power could come in dreams, but it usually had to be sought through participation in the Sun Dance or by sleeping in sacred places; pictograph sites—known as poha kahni ("house of power")—are the most sacred places. In a successful vision quest, the poha, or spirit, appears to the suppliant, bestowing skills, protections, songs, tokens, and taboos.

The shaman is known as pohakanti, or "one who has power." The shaman led group ceremonials, such as the Father Dance, the Shuffling Dance, and the Sun Dance.

JAIME PINKHAM, PRESENT-DAY NEZ PERCE LEADER

"I have heard that Native people walk in two worlds. Perhaps at one time in our history this was true. Yet, today we hear a call for cultural diversity. The reason, I believe, is modern solutions can be uncovered outside the intellectual boundaries of science and technology."

—Jaime Pinkham in Lara Evans's Winds of Change *article (spring 1995, vol. X, no. 2)*

As natural resources manager for the Nez Percé Tribe and president of the InterTribal Timber Council, Jaime Pinkham deals with issues of treaty rights and sovereignty on a daily basis. Pinkham quotes Nisqually Billy Frank, who said, "We need to be peacemakers when we can and warriors when we must."

In the tradition of Chief Joseph, Pinkham worries about what sustains leadership. "Many of our leaders leap on a treadmill that taxes their physical and mental well-being. Yet, in the face of adversity, many are sustained by the healing that must take place and by the beauty we must protect in life. Passion sustains Indian leaders." Once fearing the futility of such a monumental effort, Pinkham realized, after five years of working with the American Indian Science and Engineering Society (AISES) Leadership Conference, that he was not running out of time at all. "We wanted to incite approximately eighty students a year into continuing their leadership development. Today, five years later, four hundred students are preparing to make a difference. As long as they step forth to take the place of today's leaders, time becomes an ally."

Jaime Pinkham speaks from experience, for he took a circular path that led far from home in an effort to escape reservation poverty and to create a promising career in forestry. After working for seven years with the state of Washington, Pinkham was selected to participate in a special two-year leadership program.

Two experiences in this program—a trip to a Detroit soup kitchen, food bank, and homeless shelter and a tour of the Peruvian Andes—had such a profound emotional impact on Pinkham that he decided to return home to serve his people. In Detroit, he came to terms with a sense of abandoned pride his subjectivity had blinded him to at home. His heart poured out to these people, whose unkempt yards, run-down houses, and vacant lots reminded him of an Indian reservation. During Pinkham's second year in the leadership program, he went to the Peruvian Andes. In pointing out the extraordinary scientific and engineering achievements of the Incas, the tour guide said, "They adored nature. And that made them wise." These were words of cultural pride that Pinkham could imagine his grandfather saying.

After twelve years away, Pinkham returned home to the Nez Percé Reservation in Lapwai, Idaho, where, today, his life brings two worlds together. Symbolically, he wears his hair cut short in front for a professional look, but he wears a long braid down his back. He spends a great deal of time in suits and on the road dealing with the high technology involved in resource management; he also makes time for cultural traditions, such as learning the old songs and participating in the Nez Percé Drum society. As his uncle reminded him, when speaking of the twelve years Pinkham spent on a different path: "It wasn't that you left the circle; it was that you traveled it differently." Today, Jaime Pinkham uses the skills and knowledge he gained during those twelve years to benefit his people as he continues his journey home.

Although only men could participate in the Sun Dance, men and women could sing sacred songs and participate in the Father Dance and Shuffling Dance, a nighttime ceremony held in the autumn, winter, or spring.

The Eastern Shoshone also had timapanti, magicians or wonder workers, known for their ability to transform moccasins into bison tongues, charm an antelope herd with a hoof rattle, bring about a thaw by whirling a bull-roarer, and chase away clouds with an eagle feather.

European Contact

European contact came relatively late for the peoples of Great Basins, but once begun, the economic and political situation of the region quickly changed. By 1855, homesteaders and gold-seekers had traveled the Oregon and Humboldt Trails, and the Mormons had settled Utah. Because of the shortage of farm and ranch hands, Indians were in high demand as workers.

Beginning with Oregon in 1839 and ending with Wyoming in 1868, the federal government established reservations and regulated relations with the Indians. Because of the widely varied background of Indian agents, different Basin groups received quite different treatment from these administrators. Some peoples received distributions of material goods and others went without; some leaders were awarded diplomatic status and others were arbitrarily appointed by the government, while the real leaders went unacknowledged.

WOVOKA'S GHOST DANCE

"All Indians must dance, everywhere, keep on dancing. Pretty soon in next spring Great Spirit come. He bring back all game of every kind. The game be thick everywhere. All dead Indians come back and live again. They all be strong just like young men, be young again."

—*Wovoka, Paiute prophet and originator of the Ghost Dance*

Because spirituality is such an integral part of Native American life, it was natural for native peoples to draw upon the traditions of prophecy to cope with problems brought by European conquest. Native Americans had been isolated on reservations and denied access to the resources and freedoms they enjoyed for centuries. They suffered deep poverty and oppression; the fabric of their society was destroyed as beloved relatives died from warfare, epidemics, starvation, and exposure. With few options and no place to flee, the tribes looked to religious movements for answers to their crises. Many traditional stories foretold continental devastation and called the people to world renewal.

The first recognized religious movement in the Great Basin was the Ghost Dance, created in 1889 by Wovoka, also known as Jack Wilson, a Northern Paiute prophet. Two decades earlier, however, Wodziwob, a Walker Lake-Walker River Northern Paiute prophet—unrelated to Wovoka—had envisioned the first Ghost Dance. By the mid-1860s, the Northern Paiute had been devastated by epidemics and prohibited from using most of their aboriginal territory by white encroachment. They suffered from starvation and were discriminated against by whites. Wodziwob's vision taught that through ritual dancing, men, women, and children could ultimately restore the resources on which Indians once lived.

In 1889, after the first Ghost Dance religion had died out among the Northern Paiute, Western Shoshone, Southern Paiute, and Ute groups, Wovoka received a series of visions instructing him to revive the Ghost Dance. Wovoka's ideology, based on peaceful coexistence with whites, preached work, industry, and living in harmony. His version of the Ghost Dance sought not to change the social order but rather to transform individual states of consciousness in a group context. His basic message was adjustment to odious conditions in this world to achieve eternal happiness in a restored world.

However, the Ghost Dance doctrine that swept out of Nevada simplified Wovoka's message by guaranteeing an immediate transformation: ridding the world of whites and resurrecting the Indian dead. This message was especially welcomed by the Indians of the Great Plains, who had lost their entire nomadic way of life in the virtual elimination of the bison and their confinement to reservations. The Ghost Dance flourished there until the infamous 1890 massacre of Lakota at Wounded Knee, South Dakota.

The spirit that inspired the Ghost Dance lives on today, affirming the value of ritual to affect world change. This spirit encourages the people to practice traditional values based on the sacredness and interrelatedness of all life and to communicate this sense of the sacred to non-Indians as well.

Powwows continue to be the most public and dramatic expressions of American Indian identity in the twentieth century. Originally associated with the Great Plains, today powwows are held in nearly every major city in the United States and Canada and even in many European cities.

The Eastern Shoshone were large-scale bison hunters between 1500 and 1700. After 1700, they raided and hunted bison on horseback until they suffered a series of defeats by the Blackfeet between 1780 and 1825, which led them to retreat to the west. In 1800, Comanche Yellow Hand introduced the Sun Dance to the Shoshone, which became a major development in their ceremonial practices.

Pocatello, a Northern Shoshone, tried unsuccessfully to convince Chief Washakie and his Eastern Shoshone to join him in opposing settlers who were settling the Cache, Bear, Bruneau, and Snake valleys. The Eastern Shoshone, well organized as a distinct band with many features of Plains mounted bands, were treated with greater deference by whites than were other Great Basin groups.

In fact, they were the only Basin group not militarily conquered or displaced during the early reservation period. Their great leader Washakie welded the Wyoming Shoshone into a single band. Washakie wisely negotiated alliances with the whites and brought renewed tribal vitality to his people between 1825 and 1880. In 1867, after many requests, Washakie's people were finally granted a reservation in the Wind River Valley; however, the government later forced them to share this land with their old enemies, the Arapaho.

The years from 1880 to 1910 were among the most difficult for the Eastern Shoshone because of population losses and difficulties adapting to reservation life. Between 1910 and 1945, however, the people and their culture revitalized through innovation in their spiritual beliefs and practices. Since this period, the Shoshone population has grown and their culture has stabilized with the introduction of new occupations and urban adaptation.

CHAPTER 8

Native Peoples
of Canada

"Money is good to have, but if you have no land, then money is nothing. You have to look after the land, because it has provided for us
for many generations; if you don't look after the land, it won't provide for us for many generations."

—*Inuvialuit Elder Billy Day speaking at the Inuit*
Tapirisat of Canada Environment Workshop

ative peoples in all parts of the globe—who live
on a quarter of its lands but control little of its
resources—closely watched the negotiations of the largest
native land claim ever presented to any government. In
1976, Canada's Inuit (formerly known as "Eskimos")
submitted a land claim for a large area of the eastern
Arctic as part of a proposal to create Nunavut, which
means "Our Land" in the Inuktitut language. Years of
delicate negotiations followed, as the Canadian federal
and provincial government, the Inuit, and other native
peoples worked to resolve the issues. In
December 1991, the Inuit and the
Canadian government
signed the historic
Nunavut

Political Accord, an unprecedented agreement that yields
control of Inuit resources to the Inuit themselves.

The Nunavut agreement is unique because the Inuit
negotiated primarily for empowerment for themselves and
for their children through political control: by 1999, the
Inuit will administer a territorial government over the
entire area, which comprises a fifth of Canada. The twenty-two thousand native inhabitants are to inherit control
of the eastern and central lands and archipelagos of the
Northwest Territories, about 819,000 square miles
(2,121,210 sq km).

Left: Canadian Indians, Inuit, and Métis depended upon snow-
shoes for travel in deep snow.

Opposite: Ottawa leader and orator Chief Pontiac (1720–1769)
united diverse Indian nations against the British in the Great
Lakes region. The Huron, Illinois, Kickapoo, Lenape, Miami,
Ojibwa, Potawatomi, Seneca, and Shawnee answered Pontiac's
call to attack Fort Detroit. Pontiac called off the siege when the
French failed to deliver their promised support. Ottawa,
Ontario, named for Pontiac's people, lies in their old sphere of
influence.

The Canadian government recognizes that the Inuit own thirty-five thousand square miles (906,500 sq km) of land, including fifty-one hundred square miles (13,209 sq km) of ownership of subsurface resources and preferential and exclusive harvesting rights. The Inuit will be paid $159 million in financial compensation in scheduled payments and receive a $7.5 million Social Development Fund and a $10 million Economic Enhancement Fund. The establishment of joint wildlife management bodies and special conservation areas, the creation of joint environmental impact assessment and review processes, and a provision for economic measures to promote Inuit economic development will help them to pursue economic interests yet at the same time preserve the sacredness of their land.

The Inuit, who live in Canada's far north above the treeline, are only one of this country's native peoples, who also include various Indian groups and Métis, or people of mixed ancestry. Although the Inuit, Indians, and Métis share many common goals, they also have important cultural, legal, and political differences.

THE CANADIAN GOVERNMENT'S RELATIONSHIP WITH ITS ABORIGINAL PEOPLES

In general, the Canadian government's policies toward native peoples have been more humane than those of the U.S. government, largely because competition for land and other resources was not as intense in Canada. With more available land and a relatively smaller population, the Canadian government could be somewhat generous in treaty concessions. Furthermore, during the American

LANGUAGES OF THE TRIBES OF CANADA

1. Inuit
2. Tagis
3. Dogrib
4. Tsimshian
5. Beaver
6. Yellowknife
7. Chippewayan
8. Haida
9. Heiltsuk
10. Bella Coola
11. Kwakiutl
12. Nootka
13. Dakota
14. Ojibwa
15. Blackfeet
16. Cree
17. Assiniboine
18. Mistassini
19. Montagnais
20. Micmac
21. Algonquian
22. Mohawk
23. Ottawa
24. Oneida
25. Delaware

A Canadian Indian spears fish at Waterton Lakes National Park in the Canadian Rockies. Officially, to be an Indian in Canada, one must be registered under the Indian Act of 1876; today, there are 633 bands of Canadian Indians.

Revolution and the War of 1812, most Canadian Indians remained loyal to the Crown; in contrast to the adversarial relationship that developed in the United States between Indians and non-Indians, Canadian Indians were considered to be faithful allies rather than conquered peoples. Canadian Indians did not experience the wholesale removals and great reductions in tribal land to which their southern relatives were subjected.

Also significant in the Canadian treatment of native peoples is the pluralism that characterizes Canada. Canada has historically been a bilingual and bicultural country with a significant French-speaking population. Like the United States, Canada has a long tradition of welcoming immigrants. Unlike their counterparts to the south, however, immigrants to Canada have not been pressured to assimilate to the dominant culture. Canada is known for its tolerance for many ethnic groups.

However, today Canada's population is increasing, and the competition for land and jobs is growing. This has led to renewed pressure to exploit oil and mineral resources; these factors are contributing to more intense pressure on native peoples to assimilate into the majority culture. Canada also faces some factionalization among its native population because of the Métis people, who are of mixed ancestry but constitute a distinct cultural group.

Legally, the Canadian government has subdivided its indigenous peoples into status, treaty, and nonstatus Indians. A status Indian is a person who is registered or entitled to be registered as an Indian under the Indian Act of 1876. The government recognizes 633 bands, which generally correspond to traditional tribal and kinship groups.

Unlike the United States' system, which placed different tribes on the same reservation, the Canadian reserve system—so called because land was "reserved" for native

groups as their hunting grounds—not only kept different tribes separate but also allowed them to remain near their ancestral homelands. Most status Indians are also treaty Indians, except those who live in areas not covered by treaties, such as most of the province of British Columbia. About a third of status Indians live away from their reserves in urban areas.

Treaty Indians are registered members or descendants of members of a band that signed a treaty with the government. Nonstatus Indians are individuals who have lost their right to be registered under the Indian Act through voluntary renunciation, compulsory enfranchisement to non-Indian status, or the government's failure to register some Indian families. Canadian Indians who fought in the military during the world wars became enfranchised, losing their Indian status. For jurisdictional and public policy purposes, nonstatus Indians and Métis are classified together, and the Inuit are grouped with registered Indians.

In 1867, the British North America (BNA) Act established present-day Canada. Before this time, the Indians had negotiated separate treaties with the French and British governments; in 1867, Section 91 (24) of the BNA Act established the federal government's responsibility for Indian peoples and lands. The Indian Act of 1876 (later revised in 1951 and 1985) was intended to establish the reserve system to administer Indian affairs and, at the same time, to create favorable conditions for the assimilation of native peoples into Euro-Canadian society.

Outside the Yukon and Northwest Territories, the Canadian government owns very little land; instead, the provinces control nearly all public lands within their borders. This means that—unlike Indians in the United States—

This 1841 engraving depicts the presentation of a newly elected Huron chief. The Huron called themselves Wyandot—"People of the Peninsula"—in reference to their original homeland, a peninsula in southern Ontario east of Lake Huron. Iroquoian-speakers, the Wyandot did not belong to the Iroquois League; the Iroquois nearly annihilated the Wyandot in 1649 in a fight over control of the fur trade.

Canadian Indian bands seeking claims for lands outside their existing reserves or for lands based on traditional occupancy (aboriginal title) must negotiate with the provinces. Historically, the provinces have seldom accommodated Indian land claims; occasionally, land transfers have occurred, usually after major confrontations, such as the Kanesatake Mohawk blockade in Oka, Quebec. Difficulty in negotiating with the provincial government is a major reason that the Inuit and Cree of Quebec oppose the French-speaking separatist movement.

Despite their comparatively better treatment, aboriginal peoples remain the most disadvantaged group in Canadian society: socioeconomic conditions on Canadian Indian reserves have been likened to those of Third World countries. Unemployment rates for native peoples are far greater than those for non-Indians; Indian life expectancy is ten years below the national average. A quarter of status Indians live in unheated homes; slightly fewer live in over-crowded dwellings. The rate of violent death for native peoples is three times that of non-Indians, and the suicide rate is double.

Efforts are being made to improve Indian quality of life, however, and in the area of Indian education, in particular, some progress has been made. As the number of band-operated schools has increased each year, Indian children are staying in school longer and are seeking higher levels of education. Schools operated by Indian bands (there were more than three hundred in 1993) are a great improvement over the old system of residential boarding schools in terms of cultural survival. Usually boarding schools were Catholic or Anglican and served as a means of assimilating Indians into Euro-Christian culture. As in boarding schools in the United

Ojibwa (Chippewa) girls pose in Euro-American dress. One of the largest tribes north of Mexico, the Ojibwa live in Ontario and Saskatchewan as well as in Montana, North Dakota, Minnesota, Wisconsin, and Michigan. The Ojibwa, Ottawa, and Potawatomi formed a loose confederacy called the Three Fires.

States, teachers punished children for speaking their native languages and practicing aspects of their traditional cultures. Many children were physically and sexually abused; a recent Canadian television film received critical acclaim for dramatizing the experience of an abused young Blackfeet girl.

THE INDIANS OF CANADA

Depending on the natural resources of their particular territories, the indigenous cultures of Canada ranged from sedentary, agriculturally based societies to more nomadic hunter-gatherer lifestyles. Vast supplies of salmon and other resources made it possible for the Northwest Coast groups to live in settled villages on islands and seashores near the coastal mountains. Groups on the Atlantic coast, such as the Micmac, Beothuk, and Malecite, also lived by tidal and river fishing. In the Great Lakes region of central Canada, groups such as the Iroquois grew corn, beans, squash, and tobacco in their villages. The Blackfeet, Plains Cree, Sarcee, Assiniboine, and other

Indians of the prairies followed the migrating bison. Throughout the northern forests that stretch across Canada, peoples such as the Naskapi, Ottawa, Ojibwa, and Cree also followed a nomadic lifestyle as they hunted and fished. The seafaring Inuit continue to live on their traditional lands north of the treeline.

In some areas, such as British Columbia, native peoples traditionally speak a wide variety of languages. In contrast, much of the rest of Canada is linguistically homogeneous. All the native groups of Ontario—most of them in Quebec, the Maritime Provinces, and Manitoba—and many of those in Saskatchewan and Alberta speak Algonquian languages. Athabascan-speaking peoples dominate the Yukon and western Northwest Territories and the northern parts of Alberta, Saskatchewan, and Manitoba. The Inuit of the eastern part of the Northwest Territories speak Inuktitut. (There are also Inuit in Greenland; they speak Kalaallisut, which is an official language along with Danish.)

A national organization, the Assembly of First Nations, formerly known as the National Indian Brotherhood, represents these diverse cultures. Regional differences have resulted in internal political divisions: "treaty" and "non-treaty" Indians do not share the same path to self-government; some Canadian Indian bands are politically militant, and others are much more accommodating. At the same time, urban-based groups such as the Native Council of Canada are becoming more powerful as more native peoples migrate to cities. Despite their differences, Canada's Indian peoples unite over such issues as the 1990 land claim of the Kanesatake Mohawk in Oka, Quebec, when the Mohawk set up blockades to prevent the development of a golf course on land that the Kanesatake have traditionally claimed as their own.

Although assimilation is easier for individual Canadian Indians than it is for African-Americans in the United States, Canadian Indians have experienced a greater degree of racial prejudice than do their relatives in the United States.

This 1939 photograph shows Huron Indians on a reservation near Quebec City wearing both traditional and colonial finery in preparation for a visit from King George and Queen Elizabeth.

According to Don Collins of *News from Indian Country*, in October 1995, non-Indians tore down the sign marking the Chippewas of the Thames First Nation territory in Ontario, replacing it with the words "Kill Indians." The disturbances of recent years, which included the occupation of Ipperwash Provincial Park because it contains a native cemetery, came to a head when militant Indians invaded the Ottawa building of the Assembly of First Nations in search of Assembly Grand Chief Ovide Mercredi to relieve him of his leadership in the organization.

Many younger Indian people today feel a sense of desperation because of their frustration with the government's slow progress on issues of self-rule and land claims for aboriginal peoples. Hopelessness has led to an extremely high Indian suicide rate, as well as high rates of alcoholism and substance abuse. Member of Parliament M. Elijah Harper has met with community leaders in an effort to reconcile different factions.

"When I look at the standoffs and the frustration, and also at the problems that affect many more of our communities, like suicide, alcoholism, and hopelessness, I see… spiritual loss…people who are trying to fill an emptiness, who are struggling to find something."

Harper has called for a "Sacred Assembly" of Aboriginal and non-Aboriginal spiritual leaders to provide council. "First Nations," he said, "have lost not just our land and control over our lives, but also our connection to an ancient spirituality that has nurtured our peoples for centuries.…We must sustain the culture, values, and traditions that have sustained us for generations."

The Inuit

The Canadian Inuit live in small communities along the coasts of the Northwest Territories, on the Mackenzie Delta, on the shores of Hudson Bay, in Labrador, in northern Quebec, and throughout the Arctic Islands. Once called "Eskimos"—Cree for "raw meat eaters"—the Inuit are thought to be the descendants of the last people to migrate from Siberia to Alaska across the Bering Strait land bridge arriving in Canada around 10,000 B.C. Their supreme adaptation to the harsh polar expanses have enabled them to survive where death through exposure and starvation were constant possibilities; they live in the only area of Canada where indigenous people comprise the majority of the population.

They are now officially recognized as Inuit, which means "The People" in the Inuktitut language. Although they speak different dialects of this language, all Canadian Inuit speak Inuktitut and share a common culture based on marine harvesting. Traveling inland to hunt caribou,

fish, and waterfowl, the Inuit depended most upon seal, whale, and walrus. They lived in small groups of several families for most of the year and congregated in larger groups at sealing and fishing camps.

Not until the 1800s did the Inuit and Europeans experience sustained contact, when white whalers sailed north to hunt the bowhead whale. Inuit people became guides and crew members; whalers sometimes married Inuit women. The Hudson's Bay Company eventually established trading posts, leading many Inuit to give up hunting to trap fur-bearing animals. Many became dependent upon European goods, and the collapse of the fur trade in the 1940s led to poverty in many Inuit communities.

In the 1950s, the Canadian government finally sent relief supplies to the starving Inuit and began providing services for them. Their legal status remained ambiguous because of the remoteness of their homeland until, in 1959, the Canadian Supreme Court expanded the federal government's definition of native peoples to include the Inuit. Various levels of government administer different groups of Inuit. The territorial government has jurisdiction over Inuit

This traditional Quilleute cedar canoe is similar to those made by Canadian Indians north of the Olympic Peninsula, where the Quilleute live. Today, such canoes are sometimes equipped with an outboard motor and are used for river travel, fishing, and racing.

and other Canadians in the Northwest Territories. The Inuit of northern Quebec are governed by a regional government. Newfoundland and the federal government share the funding of government services administered by the provincial government to the Inuit of Labrador.

The Inuit's desire to negotiate a land claim with the government led to the formation of the Inuit Tapirisat (Brotherhood) of Canada in 1971. Since then, the Tungavik Federation of Nunavut has assumed the role of negotiator in the land claim.

The Canadian government employs 30 to 40 percent of the Inuit living in the North, but unemployment remains very high. Many Inuit communities still rely on traditional fishing and hunting to provide food and items to sell for income. Over the last forty years, tourism, arts and crafts, and the development of renewable and finite resources have also provided some income.

The Inuit are working to preserve the continuation of their culture through education at the elementary school level. Textbooks, newsletters, and magazines are published in the Inuktitut language. Along with Alaskan, Siberian, and Greenland Inuit, Canadian Inuit are active in international Arctic issues; the current president of the Inuit Circumpolar Conference is Canadian Inuit Mary Simon.

The Métis

People of mixed Indian and non-Indian ancestry are known as Métis, a term that originally referred only to people of mixed ancestry who lived on the prairies. Today the Native Council of Canada defines Métis as all people living in any part of Canada who claim mixed Indian and non-Indian ancestry. Although two-thirds of the Métis are concentrated in Manitoba, Saskatchewan, Alberta, and the Northwest Territories, there are Métis living throughout Canada.

Although the Métis may be phenotypically and genotypically more "Indian" than some status Indians, they have no concrete land base and have always been under provincial rather than federal jurisdiction, unlike the Inuit and Indians. They share many of the same problems faced by the Inuit and Indians, such as lack of employment, housing, and social networks, but they do not share the Indians' anxiety over the threat of termination; they have no land and few benefits to lose.

Racially and culturally, the Métis represent a hybrid people who are seeking responsible recognition of their own distinct cultural identity. A degree of mutual suspicion exists between Indians and Métis: some Métis consider it a step down to be identified as Indian. Indians are aware of this snobbery.

Many Métis say that they have all the disadvantages and none of the advantages of being officially native. They have been called "the forgotten people," and celebrated a major triumph at their inclusion in the definition of "aboriginal people" in Canada's 1982 Constitution.

The Métis have also been called "the children of the fur trade" because their ancestors were mostly born of marriages between Indian women and European fur traders. French fur traders often married Cree women on the prairies; English and Scottish traders tended to marry Dene women. European traders benefited from their close association with native peoples: not only were Indians familiar with the forests and rivers, but they also belonged to a social and political network that traders could tap into. The children of these marriages often became interpreters and middlemen in their fathers' trading businesses. Through time, the Métis developed a unique culture that combined European and Indian elements. They supported themselves as hunters, fishermen, farmers, traders, and trappers. In 1811, the Hudson's Bay Company opened land in Manitoba's Red River Valley to settlers; the resulting competition for land threatened the traditional Métis way of life, leading the Métis to develop a sense of nationalism.

These Kwakiutl Indians are celebrating a potlatch at Fort Rupert, British Columbia. Established in 1849 by the Hudson's Bay Company, Fort Rupert became the largest Kwakiutl settlement and, in time, the center of regional ceremonial activity.

In contrast to children of mixed white and Indian ancestry in the United States, the Métis were never forcibly relocated. This meant that their ties to their land and their distinctive culture were able to grow stronger through time.

When the Hudson's Bay Company sold the Métis homeland to Canada in 1869, the Métis were outraged. Louis Riel (1844–1885), the son of a prominent Métis, led the famous Red River Resistance of 1869–1870. The Métis established a provisional government under the Law of Nations and arrested several men for violating Métis law. When they executed an easterner, Thomas Scott, tempers flared and troops were sent. No blood was shed, however. The Canadian government negotiated with the Métis, leading to the Manitoba Act of 1870, which had a provision for the allotment of land to individual Métis and their children. Louis Riel even served briefly in the House of Commons in Ottawa, before being expelled.

However, conflict between the Métis and the settlers increased with the influx of more easterners who disrupted Métis culture. The Métis of Saskatchewan again summoned Louis Riel to work on their behalf. When the federal government failed to respond to Riel's petition for Métis land title, he once more established a provisional government. This time armed confrontations did occur, and eventually Canadian government officials captured Riel and tried him for treason. He was hanged in 1885.

Although the Canadian government gave the Manitoba Métis 1.4 million acres (560,000ha) of land in exchange for

This shaman and his wife belong to the Cree, one of the largest Native American groups in North America. Algonquian-speakers, Cree peoples traditionally lived in the Subarctic Shield and Mackenzie Borderlands of Canada; Cree territory stretched from Alberta in the west to Quebec in the east.

their land rights in that province, many Métis chose to continue their traditional lifestyle based on hunting. They did not want to become cash-croppers. By the 1900s, many Métis had become impoverished.

In 1938 and 1939, Alberta became the first province to recognize the Métis formally by establishing twelve Métis "Settlements" in the northern part of the province. However, with the discovery of oil and gas, some of these communities were displaced; by 1960, only eight Métis settlements remained. The provincial government reached an agreement with the Métis in 1990 that transferred 500,000 hectares (1,235,000 acres) and $310 million to five thousand Métis. Métis who live outside the settlements receive no special benefits; those who live in the settlements are governed by elected councils who deter-mine housing, land use, and policing. Although Saskatchewan Métis have "farms" with very small land bases set aside for them, such special recognition is rare.

Today Métis argue for equal recognition as one of Canada's three aboriginal peoples, along with Inuit and Indians. The Métis fight for their rights through political organizations at the provincial, territorial, and federal levels. At the heart of their agenda is the establishment of a concrete land base, which occasionally conflicts with the primary goals of Inuit and Indian peoples. Although Indians and Inuit are under federal jurisdiction, the Métis remain under provincial jurisdiction. Despite their recognition as an aboriginal people in the Constitution Act of 1982, individual Métis still fail to receive benefits through the Canadian social welfare program as an aboriginal people.

This Cree village was situated in an ideal trading location; in addition to trading with other tribes, the Cree developed early trading relations with the French and English. The canoe was indispensable to the Cree, whose lands were dotted with lakes and rivers.

The Vision of Native America for the Future

S tanding on the threshold of the twenty-first century, we cannot afford to close our ears to the message of Native Americans. Every one of us faces the challenge of survival in a time of rapidly diminishing physical resources—a global struggle that unites us all. We stand at the brink of major change and upheaval: a time when we are facing myriad critical and life-threatening issues.

Increasingly, we are realizing what it means to live in a global society. The actions of each nation—indeed, the actions of each individual—profoundly affect the environmental and spiritual well-being of everyone on the entire planet. Over the course of the twentieth century, science has vastly improved our lives with impressive technological developments in the fields of medicine, communication, and transportation, but the spiritual and human cost of these wonders has been enormous. Not only has the proportion

of the world's population who reaped these benefits been small, but even among this privileged minority, problems of alienation, violence, drug abuse, and spiritual emptiness have vastly increased, leading many to question the basic assumption that material acquisitions and technological developments determine the quality of life.

Even more alarming has been the growing evidence that we are rapidly destroying the very planet that gives us life. No longer is it possible to dismiss as isolated cases the acid-induced destruction of Germany's Black Forest or the carcasses of beluga whales floating in the Saint Lawrence River.

Above: This Kana'a-style black-on-white pottery vase is from the Early Red Mesa (Anasazi) culture and may date back to A.D. 900.

Opposite: It is now common for non-Plains Indians to wear traditional Plains dress when participating in a powwow.

The serious limitations of a worldview based on technological achievement alone are becoming clearer each day as more forests die, more rivers become poisoned, and more children kill themselves with despair over the world they will inherit.

Humans and their hominid ancestors have been on the planet for more than 4 million years, yet it has taken less than three hundred years—since the development of the fossil fuel–driven machines of the Industrial Revolution—to destroy the planet's natural resources and make uninhabitable large areas of the world. Clearly, a worldview that inspired great scientific and technological achievements at the cost of human and spiritual values is not working. A civilization's greatness cannot be measured in terms of its technological achievements, especially if that civilization destroys the continent on which its people live.

The answer lies in restoring the spiritual foundations of our relationship to the natural world. One thing that technological developments have taught us is that nothing in the outer, material world can satisfy our inner, spiritual hunger. No amount of technological wizardry or expertise can replace the threads of spiritual connectedness that weave our lives into the fabric of the natural world.

This, above all else, is what Native Americans have to teach us: a spiritual view of the world that places humans within the web of life rather than above it. Only when more and more people accept and act upon the truth that the earth is not a possession, but rather a physical and spiritual domain shared by all living things, can we begin to heal the planet on which we live.

The purpose of this book has not been the idealization of native peoples—which is as dehumanizing as racist stereotyping—but rather, bridging the gap of understanding to open paths of learning a way of being in the world based on the interrelatedness of all forms of life. Only this can ensure the planet's healing and humanity's survival as a species. Instead of reviving romantic notions from a frozen past, we can find great contemporary relevance in Native American values that hold the key to survival for all of us as we move forward together into the next century.

Clearly, it is impossible to turn back the clock on all technological achievements, nor would it be desirable. What we can do is move forward together, blending the best of Indian and non-Indian worldviews by humanizing the technological worldview. In many respects, we have let science control us; we have given away our power so that technology is our ruler instead of our servant.

The Native American worldview provides a promising direction that blends native values and knowledge with the achievements of science. We can use computers to monitor

■ 184 ■

THE FOUR WORLDS DEVELOPMENT PROJECT

In April 1995, Phil Lane, Jr., director of the Four Worlds Development Project at the University of Lethbridge, addressed the World Commission on Culture and Development at the United Nations Headquarters. Lane presented a model of human and community development based on Native American spiritual principles and values.

Lane, in an article for *Winds of Change*, recounts the history of the Four Worlds Development Project: "In December, 1982, on the high plains of Alberta, forty wise, respected, and dedicated Elders, spiritual leaders, and community members from different tribal societies across North America came together for four days and nights of in-depth, purposeful consultation. Our common purpose was to develop a model of human and community development, inspired and guided by organizing principles, values, strategies, and processes of sustainable change, healing and development rooted deep in the natural laws that are at the inmost heart and core of tribal cultures throughout Mother Earth."

Lane points out some appalling facts: "The world's population is increasing by more than 92 million human beings every year. In fact, if every human being who now lives on Mother Earth were able to experience the average economic status found in middle-income homes in North America, we would need two more entire planets."

Clearly, to continue traveling the path based on global economic competition and environmental exploitation will lead us to certain disaster. Lane proposes that by working outward, beginning with individual healing, we can heal nations and the world by ultimately developing economic systems that are life-preserving and life-sustaining.

An essential aspect of the Four Worlds Project is its underlying spirit, which is based on an important Native American principle: the spirit in which an endeavor is undertaken determines the outcome. Lane says, "As a wise Elder once told me, whenever we make economic gain on the weakness of others or unfairly exploit others for our own selfish purposes, we will pay a very high price. In essence, the hurt of one is the hurt of all, and the honor of one is the honor of all."

From a twelve-year process of reflection, consultation, and action within tribal communities across North America, members of the organization developed principles for building a sustainable world. The number four is sacred in Native American traditions; the principles of the Four Worlds Project are grouped in four categories that contain four principles each. The healing process is conceptualized as a circle, which is also sacred in Indian practices, so that change and healing begin first within each person, then spiral outward to heal family and then community levels, while continuing one's connection to the Creator. Finally, healing expands to the worldwide level.

This program calls for acknowledging the sacredness of the earth so that the world's peoples work together to reverse environmental destruction dramatically. At the same time, it is important to keep an understanding that we are all related to each other so that we treat other humans with respect.

Lane recounts the words of his grandfathers: "You know, Grandson, the Great Spirit, Wakan Tanka, has given all people wisdom. To every living thing he has given something special. Some people receive their knowledge and understanding through books. In your life, grandson, you too must read and study books, but remember to take with you on your journey only those things that bring more unity within yourself and others, that bring goodness and understanding and help us to serve one another in better ways. Wakan Tanka also gave our Native people, and all other people who live close to Mother Earth, wisdom and knowledge through dreams, visions, fasting, prayer, and the ability to see the lessons the Creator has put in every part of creation. Look at those trees standing over there: The alder does not tell the pine tree to move over; the pine does not tell the fir tree to move over: Each tree stands there in unity, with its mouth pressed toward the same Mother Earth, refreshed by the same breeze, warmed by the same sun, with its arms raised in prayer and thanksgiving, each protecting the other. If we are to have peace in the world, we too must learn to live like those trees."

the health of the earth and our split-second communication links to share knowledge about effective strategies for healing the earth.

The introduction to this book tells of the Native American belief that when the Creator made the world, the profound complexity of the Universe was so far beyond human comprehension that the Creator gave each group a tiny glimpse of the whole truth. To keep the world in balance, all groups must put into action their spiritual understanding of the world without imposing it on others. Forcing beliefs on another group upsets the natural balance; everyone has something to contribute to the harmonious balance of the world. The time has come for humankind to act according to this vision, working in concert and mutual respect for others to restore balance to the earth we all share.

BIBLIOGRAPHY

Ballantine, Betty, and Ian Ballantine, eds. *The Native Americans: An Illustrated History*. Atlanta: Turner Publishing, 1993.

Between Sacred Mountains: Navajo Stories and Lessons from the Land. Tucson, Ariz.: Sun Tracks/University of Arizona Press, 1982.

Brown, Joseph Epes. *The Spiritual Legacy of the American Indian*. New York: Crossroad Publishing Co., 1982.

Champagne, Duane. *Native America: Portrait of the Peoples*. Detroit: Visible Ink Press, 1994.

Davis, Mary B. *Native America in the 20th Century: An Encyclopedia*. New York: Garland Publishing, 1994.

Deloria, Vine, Jr. *God Is Red: A Native View of Religion*. Golden, Colo.: Fulcrum Publishing, 1994.

Eagle/Walking Turtle. *Indian America: A Traveler's Companion*. Santa Fe, N.Mex.: John Muir Publications, 1991.

Griffin-Pierce, Trudy. *Earth Is My Mother, Sky Is My Father: Space, Time, and Astronomy in Navajo Sandpainting*. Albuquerque, N.Mex.: University of New Mexico Press, 1992.

The Handbook of North American Indians. Washington, D.C.: Smithsonian Institution, 1983–1990.

Hill, Tom, and Richard W. Hill, Sr., eds. *All Roads Are Good: Native Voices on Life and Culture*. Washington, D.C.: Smithsonian Books, 1994.

———. *Creation's Journey: Native American Identity and Belief*. Washington, D.C.: Smithsonian Books, 1994.

Josephy, Alvin M., Jr. *500 Nations: An Illustrated History of North American Indians*. New York: Alfred A. Knopf, 1994.

Kersey, Harry, Jr. "Seminoles and Miccosukees: A Century in Retrospective," *Indians of the Southeastern United States in the Late 20th Century*, ed. Anthony J. Paredes. Tuscaloosa, Ala.: The University of Alabama Press, 1992.

Momaday, N. Scott. *House Made of Dawn*. New York: Harper and Row, 1968.

Native Peoples Magazine: The Arts and Lifeways. ISSN #0895-7606. P.O. Box 36820, Phoenix, AZ 85067-6820; (602) 252-2236. All rights reserved.

Starita, Joe. *The Dull Knifes of Pine Ridge: A Lakota Odyssey*. New York: G.P. Putnam's Sons, 1995.

Suzuki, David, and Peter Knudtson. *Wisdom of the Elders: Sacred Native Stories of Nature*. New York: Bantam Books, 1992.

Taylor, Colin, ed. *The Native Americans: The Indigenous People of North America*. New York: Smithmark Publishers, 1991.

Trimble, Stephen. *The People: Indians of the American Southwest*. Santa Fe, N.Mex.: The School of American Research Press, 1993.

Winds of Change Magazine: American Indian Education and Opportunity. ISSN #0888-8612. Published by the American Indian Science and Engineering Society (AISES), 5661 Airport Blvd. Boulder, CO 80301-2339; (303) 939-0023. All rights reserved. Excerpts: p. 60: Summer 1995, Vol. X, No. 3; p. 67: Summer 1994, Vol. IX, No. 3; p. 121: Spring 1994, Vol. VIII, No. 2; p. 140: Spring 1995, Vol. X, No. 2; p. 167: Spring 1995, Vol. X, No. 2; p. 185: Autumn 1995, Vol. X, No. 4.

Zepeda, Ofelia. *Ocean Power: Poems from the Desert*. Tucson, Ariz.: University of Arizona Press, 1995.

PHOTOGRAPHY CREDITS

The American Museum of Natural History: ©Edward Curtis: 6–7, 20, 21, 94, 95, 100, 104, 105, 110, 120, 123 bottom, 135, 158, 159, 165, 176, 180, 181; ©Arthur Janson: 31 top, 32; ©J. LeMoyne: 69

Art Resource, N.Y.: 2, 30 top, 33, 36 bottom, 41, 50, 54, 132, 142; National Museum of American Art/Smithsonian Institution: 14, 16, 25, 50, 161; The Pierpont Morgan Library: 18; Werner Forman Archive: 36 top, 99, 106, 110 inset, 112, 113 right, 114 both, 118, 119, 123 top, 125, 129, 130, 133, 134, 174, 182, 184 top; Werner Forman/ Smithsonian Institution: 27 inset

Corbis-Bettmann: 11, 13, 22, 42, 51, 52, 64, 66, 67, 86, 144, 150, 157 bottom, 175, 179

©Elijah Cobb: 169

FPG: ©Willie Hill: 28 bottom; ©Lee Kuhn: 39, 82; ©Frank Meitz: 128, 183; ©Jonathan Meyer: 84; ©E. Nagele: 162; ©David Noble: 90, 113 left, 127; ©A. Schmidecker: 157 top; ©Richard Stockton: 146

©Lois Ellen Frank: 5, 10, 17 bottom, 19, 68, 71, 72, 76 top and bottom, 78, 80, 85 top, 88, 91, 93, 184 bottom

©John Fadden: 43, 47, 53

Library of Congress: 59, 109, 137

Museum of New Mexico: ©Charles M. Bell: 148

National Museum of the American Indian/Smithsonian Institution: ©Jerry Farnsworth: 46, 124, 131, 149, 171

North Wind: 15, 17 top, 24, 27 top, 37, 45, 61, 75, 85 bottom, 97, 98, 153

Reuters/Corbis-Bettmann: 12, 23

©Stephen Trimble: 73, 77, 81, 87, 89, 151, 154, 166, 178

UPI/Corbis-Bettmann: 28 top, 29, 30 bottom, 35, 40, 48 top and bottom, 51, 52, 56, 57, 102, 107, 111, 116, 122, 139, 155, 157 top, 170, 173, 177

Map Illustrations by Cameron Clement: 26, 44, 70, 96, 108, 126, 152

Map Illustration by Emilya Naymark: 172

INDEX

Horses, 127, 134, 135, *135*, 138, 143
House, Conrad, 68, 89, 93
Houser, Allan, 79
Hózhó, 16, 68, 93
Humboldt Trail, 168
Hunkpapa Sioux peoples, 129, 137
Hunt, George, 109
Hunting and gathering, 10, 26, 34, 36, 44, 70, 84–86
  Apache peoples, 87
  Choctaw peoples, 31
  Chumash peoples, 99
  Huron peoples, 59
  Micmac peoples, 46, 47–48
  overhunting, 39
  Pawnee peoples, 141
  Shoshone peoples, 166
  Tlingit peoples, 117
  Walapai peoples, 84, 85
  Yavapai peoples, 84, 85
  Yuma peoples, 83, 84
Hupa peoples, 23, 94, *95*
Huron Confederacy, 56
Huron peoples, 45, *45*, 56–59, 175, *175*, 177, *177*

Iholahata clan, 31
Imoklasha clan, 31
Inca peoples, 13
Indian Emergency Conservation Work, 145
Indian "luck," 51
Indian Nonintercourse Act (1790), 60
Indian Territory, 34
Institute of American Indian Arts (Santa Fe), 121
Institute of American Indian Arts (Sante Fe), 79
Inuit peoples, 177–179
Inuktitut peoples, 170
Iron Teeth, 127
Iroquois Confederacy, 52, 56, 62–63, 65

Iroquois peoples, 42, 45, *45*, *50*, 59–60
Ishtaboli, 30, *30*, 36

Jensen, Doreen, 118

Kachinas, 72, *72*, 75, 76
Kahwan peoples, 82
Karok peoples, 21, 23
Kavelchadom peoples, 82
Kersey, Harry, Jr., 32
Kickapoo peoples, 45, *45*, 49
Kiowa peoples, 55–56, 131
Kivas, 15, *15*, 71, 85–86, *85*
Klamath peoples, 150, 155, *155*, 157–159
Klikitat peoples, 156
Kwakiutl peoples, 106, *107*, 108, 110, *110*, 111, 117, 122, 179, *179*
Kwakiutl Shamans' Society, 109, *109*

Lac Courte Orielles peoples, 61–63, 65, 67
Lakota Sioux peoples, 10, *10*, 124, 125, 129, 131–140
Land
  allotment, 145, 147–148
  annexaton, 76
  laws, 33
  ownership, 33
  power of, 17, 19
  relationship with, 59
  rushes, 40, 51
  sacred, 125
  sale of, 39
  seizures, 13
  squatting, 41
Languages, 16, 34
  of California, 96, 97
  Canadian, 172
  Great Basin and Plateau, 152
  of the Great Plains, 125
  of the Northeast, 44
  of Northwest Coast, 108

of Southeast, 26, 28
of the Southwest, 70, 73, 74, 87
of trade, 39
Lansa, Mina, 17
Las Casas, Father Bartolome de, 13
League of the Iroquois, 52
Lenni-Lenape peoples, 54–56
Lewey, Sappy, 61
Lewis, Meriweather, 159, 160
Little Bighorn National Monument, 10, *10*, 136
Lomatewama, Ramson, 72
Louisiana Purchase, 159
Luce, Nordeen Nishone, 40, *40*
Luckie, Kate, 101

Mahican peoples, 45
Maine, 45
Maliseet peoples, 45
Mankiller, Wilma, 38, 133
Maricopa peoples, 82
Marriage, 31
Masks, 23, 117
  ceremonial, 89
  Cherokee, 41, *41*
  death, 114, *114*
  medicine, 60
  portrait, 114, *114*
Massachusetts, 45
Mastamho, 83
McNeil, Larry, 121
Means, Russell, 145
Medicine men, *14*, 15, 32, 78, 100, *100*
Meganack, Walter, 112
Menominee peoples, 49
Mesas, 68
Mescalero Apache peoples, 17, *17*, 88
Métis, 179–181
Miami peoples, 45, *45*
Miccosukee peoples, 31, 32
Micmac peoples, 21, 45, 46–53

Midewiwin, 49
Milanovich, Richard, 104
Mimbre peoples, 71
Misha Sipokne, 24
Missions, 97, *97*, 99, *99*, 101, 103
Miwok peoples, 94, 96
Modernization programs, 53, 55, 59–60, 67, 89, 154
Mohave peoples, 82, 83, 84
Mohawk peoples, 45, *45*, 52, 53, 57
Mohegan peoples, 45
Momaday, N. Scott, 143
Montauk peoples, 45
Mother Earth, 16
Mounds, 24, 27, *27*, 28
Myths, 23, 49, 120

Nakota Sioux peoples, 129
Namingha, Dan, 79
Narragansett peoples, 45
Nasoftie, George, 74
Natchez peoples, 29, 38
National Center for Native American Studies and Policy Development, 55
National Museum of the American Indian, 79, 104, 138
Native American Educational Opportunity Program, 55
Native Brothers Organization, 60, 61
Nature
  balance of, 68
  harmony with, 73
  interdependence with, 15
  mastery over, 13
  relationships with, 17, 19, 37, 42
  renewal of, 23
  respect for, 15–16, 19
Navajo Peacemaker Court, 81
Navajo peoples, 16, 68, 78, *78*, 82, *82*, 89–93